Gender and Community Care

Other books by Joan Orme

Social Work Practice, 3rd edn (with V. Coulshed)*
Workloads: Measurement and Management
Care Management: Tasks and Workloads (with B. Glastonbury)*
The Principles of Case Management (with B. Glastonbury)
Managing People in the Personal Social Services
   (with B. Glastonbury and R. Bradley)

* From the same publishers

Gender and Community Care

Social Work and Social Care Perspectives

Joan Orme

Consultant Editor: Jo Campling

palgrave

First published 2001 by
PALGRAVE
Houndmills, Basingstoke, Hampshire RG21 6XS and
175 Fifth Avenue, New York, N.Y. 10010
Companies and representatives throughout the world

PALGRAVE is the new global academic imprint of
St. Martin's Press LLC Scholarly and Reference Division and
Palgrave Publishers Ltd (formerly Macmillan Press Ltd).

ISBN 0–333–61989–7

This book is printed on paper suitable for recycling and
made from fully managed and sustained forest sources.

A catalogue record for this book is available
from the British Library.

10 9 8 7 6 5 4 3 2 1
10 09 08 07 06 05 04 03 02 01

Printed in Malaysia

To my mother May and her family –
they showed me the complexities of caring

Contents

Acknowledgements

It is always problematic listing individuals who have contributed to any long-term project. The risk is that an inclusive list might be so long as to be meaningless, but a shorter list might omit someone who in the course of conversation, discussion or argument made an observation or challenged a particular perspective, and in doing so added a whole new dimension. This is especially so with this text which has been 'in production' for some five years, but is also the culmination of teaching and research over a great many more.

The book therefore owes much to the countless students on qualifying and other courses in the Department of Social Work Studies and on gender studies courses in the Faculty of Social Sciences at the University of Southampton. However special mention must be made of Simon Blyth, whose own work on gender for his PhD contributed much to my own thinking, even if he might not recognise it.

Colleagues in the Department and beyond have also generated and stimulated ideas, and provided support in particular ways at particular times. Among those who deserve special gratitude are Christine Chinkin, Bryan Glastonbury, Ian Forbes, Paddy O'Brien and Pat Usher. The Australian women who arranged the International Association of Schools of Social Work (IASSW) women's symposium at Hong Kong in 1996 and my study tour in Australia in 1997 were also a great source of strength – and fun.

Care and gender are central to the lives of each and every one of us from our earliest experiences, and these experiences contribute to the way we construct both. Hence this book is dedicated to my mother and her sisters and brother who cared for each other, and for me, in their own way. Finally, special thanks must be given to Emily and Tim who, during the production of the text, have grown into capable, caring citizens; and to Geoff, whose care has been constant.

Department of Social Work Studies   JOAN ORME
University of Southampton

Introduction

Arguments rage both with feminism and within feminism about issues of care and the influence of gender. On the one hand women have been centre stage as carers, on the other they have been ignored, subsumed into categories such as disabled people, older people and those with mental health problems or, more generically still, users. These categories are not arbitrary, they reflect the thinking about models within the delivery of personal social services. The National Health Service and Community Care Act 1990 (NHS&CC Act) developed policies of community care and introduced new concepts such as care management. In doing so it required community care plans to be produced with sections describing provision for specific user groups in an attempt to integrate health and social care services and to be responsive to the needs of users. The aim was to enable those with identified care needs to remain in the community, provided for by services commissioned from alternative sources in the independent and private sectors. But in all this attention to individual needs there was little or no acknowledgement of the writing and research undertaken within feminism, about issues of race and aspects of disability, all of which had begun to explore the complexities of difference and had come to question any notion of a coherent, homogeneous user groups.

It is the contention of this text that the provision of community care and the identification of those who are in need of it involve processes of gender stereotyping and discrimination which permeate both employment practices and welfare policies and provision. Making such a bold claim may be seen to be both foolhardy and tantamount to dismissing those who are involved in policy making and provision of community care services as being at best unthinking, or at worst oppressive towards women. To take such a negative

1

approach would not be helpful as it reflects a disregard for the work that has been undertaken and a specific and rather narrow understanding of gender. This text is optimistic and wide-ranging, because of both the wealth of literature which has been identified and the opportunity that is provided to reflect on current policy and practice in the light of interpretations and understandings of what constitutes gender issues.

The idea for the text came out of a series of units offered on qualifying social work training courses. The history of these courses parallels developments in the acceptance of first women's issues and then feminism in social work education. Teaching based on research evidence which demonstrated the differential treatment of women and men in the social services and criminal justice service led to a series of sessions along a model of 'woman and...' which parallels the early 'add women and stir' approaches to feminist research. However, as anti-discrimination and anti-oppressive practice became more mainstream in education and training curricula for social work and other related professions, feminist thought began to have influence, although not always as strongly as some would hope (Orme, 1998). The influence was not only on what topics were covered on courses, but also feminist research literature contributed to understandings of how subjects are studied, and how knowledge is disseminated.

The initial aim of the text therefore was to undertake an overview of the literature related to the practices of social and care workers, and to explore these in the context of developing feminist theory in the disciplines of social work and social policy in the first instance. However, it soon became apparent that the project was wider than this. It has been argued that feminism is both social theory and practical politics (Ramazanoglu, 1989). Feminist theory in challenging constructions of knowledge has broken down the fixed boundaries of most of the disciplines in social sciences. In its capacity to link, for example, political theory with psychoanalysis it provides a model of intellectual synthesis for the discipline of social work. Feminism and social work have much in common. Often accused of having no unique theoretical framework of its own, and of being merely applied social sciences, social work's place in the academy has been uncomfortable. Similarly, the growth of women's studies (or indeed feminist studies) has, for some time, been ambiguous.

However, both feminism and social work have the means to claim their rightful place, although, for each, the definition of that place is significantly different. For feminism, the project has been not to be marginalised as a single discipline in an academic backwater, but to ensure that it becomes a substantive part of all subject areas, not just the social sciences. As the political movement claimed, feminism has universal application: 'feminism is a political perspective on all issues of concern to human life' (Bunch, 1982: 21). In this it has been largely successful, although some have complained that in its success it is now being colonised or contaminated by men and masculinity studies.

For social work, the aim is to be recognised as a discipline which provides an interface between a number of theoretical frameworks: for example, the implications of social or economic policies for the individual, or the application of a psychological theory such as behaviour modification. It is the theorising at, or about, the interface which is the significant contribution that social work makes, and it is here that the links with feminism become apparent. As Collins (1986) has argued, the person-in-environment paradigm, which reflects the capacity of social work to accept and understand the individual affecting and affected by the social and physical environment, has echoes in the feminist claim that the personal is the political.

It was the synthesis of feminist and social work projects which led to a clearer and more positive focus for the text. The challenge was to consider the 'users' of social and care services, not only within their environment but also within their campaigns and complaints, to identify how the nature of the changes required or demanded reflected different experiences based on the gender of those users. This was not merely to advocate change for change sake or to create arbitrary divisions between men and women. The passing of the NHS&CC Act marked a significant watershed in the history of social work and social care for workers, users and carers. If social work was to survive as a meaningful activity it would have to adapt to the organisational changes, but the opportunities offered by one set of changes could facilitate others. Equal opportunities, anti-discriminatory and anti-oppressive practice had become part of the discourse of social work education and training, but were highly contentious. There was academic and political dispute about the appropriateness of this discourse, suggesting it curtailed academic freedom. At the same time it was not clear whether there had been any meaningful effect outside the seminar rooms of social work courses (Orme, 1996a). For social work to be effective as a profession and as an academic discipline, the aim is not merely to preserve the status quo, but to be consistent with the transformational praxis of both social work and feminism (Orme, 1998). Community care reforms offer an opportunity to explore how workers' understanding of gender influences their practice.

To do this it became apparent that an exploration of who provides and who receives care in the community would require an analysis of oppression in both policy and practice. While social policy studies have concentrated on the impact of community care on women as carers (Finch and Groves, 1983; Ungerson, 1987; Langan, 1992), it is argued in this text that a social work and social care perspective reveals that the gender issues of community care are more complex than that. While the attitudes which influence policy and practice affect both men and women, they are more likely to oppress women because commonly held views of femininity, that is women's capacity for nurturance and caring, have been central to the provision of social work and social care services. This text explores these views and considers how they have influenced the provision of community care, in terms of who does the caring but also in the way that services are allocated, the nature of the service offered, and who receives those services.

Hence, the text focuses on issues of gender, which involve not just women and men, but the way that the social relations between them and the constructions of masculinity and femininity have not only provided the basis of much welfare legislation, but also influenced the attitudes and practices of the front-line workers who mediate law and policy. Unless these are addressed then social work and social care cannot claim to be anti-oppressive, empowering or to be actively pursuing the value base that it espouses.

The first four chapters therefore set the context for discussions of both gender and community care and as such are predominantly theoretical. The aim is to demonstrate how feminist writing provides a useful lens through which social work and social care policy and practice can be viewed, but also to demonstrate the complexities and, at times, contradictions within that writing. In assessing the contribution of feminist theories, what is demonstrated is that they provide important commentaries on the experiences of all users of social work and social care services, not just women. Chapter 1 sets out debates within feminist thinking about constructions of gender and notions of difference. This provides the backdrop against which discussions about users' experiences will be highlighted and explored. Equally, the development of policy and practice around community care discussed in Chapter 2 provides important contextual material for the rest of the text. Both these chapters raise some overarching questions about the gender implications of both community and care, themes which are developed in Chapters 3 and 4.

In the rest of the text an exploration of research and practice literature is intended to assist exploration of how gendered assumptions have contributed to the social construction of men and women in certain client or user groups. Significantly, that distinction itself is an important construction in the process of implementing community care. The nature of clienthood has been problematic for social work, carrying with it reflections of power imbalance. The term 'user' or even customer was introduced with the rhetoric of the market which, while it espoused some notion of choice, did not necessarily change the contract of the interpersonal relationship between those who were receiving services and those responsible for identifying, assessing and providing for their needs. More accurately it confused it; within the new arrangements for care service users can also become service providers.

The arrangement of the latter part of the text into chapters related to client or user groups is further complicated because the emerging theme of the text is that each of us has a complex set of identities, and it is the construction of, and reaction to, these which influence the gendered nature of service provision. Each of the identified user perspectives brings with it its own set of experiences, its own oppressions and its own body of knowledge. While in each section there are issues which have been developed as explanations of the experiences of specific groups of users, or processes which have emerged to counteract these oppressions, they contribute to an interlocking body of theory which will be used to identify changes necessary in service delivery. At the same time, within each section the heterogeneity of the user group will be attested. Disabled people can be old, older people can be disabled or experience mental health problems.

These chapters are not meant to be merely descriptive; they are organised to reflect developments in practice which have emerged from the research and writing specific to the particular user group, and which are pertinent and transferable to other groups. So the literature on policy and practice specific to those who experience mental health problems gives enormous insights into the way gender affects the assessment and care planning process. These are themes which are equally relevant to older people, especially when it is noted that older people who use community care services are predominantly female. However, there is less attention to them in the literature on older people. While assessment of older people for community care is important, it is framed in terms of risk to themselves, and themes which emerge are about surveillance and protection. Attention to gender issues provides recommendations for political action, empowerment and participation. It is therefore appropriate to conclude the analysis of user groups by documenting the changes that disabled people have achieved in the way services are provided, but more significantly their success in changing perceptions and having their rights recognised. However, even in the positive messages from the disability movement, attention to issues of gender present challenges both for the service providers and for those who are involved in the movement. These can be summarised as the tensions inherent in recognising and validating differences while retaining a political identity.

Not only do the subjects of the chapter headings in Chapters 5, 6 and 7 intertwine, they are cross-cut by understandings of class and race, as well as gender. For workers, this presents problems of how to recognise diversity and difference but develop some kind of manageable guidelines to help inform policy and practice, which will be the focus of Chapter 8. The tension for social workers and care workers in having to respond to individual needs, but at the same time acknowledge that that individual is set within a variety of contexts, provides one of the greatest challenges for practice.

In each of the latter chapters, therefore, the notion of identity politics becomes an issue, and a form of 'identity relativism' emerges from some literature. That the experience of being old or disabled should be privileged above all other aspects of identity has led to linear thinking which does not reflect the experience of, for example, the impact of race and racism on the way that Black disabled people are perceived and treated (Begum *et al.*, 1994). Differences are either ignored, or the worker decides which aspect of identity is recognised, related to and provided for.

In working through these complexities different aspects of the relationship between service users and service providers has emerged. The literature accessed is not comprehensive, but it is from a rich variety of sources. One of the contentions of this text is that understandings are always partial, knowledge never complete, and that social work and social care practice will continually draw upon, interpret and mediate a number of theoretical perspectives. Each chapter has brought new insights to the understanding of gender relations in social work and social care which have been developed by exploring the descriptions of services provided in the light of feminist theories and explanations.

The book is therefore not prescriptive. It is not a manual of how to avoid discriminating on the basis of gender, or even how to undertake best practice in community care services, although it is hoped that one consequence of the book will be that practitioners and others will be more reflexive in their practice. It is intended to provide a theoretical context for practice, and an understanding that that context is never static but is dependent on a dialogue between theory and practice.

1

Politics of Gender and Social Care

Introduction

The aim of this chapter is to provide an introduction to the whole text by exploring the implications of focusing on gender in community care. It draws on feminist theorising about the condition of being a woman, to give an overview of how understandings of gender have been interpreted and responded to in social work practice. The emphasis is on how these interpretations do, or do not, reflect understandings of difference both between women, and between women and men. In doing this the chapter aim is to clarify why attention to gender issues, in their widest sense, is important in community care policies and practices.

The context

Feminism has contributed to debates about community care in many ways. Policy analysts, psychologists and social theorists have engaged in projects that have made women visible by drawing attention to the impact of policy implementation on women. While there has been agreement that attention should be drawn to the position of women, there have been tensions and disagreements about what that position is, the reasons for that position and understandings of which women are constructed by and within these debates. For example, feminist writers have been consistent in their analysis that community care policies have impacted on the lives of women by constructing them as carers and confining them to unpaid domestic labour (Finch and Groves, 1983; Ungerson,

8

1987). However, this analysis has been criticised for being limited in the way it addresses race and class issues (Graham, 1993), and disabled women argue that it creates a divide between women as carers and those they care for, thus denying disabled women's womanhood and their role in care giving (Morris, 1993c). Similar conclusions could be drawn from discussions which construct old age as a negative experience and portray older women as economically and emotionally dependent. Debates between women have therefore widened an understanding of the gender issues of community care but by focusing on the experiences of women, and only a select group of women. The policies, and the practices which emanate from them, impinge on women's lives in myriad ways. Women will be expected to be care givers in their own families, as friends or neighbours, as unpaid voluntary workers or as paid employees of social work; social care and nursing agencies. They will also receive care in that they constitute the greater proportion of the older population, and are diagnosed as experiencing certain mental health problems and disabilities more frequently than men.

For this reason it is crucial that social work and social care address the position of women, and reflect on practices which involve intervening in the lives of women. Women constitute the majority of social workers' caseloads, and, given in that social care and social work involve intervention in the public and private aspects of women's lives, it offers opportunities to understand, encourage and empower. Alternatively, and more negatively, it gives power to dominate, indoctrinate and discriminate.

However, the situation is more complex than this. Within both feminism and feminist social work there has been a quest to understand the subjugation of women, and to seek to redress it. Different analyses have led to the identification of different causal factors and different prescriptions and solutions (Dominelli, 1997; Orme, 1998). All have something to offer to an understanding of the position of women, and the fact that they may at times be seen to be contradictory is no bad thing. To assume that because women are theorising they should come to some universalistic conclusions may be the position of radical separatist feminists, but it denies difference and has hints of cultural imperialism which is counter to the female 'nature' that is ascribed to by those who take this stance. Also, to expect unanimity would subject feminist theorising to criticism that it is anti-dialogical, that it inhibits discussion, and as such contributes to oppressive action (Freire, 1972).

More problematic is the criticism that feminist thought and feminist social work has not addressed the position of men. This has become foregrounded by debates about the participation of men in caring (Arber and Gilbert, 1989; Fisher, 1994). Concerns about experiences of men highlight a tension for feminists who, while acknowledging that women's lives are constructed by relations with men, recognise that there is no unified analysis of how this construction comes about. More significantly, there is no agreement about where efforts to bring about change should be located. Some contend that if resources are limited, support should be given to women to assert themselves, and change their material conditions. Others argue that if men are implicated in the oppression of women, it is they who should change, and that women have the means and the capacity to bring about that change. Both these positions have within them, either explicitly or implicitly, understandings of difference between men and women. Their particular standpoint is influenced by what they consider constitutes that difference: biology, social conditioning or social construction. Reflecting a modernist position, these writers suggest that if we can identify who does what to, or for, whom and why, then the situation can be known and the conditions either accepted or changed.

For a further group of thinkers, usually described as postmodernists, the differences are not necessarily between men and women; they argue that within such categories there are differences which render the categories themselves meaningless. In this analysis the 'situatedness' of individuals in different socio-political, historical contexts mean that it is not possible to know, or prove the truth of any particular set of experiences: 'Rather than succumb to the authoritarian impulses of the will to truth, they urge instead the development of a commitment to the plurality and the play of difference' (Hawkesworth, 1989).

In examining links between postmodernism, post-structuralism and feminism, writers are concerned to explore how abandoning foundations and accepting contingency creates possibilities for a politics which is not founded on notions of universal or unified essence or identities: 'In exploring or interrogating specific possibilities of specific women in specific locations contradictions and conflict are not conditions which can be avoided or subsumed but are to a varying degree present in all of us' (Featherstone and Fawcett, 1995: 32). If there are contradictions and conflict within and between women, there is potential for differences between men and for identification and alliance between some women and some men.

In community care the potential for such alliances has already emerged in, for example, the activities of disability rights groups and advocacy groups in mental health work, where a shared identity of women and men around oppressions experienced by being categorised and stereotyped as 'disabled' or 'mentally ill' takes precedence over gender differences.

For feminists this theoretical position and emergent practice is problematic. Some have argued that it represents a (white) male academic backlash against feminist thought and action, challenging the political activity which is centred on the clear oppression of women by men (Hester *et al.*, 1996). For others it raises issues of identity politics, which have been rigorously debated between feminists within the discourses of community care. These different stances constitute a politics of gender which requires exploration before the particular position of social work and social care is discussed.

The setting apart or separatist stance of some feminist thought has been seen to deny women's positive ability to change the world, and men within it. Other positions accept the 'nature' of women, but argue that female qualities should be privileged and utilised to bring about changes in social and interpersonal functioning; to listen to women's previously unheard 'different voice' (Gilligan, 1993). These recognitions of differences assume, or create, a set of binary oppositions such as men/women or masculine/feminine. Such divisions have themselves been challenged, but in that challenge the tensions or the 'politics' of gender are reflected.

Politics of gender

Second-wave feminism explored and struggled with finding an explanation for, if not an answer to, de Beauvoir's (1972) question that 'if one is not born a woman' what is it that contributes to women's oppression. Her distinctions between the 'one' and the 'other' have provided a significant strand of feminist theorising about the causal factors for, and the outcomes of, the subjugation of women:

> [i]f the Other is not to regain the status of being the One, he [sic] must be submissive enough to accept this alien point of view. Whence cometh this submission in the case of women? (De Beauvoir, 1972: 18)

In theorising the causes of women's subjugation, and identifying means to combat it, feminist thought constantly grapples with notions of equality and difference (Evans, 1995). Some argue that while there may be biological and physical differences these should not prevent women from achieving equality with men. Women merely have to seize individual power to enable them to participate in, for example, the workplace and the democratic processes of the state and they would achieve equality. Others have seen the subjugation of women as more complicated than this.

Marxist critiques of capitalism as an explanation of the subjugation of women have been found wanting, not least because women are, and were, oppressed in pre-capitalist societies. Furthermore, the analysis of the reproduction of labour power does not explain the private oppression of women in domestic labour and interpersonal relationships (Rubin, 1975). Because of these limitations, alternative critiques expounding differences between sex and gender were developed to challenge the essentialist assumptions of natural differences between men and women. Feminist theories of gender look to explanations other than the biological: they 'seek to explain and change historical systems of sexual difference, whereby "men" and "women" are socially constituted and positioned in relations of hierarchy and antagonism' (Haraway, 1990: 131). The articulation of the sex/gender distinctions therefore argues for a challenge to the social system which creates or constructs sexism and gender. But such a challenge does not mean an inversion of power. This would merely reinforce an understanding of essential biological differences between women and men. Rubin argues that it is the very system which needs to be changed 'we are not only oppressed *as* women, we are oppressed by having to *be* women, or men as the case may be' (Rubin, 1975: 204).

Such conclusions challenge the accusations or claims that 'gender' is a synonym for 'women', but in doing so are seen to be less political, carrying no statement about inequalities or power (Wallach Scott, 1988). While offering a description of the relations between the sexes as social, nothing is said about why these relations are constructed or how they work.

Wallach Scott's criticism is not shared by all. More accurately, not all draw the same conclusions from an analysis of difference formed around understandings of gender. Those who argue that the differences between women and men have to be not only recognised but valorised, that the positive qualities of femaleness and femininity should be privileged over masculinity and maleness, identify male power, not the economic system, as the controlling influence on women in a whole variety of forms. Millet (1970) argues that men with their own culturally constituted gender roles also define the social and sexual position of women, while Firestone (1971) developed a theme of women as a class in their own right with men as the antagonistic class. The organisation of such a class structure was related, she argued, to the means of reproduction rather than production. In these analyses discursive differences between sex and gender were seen to set up polarities between male and female, masculine and feminine. For some the outcome of their analysis is that women should be separate from men. Others have rejected such a political position as arising out of the experiences of, and relevant to, only a privileged few, young, white, educated women who could make a choice about separate lives (hooks, 1987).

Essentialist or cultural feminists therefore argue that women's characteristics are static, they do not vary historically across culture, race or class, and they are benign – women are kind, women nurture and women care. De Beauvoir, for example, argues that difference between the sexes is a biological fact, not an event in history (De Beauvoir, 1972), but this does not explain why biological differences have led to the subjugation of women. This, she argues was because of social pressures to act in certain 'feminine' ways. It was the negative perception of 'femininity' which led to subjugation.

Although de Beauvoir maintained that 'woman' was a social rather than a natural construct she and other cultural feminists (Gilligan, 1993) have been accused of taking an essentialist stance, that is they assume female qualities are innate, biologically caused and as such set women apart from men. In the most recent edition of her work Gilligan responds to this charge by arguing that she is challenging the domination of male experiences: 'my questions are about psychological processes and theory, particularly theories in which men's experience stands for all of human experience – theories which eclipse the lives of women and shut out women's voices' (Gilligan, 1993 xiii). She argues that not only were men shutting out women, but women were leaving themselves out. One danger is that if, in acquiring power, women disregard men, then their analysis will be similarly partial, and that they, in Gilligan's terms, will act like men. There is a double bind here in that it might be said to be a function of the nurturing female that men should not be omitted from the analysis, but it is more rational and logical than that. Partial and incomplete analyses impact on all. Valorising the discursive voice and understanding that 'the personal is the political' validates women's experience, and for many women men are part of that experience. In the context of community care an incomplete and partial account of particular aspects of women's lives will emerge if no consideration is given to both whom they care for, and, at times, who cares for them.

A positive outcome of Gilligan's position is that she causes women to question the rules and norms by which activities are 'judged'; if justice is male, and imposed according to rational male norms, the impact on women is twofold. Hence understandings of the position of women were progressed by Gilligan, among others, because the processes of domination were analysed as well as the causes: they 'cleared a space, described a new territory, which radically altered the male normative terms of discussion about reality and experience; they forced recognition of the difference gender makes' (Bordo, 1990: 137).

That this exploration of gender permeates all disciplines is supported by Wallach Scott, who not only declares the relevance of gender to history, but argues that a historical perspective gives insight into understandings of gender as part of social relations:

> When historians look for ways in which the concept of gender legitimises and constructs social relationships, they develop insight into the reciprocal nature of gender and society and into the particular and contextually specific ways in which politics constructs gender and gender constructs politics. (Wallach Scott, 1988: 44)

For social work and social care the connections are even more evident in that workers in these spheres not only work with those very social relationships which have been constructed, they themselves contribute to, and create even more complex social relationships. The gender politics of social work has to include the relationship between the helper and those who require help, and, inasmuch as the worker is carrying out policies based on legislation, they represent the relationship between the individual and the state. It is the combination of social relations and power which makes the concept of gender useful for analysing understandings gained from community care literature: 'a constitutive element of social relationships based on perceived differences between the sexes, and gender is a primary way of signifying power' (Wallach Scott, 1988: 43). In community care, policies of predominantly male policy makers are carried out in the main by female workers, working with women in the domestic sphere in ways which impact on the lives of women and men both directly and indirectly. The failure of social work and social care workers to attend to issues of gender is documented below, but before moving on to this it is important to address concerns within feminist thought that attention to gender involves a dilution of the political project.

Identities

One criticism is that, even when theorising gender as a construction of social relations and recognising the difference that gender makes, feminism ignored other dimensions of social identity and the diversity of women's experience. This critique first brought by Black women (hooks, 1984; Lorde, 1984) was reinforced by lesbian women and led to a celebration of difference associated with identity politics.

Some have argued that women's common interests as women are effectively divided, whether women consciously experience divisiveness or not (Ramazanoglu, 1989). A general theory of common oppression of women is thought to be problematic because class and cultural differences are recognised, but feminism's theory of a shared oppression has paradoxically encouraged the elaboration of varieties of oppression which women experience. In response to criticism from disabled women Ramazanoglu argues that it is raising consciousness of women which is important not the recognition of other differences. Raising consciousness allows women to recognise other oppressions: 'while these are crucial areas of oppression for many women, they take different forms in different cultures, and so are difficult to generalise about. They are also forms of difference which could be transformed by changes in consciousness' (Ramazanoglu, 1989: 95). In this she appears to be abandoning the notion of a common political project of resistance.

In addition to 'identities' such as Black, lesbian and disabled the list of oppressions experienced by women, either as individuals or in some constituted collective identity, could be endless: reproduction, mothering, familial duties and the contradiction of women loving the men who oppress them are frequent candidates. Some of these experiences can be subsumed under, or contribute to, for example, ideologies of caring or familial ideologies, where ideologies are particular sets of ideas which shape the way most people make sense of their world. These permeate women's lives irrespective of their different abilities, sexual orientation, class, culture or ethnic background.

Furthermore, recognition of different identities leads to experiences of oppression being mediated through different groups sharing specific observable identities; the mere listing of categories often leads to unhelpful notions of hierarchies of oppression. Attempts to avoid categorisation of groups involve focusing on the processes of oppression which cover all social groups, recognising that the oppression experienced by each group is irreducible (Freire, 1972; Young, 1990b). Acknowledging diversity and difference, Young resists fragmentation of any group, or of the individual within a group, to a degree which is meaningless. She argues that it is possible to accept the illusion of 'a unified self-making subjectivity' (Young, 1990b: 45), but also to recognise that at any one time identity is constituted by an individual's relations with significant others: 'For our identities are defined in relation to how others identify us, and they do so in terms of groups which are always already associated with specific attributes, stereotypes and norms' (Young, 1990b: 46). This does not mean that groups are static, have a common nature or a substantive essence; they are defined in relation, or opposition, to other groups. More importantly, group differences cut across each other and mirror in their own differentiations many of the other groups in wider society. Thus it is possible for a Black disabled woman to be part of the disability movement as a unified project, while championing the need for all women to be free of oppression by men, and recognising the common oppressions of Black women and men. While the individual is part of a group they are not defined solely and specifically by that group: 'The individual person, as constituted partly by their group affinities and relations, cannot be unified, themselves are heterogeneous and not necessarily coherent' (Young, 1990b: 48). In this analysis Young recognises that 'identity' is not a singular, unified concept, and in doing so she provides a response to the limitations of notions of 'double disadvantage' and 'simultaneous oppressions' (Carby, 1982) which underplay the differences within Black people's experience. Reducing disadvantage to being Black and one other description can leave other complex considerations untouched and fails to recognise diversity as a central aspect of the experience of Black and ethnic minority communities (Stuart, 1996).

It is the paradox, or more accurately paradoxes, presented by and within discussions of women, gender and feminism which are central to this text. While the theoretical exploration in this chapter commenced with a focus on women, it is apparent that the category 'women' is not homogeneous, as Black women and disabled women have repeatedly reminded us (hooks, 1984; Morris, 1993a). If differences within the category 'woman' are accepted, then there would seem to be no reason to accept an undifferentiated category 'men'. If there are no fixed categories of women and men, then it is difficult to theorise essential or even acquired differences. As Bordo argues, the unity of 'gendered humanity' is as much fiction as the unity of abstract universal man (Bordo, 1990). This does not mean that theorising human experience is abandoned, it is transformed; the transformation focuses on notions of difference. Feminism, therefore, with its rich canon of theoretical explorations, offers opportunities to valorise, that is to value positively the experiences of all those who have been negatively labelled, stereotyped and disempowered by their difference, many of whom constitute users of community care services.

Difference

The developments within feminism which highlighted the importance of recognising differences between women were coterminus with postmodern and post-structural rejection of a unified subject as the agent of social or political change. It was argued that some feminist theory in recognising difference established a set of binary oppositions in which it was assumed that differences were fixed and permanent. Recognising differences between women, or within the category 'woman', can fragment any notion of a unified self. As Butler has argued 'if one "is" a woman surely that is not all one is . . . because gender is not always constituted coherently or consistently in different historical contexts, and because it intersects with racial, class, sexual and regional modalities of discursively constituted identities' (Butler, 1990: 3).

Accepting the theoretical advantages of postmodernism, some feminists recognised that the practical implications might be the loss of the concept of agency for women, the loss of coherence, and the abandonment of any project of collective resistance and therefore there could be no common political project for women (Langan and Day, 1992). The assertion by feminist standpoint theorists that the relativism of postmodernism precludes the possibility of formulating one true 'women's perspective' is at the heart of the tension. Those who ascribe to postmodernism maintain that to argue for a one true, feminist perspective, a single, universal characteristic of 'woman', denies women's diversity.

A possible solution is not to set these perspectives in absolute opposition to each other, and it has been the project of critical feminist epistemology to steer a course through the critique of different perspectives without oversimplifying the subject: 'a critical feminist epistemology must avoid both the foundationalist tendency to reduce the multiplicity of reasons to a monolithic "Reason" and the postmodernist tendency to reject all reasons *tout court*' (Hawkesworth, 1989: 556). Hence Barrett, for example, makes a distinction between difference as 'experiential diversity' and 'positional meaning'. The former equates with feminist tradition and allows for the common experiences of women to be part of a political project, while the latter emphasises meanings of differences constructed through necessarily fragmented discourses. Her conclusion is that there can be no common political project (Barrett, 1987). Positional meaning can be clearly associated with the complex identity of a Black woman who is also a user of community care service. All of these 'positions', or labels, carry with them different constructions while simultaneously being part of the individual's experience.

From another perspective, Hekman's understanding of *différance* takes into consideration understandings of 'otherness', exploring sexual difference in terms of multiplicity and plurality rather than hierarchy (Hekman, 1991). She argues that postmodernism has sought to reject dichotomies, the division into two oppositional parts, of other explanations which have led to constructed dualisms such as male/female, culture/nature. Even though they try to reject any notion of biological essentialism in the explanation of women's position or behaviour, they accept definitions and explanations which have to be set in opposition to each other. The challenge is to accept notions of difference without privileging any one set of characteristics or experiences.

Langan, recognising that the price of encouraging the concept of diversity may be a loss of commitment to change and any unified agency through which it might be achieved, recommends that a parallel project to recognising difference is to recognise interconnectedness – what is common. In doing this the complexities of women's lives can be understood: 'While different oppressions interact and reinforce one another, emphasising "difference" *per se* may lead to division and conflict' (Langan and Day, 1992: 5). This interconnectedness, the themes which resonate between the accounts of groups, has led to the creation of homogeneous categories in social work literature. Disabled people, older people or those who are mentally ill are assumed to have similarities which can be responded to. However the exploration of the experiences of users of social services will reveal different experiences of women and men within these groups, and commonalities which transcend any of the usual descriptions. It is this which will inform understandings of gender issues.

However, this is not to diminish the tensions that social workers and others working in the field have to manage. They have to work with groups defined by legislation and service organisation while recognising and respecting individuals, whatever their circumstances, within them. Additionally, categories within community care such as age, disability and mental health, challenge a simple duality of male/female identity and therefore provide insight into how understandings of gender can contribute to the practice of social care and social work. It is therefore necessary to plot the impact of feminism on social work practice.

Social work, social care and gender

Social work and social care practice has been criticised for either ignoring issues of gender, or falling into the trap of merely using gender as a shorthand or synonym for 'women'. In this process of ignoring, social work and social care have also been criticised for their contribution to the oppression of women (Brook and Davis, 1985). Although there have been concerted developments by women social work academics and practitioners to draw attention to the position of women (Hanmer and Statham, 1988; Dominelli and McLeod, 1989), progress has been slow. Generic social work texts do address gender, or more accurately acknowledge feminist theory (Howe, 1987; Payne, 1991) but the analysis is at times simplistic and rarely addresses the complexity of social relations which constitute understandings of gender. The influence on practice has been minimal and the invisibility of different women persists, particularly in their role and context as service users.

The inherent conservatism of social workers, particularly women social workers, has been cited as the reason why, in the 1970s, when the influence of feminism was growing, social work was slow to absorb the ideas and practices emerging from it (Brook and Davis, 1985). Social work literature was criticised by feminism for ignoring gender, for implying that it saw the whole family as a target for action, while actually having a largely female clientele who were held responsible not only for their own lives but also for the lives of others – dependent and otherwise. Thus social work drew attention to the central position of women in the discourse, but failed to make this overt or to theorise it in terms of the emergent feminist arguments which were highlighted by, for example, claims that patriarchal structures of the welfare state oppressed women as both service users and service deliverers (Pateman, 1989).

Within social work practice differential treatment of women and men was seen to lead to double standards, and different rules of behaviour for each influenced the way that services were allocated or withheld. It is not suggested that this was because of some deliberate oppression, but that it was a consequence of the value base of social work. One of the basic tenets of social work is individualisation, where the individual's personal experience is seen to be the valid focus for intervention. The limitation of this is that to concentrate on the individual, the private, is not only to pathologise the individual but also to inhibit any notion of public, collective or political action. As earlier commentators pointed out, casework was controversial:

> The casework relationship has been much derided by radical social work as being oppressive, pseudo-psychoanalytic, leading to the locating of problems within individuals, rather than in social structures. One-to-one work can be all these things but need not be. (Brook and Davis, 1985: 120)

The use by social workers of the concept of empathy in individualised approaches to social problems meant that at best they disempowered, and at worst oppressed, users of services. Marxist and feminist criticism of social work practice was that it was dependent upon the one-to-one relationship. Even when this relationship was not necessarily described as casework, or prescribed by the theories of Freud, it was seen to pathologise the individual in need of help, and to compartmentalise problems. The extent of need, or the ways in which factors other than personal pathology (for example, poverty, employment opportunities, welfare benefit policies or health care provision) impact on the circumstances of many were said to be ignored. The social work approaches favoured by Marxists (Bailey and Brake, 1975), feminists (Dominelli and McLeod, 1989) and others committed to user empowerment (Beresford and Croft, 1986) represent resistance to these individualised, focalised methods. They advocated community development, community action and community social work.

However, developments in community care ironically have returned the focus to the individual. As Chapter 5 illustrates, the association of social work with medical models has re-emerged in mental health practice, which continues to emphasise that the very objectives of 'clinical' practice require attention to individual cases (Busfield, 1996). Attention to an individual's particular personal characteristics has to include their gender. However, attention to gender when it does occur does not in any positive sense focus on the experiences of the individual; it is a classification system: 'universalism is a requirement of scientific medicine in which official classifications are grounded, particularism is a sine qua non of clinical medicine' (Busfield, 1996: 109).

That social work has to focus on both individuals and their environment is both its strength and its challenge. For some feminsist writers this focus has not been a contradiction. For example, in its attention to the person-in-environment social work is seen to have resonance with the project of feminism in that it echoes the feminist slogan that the personal is the political (Collins, 1986). In Collins's analysis both encourage concentration on the individual experience but see it in a wider context. Each woman's personal experience contributes to the understanding of the experience of the many, and as such can become the basis for collective action. This collective action has been associated with separatism, but the slogan also posits a separate and superior female knowledge and means of knowing, derived from oppression (Evans, 1995). As such it brings the possibility of changing the way that processes are undertaken, whether that be the process of education, or providing community care service. This has important consequences for valorising the women who are users of services, recognising them as significant in the understanding of women's experiences. It is argued in this text that it also has the potential for bringing about change for men, and for the relations between women and men in community care services.

The dual focus on the need for collective action and for personal and individual solutions can lead to tensions and misinterpretation. The slogan does not mean that the purpose of feminism is immediate liberation of individuals. As Wilson points out this would lead to unrealistic expectations and 'a belief that changes in lifestyle will in fact turn out to be the solution to the problems many women face' (Wilson, 1980: 35). The women with whom social workers work are seeking immediate liberation from their personal and individual problems, they do not necessarily want to wait for a revolution, nor do alternative lifestyles appeal to all.

Also, if the suggestion is that the collective approach is the only answer, that *all* women's experiences have to be perceived as conforming to a particular predefined explanation of oppression, then that denies each woman's individual identity. In the first instance this counteracts one of the positive aspects of the definition of individualisation – that individuals are not regarded as fulfilling certain types and paradigms but as presenting a particular problem which needs to be considered against its own particular background (Plant, 1973). It may also deny individual women the opportunity to articulate their own personal position which can further inform the political, and possibly the collective.

It is this tension between the individual, with their complex identities and their many allegiances, and the wider context of those allegiances, communities and other groupings, that provides the continuing dilemma for social work and social care practice which works at the borderland between the individual and their specific and personal needs and the wider social context where political activity is needed to bring about change. These themes are explored further in Chapter 8, but here it is necessary to document the way that feminist social work has responded to criticism.

Women-centred practice

The emergence of women-centred practice which drew attention to the particular situation of women as clients of social work, and argued for separate and specific ways of meeting their needs (Hanmer and Statham, 1988), could be seen to be a positive application of the principles of individualisation. However, it could also be seen to be part of an essentialist feminist approach in that it ascribed to a position that identified women as a specific group who require particular interventions. Interventions which might, for example, include meeting specific childcare needs constrained women in their particular roles as mothers. Such roles were acknowledged to present women as seemingly passive and dependent 'carers' in relationships, and Gilligan's ethic of care was drawn on to describe them in a more positive way (Hanmer and Statham, 1988; Hudson, 1989). Hudson's caution at assumptions about the 'naturalness' of such female characteristics highlights the possible association of women centred practice with essentialist conceptions of gender.

A further dilemma in focusing on women-centred practice is that it was seen by some to emphasise the negative position of women, confirming them in their oppressed role irrespective of whether these roles depended on natural characteristics. Wise, for example, questions the feminist project of caring for vulnerable people 'Does the "care and protection of vulnerable people" mean that women are vulnerable simply by virtue of being women and therefore need the ameliorative activities of feminist social work?' (Wise, 1990: 248). She also argues that feminist critiques of social work and social workers provide a simplistic view of women's oppression. In pointing out that women may well collude, that children do lie and men do become involved in caring she argues that this makes it difficult to accept the feminist call to 'always believe the (female) victim' (Wise, 1990). This criticism is not intended to blame women, but to recognise that a limited analysis and simplistic guidance for practice says little about women and men who fall outside the usual gender stereotypes.

The limitations of recognising diversity

More positively, women-centred practice attempts to deal with notions of diversity. The challenges to mainstream feminist theorising from the political left, from Black and other ethnic minority women, lesbian women and disabled women impacted directly on social work, a predominantly female profession which had been making certain women invisible. It had done this by ignoring their status as women but seeing them mainly as categories of users. Within women-centred practice the notion of accepting women, believing women and the problems they bring, is associated with a process of women workers identifying with female clients by acknowledging commonalities and diversities (Hanmer and Statham, 1988; Dominelli and McLeod, 1989). But even this seemingly positive approach is contentious. Mainstream social work rejected it as unprofessional: 'To recognise commonalities is thought to raise the danger of over-identification, of over-emotional involvement, thereby producing an inability to respond to the clients' problems "objectively"' (Hanmer and Statham, 1988: 9). Echoing clearly earlier feminist critiques of mainstream social work and social work theory, where the 'textbook social worker' who remains professional and uninvolved in her classic 'empathy' (Brook and Davis, 1985: 119) is seen at best as unhelpful at worst it leads to victim blaming and prescriptive responses (Hanmer and Statham, 1988). However, for feminism to reframe the individual situation into a political perspective could be seen to be equally prescriptive, especially where that perspective might in the first instance be seen to be counter to the individual's immediate need. Who is to say that an individual's identified needs should not be attended to? The response to an abused woman that she needs to be part of a refuge and to join the political struggle against the patriarchal nature of our society is as meaningless and unhelpful as the interpretation that the violent relationship is part of her individual pathology based on her early childhood experiences (Wilson, 1980).

More problematic is that for some feminists the process of recognising diversity was overshadowed by the emphasis on recognising commonalities. This exercise was seen to reinforce notions of homogeneity of women and their experiences, obscuring social and other divisions and denying power differentials between women workers and service users. Hence it risks women social workers defining what feminism means in social work (White, 1995). In a study which attempted to test the usefulness of the concepts of commonality and diversity to feminist social workers, White notes that respondents reported that they found themselves unwittingly reinforcing women as the source of, and solution to, the problems presented.

The exploration of diversity was intended to acknowledge differences among women but transcend them. Feminist social workers, in attempting to work with differences, were constrained by official categorisation of 'client groups' which focus on certain aspects of problems to the neglect of gender, that is, there were restrictions on whom they counted as 'women'. Concentrating on child care problems assumes a higher priority in the management of social work and it is only in these contexts that users or clients are identified as women (White, 1995). Older women, disabled women and those with mental health problems were not consciously identified as women by the workers. A similar process was identified in Barnes and Maple's study of women with mental health problems. When women were identified there was concern that drawing attention to them might define or underline women's failings as mothers and reinforce or exacerbate mental health problems (Barnes and Maple, 1992). While the constraints of the statutory context might be seen to be responsible for the cautious development of feminist social work practice, White's findings also suggest there are limitations to feminist social work analyses which have failed to grapple with competing diversities and identities of those who are service users.

The challenge of postmodernism

As outlined above, contributions of postmodernism to understandings of difference in social work have been the focus of feminist analysis (Featherstone and Fawcett, 1995; Williams, 1996). In her threefold categorisation, diversity, difference and division, Williams suggests that focusing on one aspect of identity might merely eclipse other differences:

> Does the process of asserting a common identity as one which is forged in its specific difference mean that, first, other facets of the group's/person's identity are obscured, and that identities become frozen into an essentialist category of difference? (Williams, 1996: 71)

Her conclusion, that while identities are not fixed in stone for the purposes of consolidation they may have to be held as fixed, temporarily frozen, is important for understandings of what political project will be served by recognising common identities. In what could be seen as a direct challenge to Hanmer and Statham's encouragement for women-centred practice to identify commonalities and diversities, she asserts: 'We cannot assume that commonalities (as women, or among different groups) exist, nor can we override difference with false consensus' (Williams, 1996: 72). However, she offers little guidance on how to move forward. Resistance to categorisation might influence her identification of diversity and difference in calls for equal opportunities and anti-discriminatory practice. Even here Williams does not make links between feminist critiques of difference and possible feminist approaches to social work and social care practice, but neither does she fall into the trap of making prescriptions for practice. She warns that while the emergence of self-help, political activism and advocacy groups are seen as an outcome of raising issues of discrimination within welfare, they run the risk of freezing differences around different forms of oppressions.

This limitation, that there is no engagement with social work practice, echoes the conclusions of Featherstone and Fawcett (1995) who suggest that abandoning grand theories in favour of 'local contextual theorising' might help to validate those who stress the complexity and ambiguity of people's lives: 'The importance attached to subjectivity and meaning could also act as a corrective to the current tendency towards analyses which eschew any focus on the individual or relational dynamics in favour of exploring structural imperatives' (Featherstone and Fawcett, 1995: 36). However, the emphasis on, and exploration of, language and terminology in writing on postmodernism is sometimes seen to be unhelpful. It represents knowledge created, or claimed, in a remote and abstracted way which makes the ideas seem irrelevant to practitioners. Language which obscures has been criticised by Ussher who argues that too much academic feminist interpretation speaks to the converted, or speaks in a way that is not helpful to many or most women:

> Feminist theorising is often unintelligible to those not steeped in its traditions, those who do not have the privilege of education, of learning, of time to unravel the complex theorising and time to learn the new and often difficult language. (Ussher, 1991: 295)

It is perhaps for this reason that White found that some feminist analysis was not helpful for practitioners. Theoretical discourses need to be comprehensible and relevant to practice. The usefulness of postmodernism for social work must therefore be explored and translated very carefully. If social work has been derided for a conservative focus on individuals, seeing them as fitting into predetermined categories, then any critique of that individualised discourse, or construction of an alternative discourse, must be relevant to the circumstances in which social work and social care operate. It must deal with the lived experience of those for whom the services are, or should be, available. These may be recognised by reference to their experiences of being defined and categorised as 'men' or 'women', but it is more likely that they are constructed by other definitions such as 'older people', 'disabled' or 'mentally ill'. The subjectivity and meaning of the lives of users of community care services, or indeed any social work or social care service, could include many descriptions which recognise the complexity of people's identities and the diversity of their needs.

Ussher for example sees 'madness' as a signifier which positions people as ill, and she suggests that there is a need to look to the discursive practices recognising connections between discourses. The notion of discourse is used in the Foucauldian sense of regulated systems of statements which have a particular history (Ussher, 1991). Hence the way madness is understood varies at different historical moments, and would also be described differently in medical and sociological writings. Busfield, a sociologist writing in the field of mental health, accepts that there may be a plurality of languages, meanings and interpretations, and consequently explanatory accounts, but does not accept the postmodern conclusion that there is no independent reality. She suggests that there can be a world of agreed fact within the framework of shared meanings, and that postmodernism directs attention away from analysis of social structures and material resources. Its underlying assumptions, that everything is in fragments, destroys the basis for political action and intervention and constitutes a highly conservative framework (Busfield, 1996). The individualising tendencies of postmodernism have, according to Busfield, led many of those involved in the care of mental health disorders to ignore the importance of the social and material conditions of individuals' lives that are often conducive to mental disorder. What is required is an analysis on the basis of gender which is not solely about women. She offers a 'Theory of Gender' which consists of six underlying assumptions which she suggests must:

i. be based on feminist foundations, i.e. take a concern for women's lives as a starting point;
ii. reject epistemological relativism, a return to knowledge that accepts the existence of a real world that is potentially knowable ('a realist philosophy of social science'), and accepts the superiority of some claims over others;
iii. give proper attention to economic and material conditions, as well as to the realm of meanings, symbol and culture;

iv. involve systematic examination of the sources of power and of power relations, including the material bases of power, i.e. women's and men's relation to the labour force;

v. give proper attention to historical, cultural and material specificity – to help facilitate understanding of historical developments, and how these frame and inform understandings; and

vi. treat gender as an all-pervasive dimension of social relations and social institutions (Busfield, 1996: 48ff)

Her clear focus on women within an analysis of gender contrasts starkly with the conclusion of some postmodern feminists that what is necessary is jettisoning the category women (Butler, 1990). This latter theoretical position is probably not helpful for social workers who have to work with women who are both categorised, and categorise themselves, not only as women but as fulfilling particular roles, e.g. mother, wife, carer. On the other hand it may be helpful to those who have to work with women who do not conform to 'feminine' stereotypes, for example women who are violent or abuse children.

Despite the problematics posed by postmodernism, with its denial of a unified subject, its contibution has been to revisit definitions of gender. Those definitions which include the social relationships between women and men have influenced feminist social workers to widen both theoretical analysis and practice to include work with men.

Working with men

That men have featured in the work of feminist social work over time is not disputed, but this has usually been as the source of the oppression of women (for example, in situations of child abuse and domestic violence), or as non-contributors to the conditions with which women have to cope, such as child care and poverty. Attention to gender in social work has focused on the effects of sexism on men and has led to conclusions that the responsibility for change has been seen to lie with women (Thompson, 1995). One consequence of this is that men's behaviour has gone unchecked. The rationale for feminists working with men therefore has to go beyond incorporating feminist ideas about men into theoretical frames of reference, but to initiate change (Cavanagh and Cree, 1996).

This stance is not uncontentious, nor is it particularly well theorised in social work. In a rather simplistic essentialist definition, Thompson argues that masculinity is a social construction that establishes a set of gender roles, which in turn both define 'normal' behaviour for men and privilege that behaviour as the norm against which other behaviour (particularly that of women) is assessed or judged. In highlighting that duality of male/female behaviour, he argues that ' "anti-sexist" social work can have a role in breaking down gender stereotypes and releasing people from the restrictions and limitations inherent in patriarchal social relations' (Thompson, 1995: 464).

However, there is a tension between approaches highlighted by competing prescriptive lists, or codes of practice. Thompson draws attention to the negative effects on men of being cast in the role of oppressor (Thompson, 1995), while Cavanagh and Cree's starting point is that women are oppressed and that men inhabit privileged positions in relation to women. They see 'unsettling men' as their project (Cavanagh and Cree, 1996: 183).

In community care such a project may seem contentious. In working with male users of services who are older, disabled or experiencing mental health problems, to unsettle them on the basis that they enjoy the privileges of their male identity, ignores their shared experiences of oppression and powerlessness with women users of services. There would, for example, be little sense and not a great deal of empathy in challenging definitions and gendered assumptions with older people, male or female, who are already disoriented and confused. There is some evidence that men are more willing to take on domestic chores in later life (Arber and Ginn, 1991), but there is little to be gained in demanding this of all older men requiring care services. Such approaches in the area of race have been labelled as 'political correctness' by critics of social work, and have been cited in attempts to discredit social work education (Orme, 1994).

A more significant project may be to clarify how understandings and constructions of femininity and masculinity have influenced the way that services are provided and serve to perpetuate stereotypical assumptions which oppress and constrain both women and men.

Gender and community care

Acknowledging that there exist power differentials between professionals and service users, between those cared for and those providing care, and between those who theorise care and those who are being theorised about (both carers and those cared for), constitutes elements of the politics of care debate explored specifically within feminist literature (Evans, 1995). However, this debate has taken place predominantly around the process of caring (Finch and Groves, 1983; Ungerson, 1987; Graham, 1991).

It is difficult to engage in discussions about care without generating certain stereotypes or, in the parlance of postmodernism, particular subjectivities. The emphasis on the caring relationship from the perspective of who does the caring and what it entails has to a large extent ignored the experiences of those who receive the care. The imperative to recognise these experiences comes not from policy instructions associated with the NHS&CC Act to involve users, but from pressure from people (predominantly women) to hear the voices of those whose identities are constructed variously as clients, users, or who have been categorised as 'the disabled', 'the elderly' or 'the mentally ill'. Listening to the diverse experiences of people thus described has contributed to understandings of how those differences are constructed. That the voices have not been heard, even by feminist academics, has been argued strongly (Morris, 1993a). Morris's critique of the academic research process recognises other power balances, the divide between researcher and those who conduct the research. The power of the research process and the gatekeeping of who undertakes it has been significantly challenged by feminist research (Orme, 1997), but research findings have to be seen in their historical context. Morris rightly argues that early debates focused solely on the impact of community care on the lives of non-disabled, non-elderly women who were identified as shouldering a 'burden of care' (Morris, 1993b: 42), but getting women on the research agenda in social care was an achievement. The unintended consequences of conclusions drawn about impairment, that age and disability constituted a 'social death', reveal, according to Morris, unspoken prejudices and silence the voice of disabled women. Similarly, Dalley's description of 'dependent people and the women who usually care for them' (Dalley, 1988: 1) denies disabled women and older women identities as women. The assumption was that the category 'woman' was non-disabled and non-elderly (Morris, 1993b).

However, feminist contributions to community care are more positive than this. There can be a commonality in the projects to be pursued, but it is as yet unrecognised. The focus seems to be on emphasising conflict. User groups, especially in the field of disability, have influenced the policy agenda and have challenged early feminist assumptions:

> Debates about the nature of dependence, independence and interdependence, and related to these issues of power, choice and control have been central to disabled people's arguments. These are the very areas, however, which bring the disabled people's movement and the feminist analysis of informal caring most obviously into opposition. (Parker, 1996: 252)

These debates reflect conflict between attention to the needs of carers, and specifically women as informal carers, and the rights and needs of users which is at the core of much of community care policy and practice. Arguing that it is possible to work with the contradiction that women are simultaneously united as a group and also divided, Ramazanoglu (1989) emphasises active resistance rather than passive victim roles for women. This presents a challenge to social work practice where the notion of the term client, user and even customer has to date not suggested either political activity or resistance. The nature of clienthood has always been problematic for social work, carrying with it notions of power imbalance (Hugman, 1991). The introduction of care management in community care into welfare provision, based on the concept of the market, was intended to reflect some notion of choice. However, it does not necessarily change the power balances within interpersonal relationships. In fact it has been argued that community care, with its attendant emphasis on contracts and quality assurance, involves a rationalising and formalising of care while providing payment for care has created a professionalisation of informal care which has led to the loss of the 'caring' element of the relationship (Fox, 1995). Equally, a consideration of the processes of caring must involve an analysis of who does it and who receives it, otherwise women may be constrained to continue caring, or be expected to care, while men will have neither the injunction nor the opportunity to care. All of which has implications for the gendered analysis of care which has been at the heart of feminism.

Similarly, community care reforms with their emphasis on consultation, user involvement and choice have stimulated a discourse on empowerment. An aspect of empowering practice is to validate an individual's experience and find ways of linking this with others who may have common and shared experiences without losing the

particular individual identity or fragmenting the responses down to
a level that is meaningless. While recognising the limitations and
tensions of the relativism of postmodernism, and the lack of a
concrete agenda for action that such theoretical deconstruction
offers those who are feeling powerless, questioning and redefining
identities offers more positive opportunities. Feminism's engagement with notions of diversity allows for alliances between women
as carers and cared for, and between women and men who are
disabled, older or experiencing mental health problems. Challenging
how gendered assumptions have contributed to the social construction of men and women in certain client or user groups, it is also
possible to acknowledge the caring roles of men.

   While the preceding discussion illustrates that challenging stereotypical assumptions occurs at the level of the theoretical, it also
requires political and practical activity in social work which is
involved at the interface of the individual and the state.

Conclusion

This chapter has sought to provide an overview of the impact of
feminist theory on social work, social care and community care
practice. The influences have been progressive in that early feminist
analysis focused on women, and what was specific to their experiences and their ways of being. For social work this both challenged
traditional practice and stimulated the development of women
centred practice which sought to reduce the differences between
women workers and users and highlight their shared experiences
of oppression. In particular, women's caring capacity, and the
expectations that they would or should care, is seen to be a common
theme within both mainstream feminism and social work. While this
is introduced in this chapter, it is explored in greater detail in
Chapter 4.

   Putting women's experiences in the foreground in social work
was a significant step in the development of feminist social
work, but the analysis had its limitations. Attention to the diversity
of women's experiences as users of social work and social care
services, and how these may be shared with men who are service
users, leads to a consideration of how identities are structured by
experiences of oppression. Such considerations have resonance with
postmodernism, but the limitations of a highly theoretical and, at

times inaccessible, analysis are noted. It is suggested that a more helpful approach is to recognise how different experiences of women and men as users of social work and community care services helps to clarify understandings of constructions of masculinity and femininity. The questions raised about whether gender or other identities are the most significant descriptors have been raised by disabled feminists who have highlighted the limitations of feminist theorising about community care policies. Before looking in detail at research and practice evidence relating to disabled people which have resulted from this debate, it is necessary to outline the community care policies which have precipitated the analysis of this text.

2

Community Care: Policy and Practice

Introduction

Community care as a policy initiative was made explicit with the National Health Service and Community Care Act 1990, but some notion of community care has been present throughout the history of welfare provision. This chapter addresses the policy developments which led to the 1990s legislation, and their implications for social work and social care practice. In doing so it focuses on gender, analysing the way in which policy has impacted on women and men, and the way assumptions made about gender in the organisation of community care influence the processes of service delivery.

There are three strands within policy development which influence understandings of community care. The first is that the notion of community care carries with it implicit and explicit understandings of where the care should take place. Early notions of 'indoor' and 'outdoor' relief translated into institutional or residential provision as opposed to community care. However a further distinction was made in the 1970s between care 'in' the community, which might include small fully-staffed residential units, day centre provision or qualified domiciliary care, and care 'by' the community, which involves individuals being dependent upon the goodwill of family friends and neighbours: 'the provision of help, support and protection to others by lay members of societies acting in everyday domestic and occupational settings' (Abrams, 1977: 151).

This second strand, the distinction between the provision of care by state-funded workers and care by others, is often identified as the difference between formal care and informal care. In the reforms associated with the NHS&CC Act a third distinction in care provision has emerged. The introduction of the purchaser/provider split based on a market approach to welfare provision meant that more formal care was provided by voluntary and independent sector agencies, operating on a contractual basis, to provide packages of care arising out of assessments by local authority employees described alternatively as care managers or social workers.

It is these developments, the increased use of informal care and the broadening of formal care to the voluntary and independent sector, which have given impetus to the process of identifying a value and professional base for social care workers. As part of that value base attention to issues of gender are fundamental, impacting on analyses of who is involved in assessing for, identifying and providing care. The way that gender has influenced those who have been the recipients of services, those who have been identified as having need, or indeed who have been denied services, has been less apparent in the literature. This chapter, in trying to make this more explicit, therefore serves as part of an introduction to the rest of the text.

Beginnings of social work and social care in the community

Most commentators identify the beginnings of social work and social care with the reforms of the Poor Law. Although the emphasis is often on the Charity Organisation Society as the precursor of modern casework, it is also possible to identify the beginnings of community care policies in the work of its members.

Outdoor relief

Under the Poor Law the workhouse was available for those who were unable to support themselves, or be supported by friends and relatives. In the nineteenth century a gendered perspective as a determinant of practice was implicit and unquestioned in the organisation of services based on a model of familial and other support. The family unit comprised men and women in marital relationships and the expectation was that men would work until they died, and that women would be in relationships with men who would support them financially. Women, while engaged in labour in, for example, fields and factories, were also responsible for the production and care of large families, through childhood, and beyond if the family member was not able to become independent because of illness or impairment. Women became tied to their marital relationships, and often ended up in the workhouse if they were unable to achieve or maintain marital status; literature is scattered with accounts of the demise of young girls who gave birth to illegitimate children, for example. Other women who came to the attention of the Poor Law officials were those who were unable to cope with the exhausting grind of work, childbearing and poverty (Brook and Davis, 1985).

The provisions of the Poor Law also included 'outdoor relief', that is domiciliary or parish relief which constituted an early form of community care. Arguments for and against such relief, such care in the community, were subject to economic pressures, rather than decisions being made on what was best for the individual or the community. The dilemma was that although 'outdoor relief' was no more expensive than residential care it was more attractive and as such might encourage more people to apply for it, therefore increasing the overall bill. This outcome was not in line with a philosophy which ascribed to notions of deserving and undeserving poor, and which supported a policy that funds should be administered in such a way as to put off all but the most desperate.

The family and the Poor Law

In such policy initiatives the community was represented on the one hand by the immediate relatives who were expected to provide for the person if they were able to care for themselves, to prevent them requiring 'relief'. On the other hand, the community was represented by the smallest administrative unit, the parish. The Poor Law was gendered in its approach, but significantly gendered expectations were overlaid with class distinctions. The parish, and those who administered the 'relief' were in the main men, or women from upper-class backgrounds, who either through belief or compliance subscribed to the views reflected in the system and the way that it was administered. In assuming that paupers should suffer from their condition, harsh judgements were being made about those who, for whatever reason, were unemployed. Lifetime paid employment was an expectation of males, and while women's role in childbearing was recognised there is evidence that working-class women were expected to contribute to the economic solvency of the family unit, when that was necessary. Those who could make no contribution to the family unit became dependent on relief and the workhouses quickly filled up with orphans, elderly people, those who were sick and disabled, mentally ill people and those now described as having 'learning difficulties' (Sapsford, 1993). It is in this organisation that the beginnings of society's oppression of particular stigmatised groups can be plotted. Policies have been developed throughout the twentieth century which ultimately led to 'welfare' approaches to such groups which maintained them in a state of dependence, and often inappropriate residential accommodation.

Charitable relief

The harsh criteria of the Poor Law led to the proliferation of charitable relief, but this developed in an uncoordinated way with no apparent criteria for the help given. There was concern, not at the inequity of a system which meant that some people did not get help, but that the indiscriminate giving of charity might weaken the 'will' of those in receipt of help. Both the Settlement Movement and the Charity Organisation Society depended upon a belief in the civilising effects of the personal relations between the classes (Brook and Davis, 1985: 8), but these were also gendered in their development. The former was based on 'paternalistic enlightenment' involving the imposition of a set of cultural values and moral leadership. The involvement of women was limited, primarily because of the association of culture, values and morals with males, but also because the organisation and constituents were drawn from male undergraduates. There were also gender differences in their approaches to their work. Those women who did participate were the ones to venture out into the community to undertake service to individuals and families, while the men gave lectures and formed clubs (Lewis, 1991).

Women, men and charity

Workers with the Charity Organisation Society (COS) were predominantly women, albeit whose activities were being dictated and circumscribed by committees of men. With Octavia Hill as the figurehead, the 'traditional' female values of support and enriching personal experience were transmitted through the use of visitors, and the organisation of charity which enabled individuals and families to survive within their communities, despite the paradoxes of class and personal experience (Wilson, 1977). The aim of workers in the COS was to secure self-maintenance of those applying for assistance by demanding that men provide for their families, and that women exercise careful housewifery in support of men's efforts. Thus Octavia Hill, along with other women involved in social action, attempted to impose upon poor families a bourgeois family form with its gendered expectations which had different expectations of responsibilities within the family for women and men (Lewis, 1991). Additionally, the interventions were mainly through home visits, which meant that the involvement of women as recipients was greater than that of men. These women therefore became subject to regulation and were held responsible for the behaviour of the men.

Meanwhile, while some women were providing services, and being managed by men, the communities in which they worked were being analysed and defined by men. The social research of Joseph Rowntree and Charles Booth, for example, not only described the state of communities with statistical evidence but in doing so prescribed the nature of aid to be provided. In this distribution of effort is reflected the differential involvement of men and women in communities and organisations, and the different outcomes of that involvement. While these are explored in greater detail in the next two chapters, it is significant to note that the work was divided between the emotional, feminine caring, as exemplified by Octavia Hill and her workers, and the masculine rational analysis represented by the preoccupation with statistics and technical approaches. Some women, such as Beatrice Webb, were involved in social investigation which involved 'the study of aggregates rather than individuals' (Lewis, 1991: 15) and were therefore deemed to adopt a masculine rational approach.

The polarisation of masculine rational–feminine caring was therefore not always helpful. For example, the aggregated data of surveys such as that undertaken by Booth, recorded in *Life and Labour of the People of London* (1883), was reinforced by data documented in the individual case records of the COS and Settlement workers which reflected the more subjective accounts of the workers. Interestingly, the outcomes of such surveys were interpreted differently. Those involved in direct work, such as Hill, ascribed drunkenness, poverty and other social ills to individual moral failure. Others, including the Webbs, identified that social conditions reflected the failure of ruthless employers and landlords, and required collective public action (Younghusband, 1981). Significantly the unspoken (or unwritten) commentary is that in this analysis those predominantly held responsible are male. Equally important is that attention to the split between the individual and the collective response is a recurring feature in debates about social work and social care and has already been identified as a concern of feminist theorising.

The beginnings of social work and social care therefore involved women of social action, but with differential involvement of different social classes. For working-class women their duty and responsibility to both themselves and to social progress was achieved by fulfilling their 'wifely' duties. This suggests a circumscribed notion of social progress for working-class women whose involvement in the community or state was to be mediated through the family. Middle-class women who became involved in social action were inspired by their sense of duty which enabled them to fulfil their obligations as citizens. Social action not only involved women in work in the community, through the settlements by linking with fellow workers, or through membership of organisations, it also gave women, especially unmarried women, a sense of community (Lewis, 1991). Understandings of the relationship between community involvement and citizenship are significant for a gender analysis of community care and are the subject of the next chapter. The dual theme of development of welfare services based on particular conceptions of user, and the impact of that development on those involved in service provision is the focus for the rest of this chapter.

Women, men and welfare

Throughout the twentieth century changing demographic patterns have led to greater attention to the needs of different groups who are deemed to be in need of welfare. While women have been a continuing focus of those providing the services, the needs of men have overtly or covertly led to significant policy decisions which have impacted on the role and treatment of women within them. For example, the ageing population has become more dominated by females because of reduction in perinatal death rates, women's greater longevity and the loss of male lives in the Second World

War. The composition of the population of disabled people was similarly influenced by the Second World War, with a greater number of young men disabled as a result of it. This latter effect significantly influenced the development of the welfare state which sought to provide, among other things, a land fit for heroes. The Disabled Persons Act 1948 and other social reforms were driven by the need to maintain standards for a male workforce to sustain the economy, as well as a need to recognise, if not glorify, the contribution that men had made to the protection of the independent state. Women did not contribute directly to war because it was deemed to be 'not their way'. The impact of war on women is integrally tied to assumptions about women's role in caring for returning warriors, reflecting the care work explored in Chapter 4. It was difficult to justify women's involvement in war in any other way. The argument that they should sacrifice themselves 'for their country' made little sense when they were excluded from the means to citizenship and therefore did not feel a commitment to the country (Woolf, 1938).

Women and service

Women did, however, make their contribution and the two world wars marked the beginnings of women's paid involvement in the caring professions. They participated indirectly in war, working in hospitals as well as providing other 'service' industries such as drivers, landgirls and munition factory workers. Middle- and upper-class women, who were deemed 'surplus to the requirements of the male population' (Brook and Davis, 1985: 7) became involved in tasks such as hospital almoner which included interventions later identified as social work (Walton, 1975).

The Second World War was significant in that it claimed many more civilians as victims, and involved the evacuation of women and children from vulnerable cities. Social workers were called upon to deal with a range of practical and other problems: 'the tales of woe: children with lice infested heads, bed wetting, beer drinking mothers (seen as a rare phenomenon in country areas), and the rich variety of social and psychological problems one might expect when an urban population is displaced and families are disrupted' (Aves, 1983: 5). The emphasis changed to working with people in communities, however they might be prescribed; displaced communities or those created by the very process of evacuation.

Community provision

At the same time, emergent legislation such as the National Assistance Act 1946 influenced provision in the community. Informal purpose-built homes were gradually replaced Poor Law institutions. To facilitate integration people from the local community were encouraged to bring in outside interest and friendship. Statutory requirements under the National Assistance Acts encouraged better provision for those who were then deemed 'handicapped persons', but the emphasis was on material services, not so much on social work as a necessary element, while services for older people were not seen as a statutory responsibility. At this point the existence of separate welfare and children's departments symbolised the different emphasis in attention given to groups of people, with the needs of groups who now constitute the users of community care services being of lower priority to those of children. Women as mothers remained in the full view of workers' critical gaze, while in other services women were rarely acknowledged, other than in negative ways. Men rarely featured as the focus of the social work gaze or investigation.

Ironically, this emergent provision marks the beginning of the 'history of neglect' in both residential services and services necessary to maintain people in need in the community (Means and Smith, 1994). For example, neglect was evident in the use of large inhuman asylums for people with mental health problems. The differential impact on women and men of this neglect was apparent. However, a feature of the neglect was the denial of individual identity and agency. Therefore, it may be that the discrimination was inadvertent rather than directly gendered.

This was not so for all groups. The categorisation of those with learning difficulties under the 1913 Mental Deficiency Act and their separation from their families was to protect them from exploitation, but also to protect society from the moral threat they posed. This was particularly so in the case of women who by virtue of their low intelligence were assumed to be prone to loose morals, promiscuity and liable to carry disease (Abbot and Sapsford, 1987). The consequences of 'loose morals' were not so apparent for men with low intelligence who, despite being more prevalent in the population, did not experience negative labelling in the same way and were not institutionalised to quite the same extent (Williams, 1992).

Institutional care

The treatment of those in institutions and groups marginalised in other ways became the subject of research reports and public scandals which led to theoretical questioning of the appropriateness and effectiveness of institutions (Goffman, 1961). For some the focus was on the interaction between society, the individual and the institution and the functions of institutions as controlling those perceived as deviant (Foucault, 1977). Significantly, in observations which illustrate the gender-blind research which has been the subject of feminist criticism discussed in the previous chapter, Jones and Fowles claim the social control mechanisms operating were arbitrary but were 'class biased, penalising the poor, the black and the immigrant' (Jones and Fowles, 1984: 11), but with no mention of gender. This conclusion either ignores women's experience, or assumes that they did not have the capacity to be deviant, or, if they did, suggests that society would be too paternalistic to confine them in institutions. The latter was patently not true. Institutions were warehousing significant numbers of women. It was not only that women were being constrained in institutions, but often this occurred because of assumptions about their womanliness. Either they were not behaving in ways which were expected and accepted, they were being deviant as women, or they had failed to arrange their lives in ways that meant that they could be provided for by others, that is men.

Similarly Means and Smith explain the history of neglect of older people, people with disabilities and people with mental health problems by exploring a variety of perspectives, including political economy perspectives, the power of institutions, and the politics of implementing community care, but in none of these do they suggest that gender was a feature. It is only when addressing informal caring and cultural stereotypes that they make explicit reference to gender issues (Means and Smith, 1994: 38f). Gender issues are seen to be significant only when considering those who provide the care, and by default only women are implicated. This denies that all aspects of social care, including those who provide it and those who receive it, are imbued explicitly and implicitly with understandings and assumptions of gender differences and that these differences impact on women and men.

Social care

With greater attention being given to residential care the emergence of social care as an aspect of social work became significant. The distinctions between social work and social care have been the subject of much debate, and while the analysis of the strands of the activities is not the prime purpose of this text, what is significant is that debates about the role and function of a predominantly female profession call into question the skills and expertise necessary for its performance. Younghusband notes that those who feared that the reforms brought about by Beveridge would kill social work as a profession failed to recognise that what she calls social care was something much broader than financial help alone. Throughout her short history of social work she identifies a strand of social care, or personal social services, which she sees as an absolute requirement of the performance of social work (Younghusband, 1981).

Ironically it was the female involvement in providing these services which Younghusband had criticised in her earlier report (1947). Social work and social care provided in the community as the precursor of community care were seen as female activities, so much so that Geraldine Aves in an Eileen Younghusband Lecture claims that in the 1950s social work was an exclusively female profession, and that when Younghusband insisted on recruiting men, this was seen by the then Ministry of Health as a 'curious aberration' (Aves, 1983).

Within the context of a history of care, it is interesting to note that social care involved a laudable requirement that 'individuals of any age must grow and be sustained as whole people if they are not to atrophy or become distorted as persons' (Younghusband, 1981: 18). Identified means of social care, of helping people to grow in their social relationships, included self-government, self-help groups and active involvement of clients in decision making in the services they received. Younghusband (1981) suggested that this notion of care also operated within the work of some individuals within residential care, and she claimed that by the early 1970s it permeated services and professions other than social work. These observations provide a significant precursor to the language and philosophy of the 1990s community care legislation.

Social care, in Younghusband's view, was therefore a positive which needed wider application. However, this position provides a problematic which continues to vex writers on anti-discriminatory practice: if social care was such a good thing why was it to be preserved only for those who, in Younghusband's terms, were considered 'underdog'? As a means of self-fulfilment it is presumably desirable for all, but it was only provided for those who were deemed not capable of providing for themselves. Individuals and groups in receipt of social care were traditionally those who were institutionalised, and who subsequently became the centre of community care policies, but as such they have been identified as experiencing oppression and discrimination by virtue of being in receipt of services, of being clients of welfare agencies. If social care was to reflect or make available to some groups a sense of self-worth, it is an irony that social work did nothing to prevent the sense of worthlessness experienced by some because of attitudes towards them, attitudes which were exacerbated by the existence of social work as a profession created to 'deal' with them.

Community care

With the emergence of the welfare state the notion of community care became more concretised in legislation. The Mental Health Act of 1959 and the 1962 Hospital Plan sought to close large mental hospitals, and assumed a network of services to be provided by local health and welfare services and available to those who would subsequently be placed in community provisions. Similarly in work with older people, the notion of community care involved a move away from hospitalisation, but more explicit expectations that local authority residential care was part of community provision (Aves, 1964). Care in this sense was 'in' the community, but did not require anything of the community, other than an acceptance of small residential units in the neighbourhood.

Marking this 'community phase' of the development of community care (Payne, 1995) was the implementation of the Seebohm Report (Seebohm, 1968). Reflecting the social democracy of the 1960s and imbued with a liberal commitment to enhancing social citizenship, the Seebohm Report argued for the creation of a community-based family service provided by local authorities and assumed the existence of a network of reciprocal relationships which, among other things, would ensure mutual aid and give those who experienced it a sense of well-being (Langan, 1993). While independent sector organisations such as the Cheshire Homes had developed the concept of the 'family home' for young physically disabled people, the focus of Seebohm was on non-residential services, that is services for people in their homes, supported by family members, rather than the organisation of residential services along family lines (Means and Smith, 1994).

Representations for community-based services were made on a number of grounds. The cost of residential and hospital provision was certainly a powerful influence, but concern about standards of care was also a significant factor (Means and Smith, 1994). However, the status of the particular groups who were subject to residential care was seen to be important, not least in recognising the need to have services provided in ways which entitled them to the rights of other citizens. Developments were slow and the main impetus of the mid-1980s came from the involvement of the private sector in the provision of residential and nursing home facilities, predominantly for older people.

These developments drew attention to the way that care provision in the community would be organised and the implications of this for women. What emerged was a series of contradictory expectations. There were implicit expectations that women would be both providers and receivers of the emergent social services. They were to contribute to the needs of the state and immediate communities by their involvement in paid work in the developing facilities, but when they did so they were criticised for not demonstrating or fulfilling the expressive, emotional and natural feminine characteristics associated with a performance of motherhood which involved full-time child care (Brook and Davis, 1985). It was the assumptions of the naturalness of motherhood which meant that women were also called upon to provide the informal care which was an important feature of the emergent community care policies. However, it was predominantly in the field of child care that women were recognised as receivers of social services, when they were subject to the inspectorial gaze of social workers if they failed to meet the requirements of 'good enough' mothering (Hanmer and Statham, 1988). Men are significantly absent from these discourses, either as recipients or as formal or informal providers of care.

Beyond state welfare

By the early 1980s community care policies were about keeping people out of hospitals and homes. The shifting emphasis was also away from state provision to informal and voluntary provision, and the distinctions between care *in* the community and care *by* the community were already being drawn (DoH, 1981). The growing government unease at the mushrooming private sector paralleled the concerns in the late nineteenth century at the disorganisation of the charitable organisations. Hence for the Conservative government of the 1990s community care became a means of moving away from direct state provision towards the recognition of a mixed economy of welfare.

The Barclay Report

The Barclay Report had been commissioned by an incoming Conservative government to review the organisation and delivery of personal social services by local authorities. In undertaking the review it introduced notions of community social work which drew on research evidence about the effectiveness of services organised on small geographic units of 'patch'. In doing so it added to the understanding of social care by making distinctions between social work activities such as individual counselling and 'social care planning'. The latter concept was linked to a notion of 'brokerage' which involved putting together packages of care at the 'street or village level' drawing resources from statutory, voluntary and informal networks (Barclay, 1982: 198ff).

Community social work

This brokerage was accompanied by notions of community social work, which was distinct from earlier understandings of community work. Community social work involved formal social work which was problem-focused, but worked with local networks of formal and informal relationships to help resolve those problems. In this way it was unlike community work in that workers would retain their statutory responsibilities (Barclay, 1982: xvii). The proposition in Barclay was that there would be community social workers who would engage more closely with communities, and in being more accessible would receive different kinds of referral; they would specifically discourage dependency by not opening cases precipitously or keeping them open unnecessarily. They would draw on informal and community sources of support in offering help and to avoid involvement of statutory workers (Fuller and Tulle-Winton, 1996: 682). All of these clarifications of community social work rested on the Committee's understandings of the nature of community which is discussed in greater detail in the next chapter.

In their recommendations the Barclay Committee could be seen to be preparing the way for the more fundamental changes to state welfare provision which were brought about by the 1990s legislation. The proposals were never directly implemented but were mediated through several stages of review before being introduced in a far more radical form. In the light of the subsequent history of social work it seems ironic to observe that the changes envisaged by Barclay were seen to be threatening to the profession of social work. Part of this threat was from the introduction of informal support such as volunteers. It was the threat to professionalism rather than any acknowledgement of such changes in service delivery which was the focus of social work concern.

Even those who argued for the role of volunteers (Aves, 1983), both as a positive contribution to the means to meet the ever-increasing demands for social work intervention, and as a way of validating the work of many who were involved in voluntary action, did not identify who would be the volunteers. There were difficulties in recognition and definition:

> Recognition of who in contemporary society volunteers are demands a very broad approach. There are difficult issues associated with the question of unemployed persons being volunteers; there is need to appreciate the part played by neighbours whose contribution to meeting social need cannot be over-estimated and who certainly do not see themselves as volunteers. Great care must be taken not to tarnish the spontaneity of their help by any effort to systematise it. There is too the question of the extent to which it is reasonable to describe people as volunteers when they achieve some financial reward for their services. (Aves, 1983: 13)

Significantly no mention is made of the fact that the unemployed persons, the neighbours and others who are the volunteers were invariably women, and as with the workers in the Charity Organisation Society, women of a certain class. Equally the dilemmas about payment for care are complex. Baldock and Ungerson's research indicates that there are taken-for-granted arrangements between family, friends and neighbours which involve payment in both cash and kind, but that those involved would not see themselves as volunteers or carers (Baldock and Ungerson, 1994). However, that these arrangements exist provides an added dimension to the debate in feminist social policy about the implications of payment of women for informal care. The resistance is not to the transfer of money or goods as a recognition of the service provided, but to the formalisation of such arrangements in ways which would both deny the female carers' choice, transforming it into an expectation or duty, and thus changing the nature of the relationship.

Mixed economy of provision

The Audit Commission Report (1986) represented a tightening of policy initiatives begun with Barclay. While the community social workers described above developed on a small scale, they almost disappeared by default rather than design because they became victim to a series of economically driven reforms from central government policies: 'which combined at the end of the 1980s and in the early 1990s to reduce local government autonomy, cap spending, prescribe essential separate services for children and other service users, and introduce market mechanisms' (Hadley and Leidy, 1996: 825). The Commission highlighted the slow and uneven responses to community care provision, identifying six features of positive schemes and effective innovation: strong and committed local champions of change; focus on action not bureaucratic machinery; local integrated services; focus on local neighbourhood; team approach, and partnership between statutory and voluntary agencies.

The barriers to community care were seen to be in the resistance of social services and health authorities to innovation and delegation. Tensions and rivalries between the health services and social services in the provision of care were said to have led to an emphasis on services not clients, and the criticisms of the duplication of services provided by different agencies, accompanied by risk of people falling between services, echoed those made prior to the setting up of the Seebohm Committee. However, while the rhetoric of the Audit Commission sounded sympathetic to the philosophies of community social work, the policy outcomes led to, among other things, services fragmented by group specialisation and the purchaser/provider split; increasingly prescribed methods of organisation, and the reduction of professional autonomy and local discretion (Hadley and Leidy, 1996).

Despite the commitment of some to its principles (Smale *et al.*, 1988), community social work was not necessarily all positive. Feminist criticisms of many forms of community action in the 1970s and 1980s highlighted the expectation that women contribute actively to community developments by, for example, providing access to local networks, while the direct needs of women in the community were not met (Dominelli and McLeod, 1989). Although community social work is distinct from community action, it could be subject to the same criticisms. Additionally, identifying the positives of early detection and prevention of, for example, crises in child care, ignored a consequence of community social work that women were pulled into the welfare net, and their function as mothers and carers was monitored in a way that male roles in families were not. Meanwhile, injunctions to involve local people in planning and support took no cognisance of the different participation of women and men in community action, nor of the specific arrangements which might have to be made to ensure the involvement of all women, and of Black women in particular.

Packaging care

It was with the Griffiths Report (1988) that the significant changes to arrangements for community care were introduced. The major relevant recommendations for local social services authorities included the requirement to liaise with health and the voluntary sector for planning purposes. Individual needs were to be identified and assessed, taking into account personal preference, and packages of care were to be designed which were best suited to enable the consumer to live as normal a life as possible. These packages of care would be delivered by building on available contributions, in the first instance from informal carers and neighbourhood support. To avoid the expensive use of residential care domiciliary and day care would be offered before residential care was provided. While local authorities retained the lead role in community care provision, Griffiths was explicit that the new arrangements were likely to change the way in which professional social workers operated, and make more use of staff who were not qualified as social workers (Griffiths, 1988). Local authority social workers would act as designers, organisers and purchasers of non-health care, but not as direct providers. They were to make maximum use of voluntary and private sector bodies to widen consumer choice, stimulate innovation and encourage efficiency, thus using managerial functions and skills needed to buy in services.

Like much policy and legislative documentation the Griffiths Report was not explicit about the implications of such a shift in the organisation and delivery of community care. The closest it came was to recognise that skills transfer from professional staff to informal carers would be overt, without acknowledging the impact of a transfer of function from a professional workforce which was predominantly female to unpaid informal carers who would also be predominantly female. It could be argued that because this was a shift of emphasis between different groups of women it was neither gendered nor discriminatory. However, the analysis is more complex than this. If the 'community carers' identified in the Audit Commission were not to be social workers, but unqualified low-paid workers, or unpaid volunteers and family members, the shift would be in the way that work undertaken predominantly by women was recognised, valued and remunerated. As such it provides a prime example of how issues to do with women, based on taken-for-granted expectations of the different roles of women and men, were not being addressed in policy and legislation, even though discrimination legislation dealing with race and gender had been in place for some fifteen years.

Equality of opportunity

The White Paper *Caring for People* (DoH, 1989) in the main followed the proposals of the Griffiths Report. In transforming the role of social services departments from that of service providers to 'enabling agencies', and emphasising the government's aim to 'promote choice as much as independence' and to 'make maximum use of the independent sector', it introduced community care planning and care management, both of which were imbued with notions of user consultation and involvement. The White Paper made explicit, but passing, reference to the need to consult with members of ethnic minority communities to ensure services were responsive to their needs (DoH, 1989), thus responding to the reviews of social services which had been carried out in conjunction with the Commission for Racial Equality in the wake of the Race Relations Act 1976 (ADSS/CRE, 1978). However, although there had been parallel legislation to counteract discrimination on the basis of sex, there was no positive or explicit reference to issues of gender. Indirectly, the acknowledgement that the bulk of informal care is carried out by friends, neighbours and kin, carries with it recognition of the gendered divisions in care work, but there is no reference to the potential for the different needs of women and men users of the service, or explicit requirements that women as users and carers should be consulted as part of the community care planning process.

The limitations of the 1970s discrimination legislation are that it gives stronger powers to local authorities to intervene in matters to do with race but not sex (Section 71 of the Race Relations Act), and its emphasis is on formal equality. Welfare and family legislation are exempt from the remit of the Equal Opportunities Commission (EOC) which means that it does not impact on the most powerful aspects of women's lives: 'For most women, the sexual division of labour within the home is a central reality of their lives and yet this has been specifically excluded from the terms of reference of the Sex Discrimination Act' (Gregory, 1987: 22). The reasons given were that the government did not want to intervene in the private relationships of citizens, yet in both the intended and unintended consequences of community care legislation the government has made significant impact on the lives and private relationships of citizens, both women and men. That is, of course, if it is taken as given that older people, disabled people and those with mental health problems do have the status of citizenship, an issue which is discussed in Chapter 3.

To go beyond formal equality, to acknowledge the substantive inequalities which prevent people from competing on equal terms, raises dilemmas in discussing the treatment of women in the context of gender. Laws which offer women special protection purely on the basis of their sex may perpetuate and reinforce myths of female inferiority. To have legislation which purports to provide equality in the workplace, but at the same time to introduce legislation which perpetuates the stereotype of women as dependent on men and available as care givers to all, denies, or at least creates barriers to, access to the workplace. This suggests either hypocrisy or a gross misunderstanding of the processes of discrimination. Welfare legislation is rarely explicit in its gender assumptions, it merely reflects and reinforces attitudes which are generally held (Orme, 1992). While women were becoming more apparent in the workplace (and not just in schools, hospitals and social services departments) they continued to shoulder the burden of child and family care (Hewitt, 1993). This reflects a set of assumptions reminiscent of the philosophy of the Poor Law, that men are required to be the bread winners, and that they have limited capacity to care. Not only are women discriminated against because of their lack of status in the paid labour force, but men who wish to make a contribution to the caring may be perceived as uncommitted workers. To make inroads into this requires raising awareness at all levels, and ensuring welfare legislation policy be 'equality proofed' to prevent it inadvertently impacting differentially on women and men. A consequence of this may be that the positive statements which are beginning to be made to counteract discrimination on the basis of race in, for example, the Children Act might also address issues of gender.

A further limitation of the equality legislation was that it only applied to 'market place activities' and so excluded a number of government activities. Therefore, while it can be invoked in employment practices of social services, it does not extend to services; the actual practices of social services departments are not open to scrutiny. Through training, the Central Council for Education and Training in Social Work (CCETSW) has made some impact on the attention paid by social services to issues of discrimination especially on the basis of race (Orme, 1991), and most local authorities have equal opportunities' policy statements. The community care reforms could be scrutinised and perhaps challenged as discriminatory because they constitute a move from qualified to unqualified staff, and therefore contribute to a reduction in the status of a predominantly female workforce, but it is unlikely that such a challenge would get very far. A more interestingly complex issue is the impact of the move to the 'market place'. Such a move could enable social services departments to commission services only from provider agencies who demonstrated they were working within the spirit and the letter of all anti-discriminatory legislation. However, local authorities, through local government legislation (Local Government Act 1988) introduced under Margaret Thatcher, were prevented from imposing 'non-commercial' conditions on contracts. This effectively curtailed contract compliance in relation to employment of racial groups and made it illegal in relation to women (Gregory, 1987). Under the New Labour administration compulsory competitive tendering has to be governed by principles of 'best value'. It could be argued that the notion of value could include the principles of equality of opportunity, but in the main the emphasis is on economic value.

The responsibility to ensure that services are fair, that there is equality of access and appropriate response to need, that services acknowledge difference but do not discriminate unfairly on the basis of those differences must operate, at all levels in the care management process.

Care management in community care

The National Health Service and Community Care Act 1990, which was passed very quickly after publication of the White Paper, was not accompanied by the repeal of previous legislation; it did not seek to replace it but to impose upon the delivery of social and care services a particular ideology. Specific legislation in the field of mental health, disability and complex arrangements for the provision of statutory residential and domiciliary services remain, but in considering the gendered aspects of the delivery of social work and social care services, the introduction of care management is a focal point in the changes to delivery of service.

As has been argued, the changes brought about impact upon employees of the statutory, voluntary and independent services commissioning and providing care, and on individuals and families providing care in the community on an informal basis. The rhetoric was that the changes should benefit users of the services, emphasising the government's aim to 'promote choice as much as independence' (DoH, 1989). However, in promoting choice and independence an important group to be considered are those who might require services but, for whatever reasons, do not receive them. It is often in the latter categories that the impact of assessments for services based on stereotypical gender assumptions is greatest.

Care management can be both a method of social work, a way of intervening in the lives of those who have identified needs, and a form of managing, of organising the delivery of services to individuals and groups of users (Orme and Glastonbury, 1993). The major processes for care management include: identification of people in need, assessment of care needs, planning and securing delivery of care plans, monitoring the quality of care provided and reviewing client needs (DoH, 1989, 3.3.4: 21), but despite specific guidance there is a multiplicity of models of implementation for care management (Lewis *et al.*, 1997). The gender implications of the various aspects of the process can be identified at a theoretical level, but this text, in assessing the literature on specific groups, will analyse how the complexities of attention to issues of gender provide the means to review the value base of social work and the practice implications as influenced by policy and legislation. First, an overview of the processes of care management may help to clarify the potential ways in which gendered attitudes might influence practice.

Identification of people in need

Information is required for budgeting purposes by purchaser organisations, namely the local authorities and health services, and can be gathered from large-scale data sets such as demographic, census and referral data. This can be used to ensure flexible services by stimulating voluntary and independent sector provider agencies. If the process of identifying need is not undertaken comprehensively, it will both limit the funding that can be made available for individual packages of care, and restrict the range of services available. For example, if due note is not taken of the ethnic composition of a particular geographical area, then the facility and finance for professional, independent interpreting services will not be available. Equally, if the demographic changes brought about by an ageing population do not recognise the predominance of women in the older age groups, then the information will not be put to best effect. However, while there are some obvious systems that are needed to meet the needs of Black and ethnic minority groups, the existence of systemic discrimination suggests that organisations are not good at addressing fully the needs of discriminated groups because they are often imbued with cultural assumptions which may indirectly exacerbate oppression and discrimination (Young, 1990b).

Collective responses

There is potential for a shift from the individualised culture of social work provision to one of pooling information through the identification of needs. If this occurs it could lead to responsive and innovative services designed to both identify individuals with similar needs and recognise the resources to meet those needs. Truly innovative services could allow for contracts to be given to cooperatives, or groups of users who themselves could meet identified care needs. Feminist critiques of social work described in the previous chapter led to suggestions that women's needs might best be met outside the welfare system (Wilson, 1977). Ironically, community care legislation meant that this radical shift might be met by changes brought about by a conservative ideology of the market. Opportunities could arise for collectives of, for example, older women to respond to identified need (Dalley, 1996) and to set themselves up as provider agencies. However, the tendency of purchasing agencies to engage in block contracts with larger voluntary and independent sector agencies has meant that opportunities for innovation, or user-led organisations to become provider agencies have been limited. More significantly campaigning feminist and anti-racist groups have been constrained in their capacity to act as advocates if they wished to become provider agencies (Langan, 1992). Meanwhile, provision which had been user-led was threatened by moves towards a purchaser/provider split to the withdrawal of government funding on the basis of grant aid. Such moves created which led threats to the collective provision by women in organisations such as Women's Aid and Rape Crisis who have had to form themselves into limited companies in order to qualify for financial support.

Assessment of care needs

The assessment of need is pivotal to care management but is only part of the total process. Assessment contributes to identification of global needs, it informs decisions about whether an individual package of care should be provided, it specifies the component parts and level of service delivery within that package. As such it becomes the action plan for the service providers, the budget indicator for the purchasing agency and the blueprint for quality assurance processes (Orme and Glastonbury, 1993).

Policy guidance that the assessment has to be an integrated system, separated from the provider services in order that it is consistent with a needs-led approach, but at the same time mindful of definitions of need and limitations of resources, is fine in principle but difficult to achieve in practice. The need to be engaged in a process, but to be totally unaware of, or agnostic about, the services that are or might be available is unrealistic. However, it is the practice of fitting assessment of need into available services which has had the greatest impact on the gendered allocation of resources, in terms of the nature of the services allocated, to whom, and who provides informal care.

The outcome of the assessment, an individual care plan, is closely linked to the process of producing it and, more significantly, who is involved in that process. Assessments should be interdisciplinary and involve users and carers. The involvement of both these groups can lead to a conflict of interests, and it is in these negotiations that competing rights of service users to choose what kind of care they would like, and the right of women relatives not to have to care, have to be addressed by the person undertaking the assessment. Assumptions about the nature of care arrangements have to be avoided, or at least challenged, if they perpetuate stereotypical assumptions about the differing caring capacities of women and men, in terms of caring for themselves and others.

Planning and securing the delivery of care

Once needs have been assessed, workers negotiate how these can be met, and in doing so will engage with whatever managerial and budgetary devolution arrangements are in place to ensure the provision of care packages. During this process, as will be demonstrated in the later chapters of this book dealing with the perspectives of particular user groups, gendered assumptions by care givers and care receivers may influence the allocation of resources. Systems will be required to ensure that services are available and these involve the process of commissioning.

Commissioning

In the first instance the services provided will be influenced by the views of those who commission the services. The commissioning process operates on a continuous basis to ensure that a range of services are available to meet the requirements of care plans, and contractual arrangements with voluntary and independent sector providers are central to this. Without innovation and imagination there will be limited choice for meeting needs, and services will be offered on the same lines as they were before the legislation, with users having their needs defined by what is available rather than by innovative and flexible responses. Commissioning has to respond to both identified needs from demographic data, and aggregated data from care plans. Provision can be made by recruiting volunteers, contracting with voluntary and independent sector organisations for service provision or creating an internal market within the statutory sector. However, if the notion of choice and user empowerment is to be fully realised, then the potential for one-off resources to respond to the particular need of an individual also has to exist.

As with assessment, awareness of the potential for discriminating on the basis of gendered assumptions is ever present in the commissioning process (Arber and Gilbert, 1989; Boniface and Denham, 1997). Who receives day centre places, and the allocation of resources from personal assistants to meals on wheels will influence the number and nature of contracts and the expectations of providers within those contracts. For example, if staff in a particular day centre for disabled people assume it will have predominantly female users, they may decide not to have workshops which provide technical skills, but to confine activities to those which are traditionally 'female' such as handicrafts and soft toy making. Equally, because of assumptions about the 'naturalness' of women to provide personal care, local authority managers may automatically recruit a female workforce of personal assistants, thus not providing male users with the choice of having a male personal assistant.

Consumers of care

Critiquing assumptions of empowerment and choice in a consumerist model of social care, Walker concludes that the only way frail and vulnerable service users can be assured influence and power over service provision is if they or their advocates are guaranteed a 'voice' in the organisation and management of services. A consumer-oriented model is contrasted with the user-centred or empowerment approach, the intention of which would be to 'provide users and potential users with a range of realisable opportunities to define their own needs and the sorts of services they require to meet them' (Walker, 1993: 222). The gendered implications of this are that services must be able to respond to the identified and articulated need, but be aware of the influence of constructions of gendered lives among those who are in receipt of services. The requirement for a change of attitude to reflect professional values which regard cooperation and partnership as a normal activity has to be accompanied by an awareness of the heterogeneity of user group categories. Walker underlines the need to challenge existing practices including: 'the traditional basis of professional status and providing for the input of informed user knowledge and preference, which means finding ways for community members to take part in the development of community care policy – in short, power sharing' (Walker, 1993: 223). However, such power sharing has to be mindful of the different ways in which power operates between men and women.

Monitoring the quality of care provided

Having contracted with provider agencies, individual carers and volunteers for the provision of the component parts of the care package, the care manager has to monitor the quality of care provided. As has been stated, the assessment document provides the blueprint in the first instance, in that it identifies the nature and level of the care required. Care managers can work to service agreements with provider agencies to ensure levels of care, and may need to invoke contract compliance in situations where standards are not being met. More significantly, systems for involving the user in monitoring and assessing the quality of care will be essential for feedback to the care manager who will not be in constant attendance.

Such systems could include straightforward logging of contact by those providing the care, confirmed by those receiving it. Similarly, performance indicators based on the length of time it takes for an agency to respond to a request can be accepted as measures of quality. What is more complex is the assessment of quality which can be influenced by individual perspectives of what is required and when. The rejection of a service offered by an individual volunteer might be based on real limitations of that volunteer, or it may be the result of a personality clash with the user of the service. The task of the care manager is therefore to balance the expectations of the user with a realistic appraisal of what it is possible to provide. In the process significant weight might be given to the ways in which assessments, complaints and criticisms are made. Work on the provision of care has suggested that male carers have received more services, perhaps because they make assumptions about their rights or are generally more assertive because of experiences in the work-place (Ungerson, 1987). Alternatively, stereotypical assumptions about older women identified among caring staff could have paral-lels in the attitudes of domiciliary staff, so that their complaints or criticisms may be trivialised or ignored.

Review of client needs

The process of review is part of an ongoing assessment in that procedures are established to ensure that the requirements of the original care plan are met and are still relevant to the needs of the individual user. This last point is crucial in that care plans are made for individuals who have the potential for rapid changes in their situation. Older people and those with mental health problems are likely to have unpredictable changes in their situations, while adults with physical disabilities might present more stable circum-stances. The responsibility of the care manager is to keep a watching brief and to be alert to any changes. These can be identified by periodic visits to the individual user, but this may be perceived as being intrusive and bureaucratic. Alteratively, they may be ensured by a system of feedback from the service providers. A programme of regular or periodic reviews is essential for maintaining standards and ensuring that needs are met. These reviews can take the form of mini-assessments or reassessments. However, the potential for reviews precipitated by changes in the situation of the user must also be instituted, but it is this aspect of the policy which has fallen by the wayside because of the high workloads involved in care management (Lewis *et al.*, 1997). Reviews, if they occur, are carried out by less skilled staff in providing agencies or by non-skilled relatives and others alerting care managers to perceived changes in the situation. As Busfield points out, the implications of this form of deprofessionalised assessment may have significant implications, especially for people with mental health problems (Busfield, 1996). Chapter 5 explores the consequences of behaviour associated with mental illness being interpreted incorrectly on the basis of gendered assumptions, unfamiliarity with symptoms, or because of concerns about risk either to the user, or those involved in their care. Addi-tionally, the point made above about the different ways in which needs are attended to could impact on older women who might not daw attention to their deteriorating circumstances.

Impact of care management

As well as impacting on the provision of care, changes identified with care management occurred in the organisation of social services departments. These include a flattening of the job hierarchy, which led to a depression of wages (Lewis *et al.*, 1997). It is significant that this occurs in a profession which is predominantly female and is accompanied by changes in approaches to education and training for the profession which depends on technical competencies (Ford and Hayes, 1996). This diminution of the status of formal care work is accompanied, through developments in payment for care through such legislation as Direct Payments (Services) Act 1996, by the commodification of care in the informal arena, that is payment for acts of caring which can depersonalise the process and make it subject to market forces. The implications of such policies for the gendered nature of caring is discussed in Chapter 4.

Users and carers

It has been argued that some of the weaknesses in the implementation of community care policies relate to continuities of assumptions rather than negative impact of radical change (Means and Smith, 1994). For example, the assumption that efforts should be made to support carers in their caring functions, rather than giving carers choice in whether they want to care, and users choice in the methods and means of care they prefer, is exacerbated by the lack of resources to ensure high quality alternative caring provision. While many recognise that the development of effective community care provision depends on levels of financial and other resources made available, it is argued that changes in organisation for service delivery, in particular the involvement of users and carers in decisions about the nature of provision, will be significant and will produce enough positive change. The Carers (Recognition and Services) Act 1995 made a distinction between carers and users, acknowledging that they have different needs and competing rights However, if the practice of social and community care fails to recognise the distinctions within categories such as 'users' and 'carers', not least that an individual can be both a user and provide care for others (Manthorpe, 1994), then it will continue to oppress. When individuals are categorised according to user groups, such as people with disabilities, older people and people with mental health problems, the differences and the similarities are seen to be significant. But a further deconstruction of these categories reveals the complex identities of those who are recipients of services, that they are not members of homogeneous groups of older people, people with learning difficulties or those with mental health problems, but are men and women from different class, ethnic and religious backgrounds.

Conclusion

This chapter has plotted policy developments which led to the organisation of service delivery around community care with a cursory overview of the processes of care management. It has been noted that gender has not been overtly referenced in the formal policy statements but impacts at all levels in service provision, on formal and informal care providers and recipients.

The greatest acknowledgement of gender in debates about community care has been the impact on the lives of women as informal carers, but as will be seen in the later chapters of this text, the influence of gender is more far-reaching than this. Before charting this influence within the different formal categories of users it is important to address some of the assumptions which have underpinned the policy and practice developments outlined in this chapter. In particular, understandings of both community and caring by policy makers and some theorists have ignored the complexities of a gender analysis either by focusing predominantly on the experiences of women, or by analysing and theorising in ways that have privileged undisabled white male experience as the norm.

3

Community, Citizenship and Community Care

Introduction

The previous chapter described the concept of care in the community which developed during the decade before the passing of the National Health Service and Community Care Act 1990. Early formulations of community work involved activity which was separate from, but complementary to, social work predominantly in the voluntary sector. The concept of community social work introduced by the Barclay Committee as the immediate precursor to the NHS&CC Act represented a shift in thinking about the role of statutory social workers in the community.

Care management in community care, by reframing further the role of the statutory social worker, brings attention to both understandings of 'community' within social work and social care, and the role of citizens within the provision of welfare. In doing so it provides opportunities to analyse how constructions of gender operate in community care, how distinctions between women and men are perceived and influence service delivery. Although policy does not directly address distinctions between female and male experience, definitions and assumptions impact differentially on women and men when they become users of social and community care services. Biographies, assumed status and different roles performed within the community before and after intervention by social, health and care workers influence the services provided, and the way in which they are provided.

In this chapter, therefore, changes brought about by the NHS&CC Act are first examined in the light of the literature on 'community'. The starting point is the sociological literature which highlights that the definition of community has changed over time. Feminist literature has made a significant contribution to discussions of community as a contested concept. Simple distinctions between notions of community, as either spatial or dependent upon networks, have been replaced by notions of community as the site of individual action, the arena in which constructions of identity are negotiated. Those involved in social work and social care are central actors in these processes.

Furthermore, this emphasis on individual action has implications for definitions of who is perceived to be, or can achieve the status of, citizen. Such definitions have gendered overtones which are significant for all those who are defined as users of community care. This is the second theme of this chapter.

Context

Chapter 2 described the arrangements made for service delivery after the implementation of the NHS&CC Act and the impact that these had on a profession which was predominantly female. Underpinning the legislation was a set of ideals, framed within the rhetoric of the market, which emphasised for users freedom from unnecessary state intervention and freedom to choose services which were appropriate to their needs (DoH, 1989). While these were laudable goals there was concern that because they were linked to the operation of the market they would not be upheld. It was anticipated that assessments would continue to be resource led or that, by default, those who had traditionally been excluded from access to services, namely Black and ethnic minority people, would continue to be ignored or deterred from accessing services. The emphasis on choice meant that, for good or ill, the focus was changing from the providers of services to the recipients/users of those services.

Other changes in the delivery of services to adults in need of care because of illness (both physical and mental) and disability did have implications for providers of services. The move to a purchaser/provider split with the encouragement of a mixed economy of provision meant that services were more likely to be provided from the voluntary or independent sector, with an anticipated growth in the latter. In the light of the history of the introduction of other welfare reforms, the conservatism of organisations, and individuals within them, might mean there was resistance to these

changes Such resistance might be exacerbated because the legislation was underpinned by the seemingly unacceptable ideals of the
market and consumerism (Orme and Glastonbury, 1993). Alternatively, the changes provided opportunities to respond to criticisms,
which came equally from radical commentators and feminists, of
the way that social work and social care had previously created
conditions of dependence, oppression and stigmatisation for users
of services.

It was not the legislation itself which provided these tensions but
the political climate in which it was introduced and, just as importantly, the changing political climate in which it became operational.
The move towards provision of welfare outside the statutory sector
reflected a clear commitment of a Conservative administration to
introduce market principles into welfare. In attempting to counteract the worst exigencies of a totally individualised market approach
without committing themselves to universal statutory provision, the
Left explored the legitimacy of individual rights to welfare (Coote,
1992). Although alert to party political allegiances and the ideologies underpinning them, notions of 'individual' rights, however, are
often debated, in terms of gender politics, in an apolitical way. The
individual, the subject, is usually assumed to be a white, undisabled
male. Even when this is not explicit, different constructions of
personal experience which might impinge upon rights afforded to
individuals, or the way that they can utilise such rights, are rarely
addressed.

However, claims of unifying characteristics which produce or
determine rights for groups such as women, disabled people or
Black and ethnic minority people are limited because they do not
experience these rights. Of greater concern is that some within the
groups are prevented from asserting their rights effectively because
of the characteristics which are said to unify them. The assumed
homogeneity of the group may deny individuality. For this reason,
recognition of differences and diversity has informed debates within
feminism and ethnic and racial studies about citizenship and community participation (Ahmad and Atkin, 1996; Yuval-Davis, 1997),
and in doing so has led to challenges to descriptions of unified
categories. Significantly, while focusing on minority and oppressed
groups, such debates also challenge assumptions that there is a
unified category of white undisabled male, which infers that all
those thus described will have similar personal histories and experiences.

This means that focusing on gender recognises difference, but seeks to explore the implications of both the construction and impact of the perceived differences for women and men. It is within this context that the concepts of community and citizen need to be examined

Community

The task of the social worker, or any other worker, as care manager to stimulate services in the community in order that there can be a response to identified need depends upon agreement about what constitutes 'the community'. The shifting concept of community reflects the different ways in which the term has been used and leads to ambiguities in its usage. This may of course be deliberate in that the different meanings of community have been appropriated by different interests at different times to justify politics, policies and practices (Mayo, 1994). Understandings of what constitutes 'community' in community care, carry with them assumptions not only about where the care will take place, but also about what can be expected from a community, or the citizens who are its constituents. These understandings and assumptions beg questions about who is available to make community-based provision, and on what basis. This reinforces the dichotomy set up between those who require services, and those who provide them, either as formal workers, voluntary workers, volunteers or informal carers.

What is 'community'?

It has been suggested that the term community has so many meanings as to be meaningless (Bulmer, 1987). Examining the variety of meanings offers the opportunity not to arrive at some sterile definition, but to explore the differential impact of the definitions on women and men, and on users of services constructed by other definitions.

There is difficulty in achieving a consensus about the term community; it is a contested concept. An early analysis of the use of the term indicates that studies of communities highlight a distinction between normative descriptions of what sociologists, among others, think community should be and empirical description of what is observed (Bell and Newby, 1971).

A common starting point is the distinction between *Gemeinschaft* and *Gesellschaft*. There is some agreement that the former translates as 'community', but that the latter is more contentious. Alternative interpretations include 'association' (Mayo, 1994: 51) or 'society' (Bell and Newby, 1971: 24). Linked to the notion of social change, *Gesellschaft* refers to the large-scale impersonal and contractual ties which were seen to develop at the expense of *Gemeinschaft* the latter being constructed by social relations which were small scale and personal – kinship, neighbourhood and friendship incorporating a shared sense of identity.

This dual definition of community was the focus of empirical studies of the 1970s (Bulmer, 1987). The loss of community identity documented by these studies was thought to be caused by the effect of post-war policy implementation, for example, physical relocation of populations brought about rehousing programmes. Those that continued to exist did so in some form of 'urban villages' and these geographical communities had strong social ties within particular neighbourhoods. Significantly, they were said to depend upon a 'mum' figure, a person, usually female, at the centre of local inter-action functioning as combined information exchange and transit depot. At the same time studies described mother–daughter rela-tionships as a key link in traditional working-class extended families which were at the hub of community, thus recognising the female-ness of community (Young and Willmott, 1957). It was these to which the Barclay Committee seemed to be alluding in their defini-tions of community social work, but the dependence of the report on these early empirical studies has been criticised for not recognis-ing that the conditions which created those communities had chan-ged in ways which made the project of community social work invalid:

> With changing material circumstances – increased living standards; improved housing; greater mobility; the greater employment of married women etc– the basis of the solidarities described in the traditional studies have with-ered, and cannot in consequence be easily resurrected–even with the aid of fully trained social workers (Allan, 1983: 422)

Allan goes on to highlight a distinction between 'kith' and 'kin' in the studies usually drawn upon. This distinction hinges on the public/private dichotomy of relationships which is central to the provision of care, or more accurately the nature of care provided.

It also influences the perceptions of the contribution women and men make to the community.

Women and community

One consequence of recognising confusions in definitions was to abandon the use of the contested term community and to focus on process: 'to conceive of the relationship between individuals as the links in a social network' (Allan, 1983: 420). Networks are the outcome of the interactions between individuals, and focusing on their operation has echoes of Young's 'mum' figure. Feminists who identify women's work as community work analyse skills in networking as the basis for women's involvement in community action. However, as Chapter 1 outlined feminist analysis does not necessarily provide agreed definitions or explanations.

Alternatively, involvement of women in the community is not always synonymous with feminist practice. Descriptions of feminist community work, involving campaigns and networks as initiatives that emerge when a group or groups of women cooperate or organise collectively around issues aimed specifically at tackling gender oppression, are limited and do not recognise the breadth of the contribution women make. It is neither helpful nor appropriate to assume that when women are involved in the community they are only concerned with 'women's issues' which are traditionally defined as matters to do with child care.

Some writers make a distinction between groups which challenge the determinants of women's inequality, and groups and campaigns run predominantly by women which concentrate on helping women cope with the status quo (Dominelli and McLeod, 1989). In doing so they argue that it is either the focus of the work or the ways in which the work is done which identify it as feminist.

There is a danger that arguing for a specifically feminist community work or community action assumes that there is some essentially 'feminine' or women's ways, as opposed to male ways, of working. To adopt such a stance, that either through nature or through a learned collective response to the oppression of male ways women work differently from men, denies the efforts that women have put into such collective ways of working.

Despite the association of women and networking, community action of itself is not inherently feminist. It has been criticised for paying insufficient attention to people's emotional problems, and failing to engage with the importance of gender in its theory or in its programme of action or employment practice (Dominelli and McLeod, 1989). Equally, when feminists are involved in community action they do not confine themselves to campaigning for issues which are traditionally defined as 'women's issues'. While women's involvement in Greenham Common and the Northern Ireland peace movement can be labelled as women's ways, because of their association with cessation of violence and protection of communities which include children, accounts of women's role in, for example, miners' strikes, and others' perceptions of that role, highlight dynamic processes of community identification and women's involvement in them (Mayo, 1994).

Whatever the topic or focus for action, to define community or collective ways of working as the prerogative of women, abrogates men of their responsibility to try and work in this way, or, as those in the men's movement have observed, invalidates it when they do try.

However, community action was not the only contribution that feminist analysis made to ways of working with communities. For some feminists, to work collectively and to organise outside statutory services was the only option in the political campaigns to bring about positive changes for women in the state provision of welfare. Practice which evolved out of consciousness-raising involved collective political action which included setting up collective self-help organisations such as the Women's Aid movement as a response to domestic violence (Wilson, 1980). However, advocating radical change in both the organisation and means of service delivery was not universally acceptable. Women who were users of state services were often overwhelmed by their individual problems and had neither the time nor the energy to act collectively. While the early studies of communities had highlighted the capacities of working-class areas to provide systems to support and nurture each other, when these systems broke down, or when individuals were excluded from them, the resources of the state were sought. This could lead to women- blaming in that they had not provided the support or cohesion necessary to prevent state intervention.

Also, calls for collective action could be alienating to some groups of women. Advocating changes of lifestyle to offer a sense of community and connectedness made little sense to Black women and women from other ethnic groups whose cultural experience was one of shared identity. hooks (1984) argues that offering such suggestions for change of lifestyle are attractive and realistic only to those women who are middle class, young, educated and unmarried, thereby alienating most if not all women who are the users of social services.

These debates within feminism are important because they illustrate different meanings for different women, and hold them all as equally valid. However, this acceptance of the personal as the political among women which recognises that Black women, lesbian women and women of different class have different experiences becomes problematic if it is universalised to include the experiences of men. Yet for some women it is as important to recognise shared oppressions. In an essay expanding the answer to the question: 'If women want equality with men, with which do they wish to be equal?', hooks (1987) argues that to stay with the personal limits the contribution feminism can make, and that both the personal that is political and the politics of society have to be part of the broader perspective of feminism (hooks, 1987).

The dependence of the Barclay Committee on understandings of community suggests that it is important to look a little more closely at the use of the term community in social work and social care and within this the politics of society.

'Community' in social work and social care

Early social work writings on communities rely heavily on an understanding of community as location (Hadley and McGrath, 1980). Area-based organisation such as a patch system could, it was argued, change the relationship between statutory social workers and the catchment areas in which the workers were operating. With policy developments, basic notions of community social work were introduced and social services departments were required to encourage, support and promote voluntary effort and engage in 'assisting and encouraging the development of community identity' (Seebohm, 1968: para 477). The principles were more fully explored by the Barclay Committee for whom community social work involved elements of locality, attachment, social cohesion and shared interest (Barclay, 1982: xvii). It is this definition which has underpinned the development of community care predicated on assumptions that there are networks within geographical locations which would provide the means to care for people within the community, which is distinct from notions of the community defined as 'not in an institution', where the assumption is that resources such as buildings and staff would be provided to enable people who had previously been institutionalised to live independent lives within a geographical area.

Community social work, it was argued, would involve the inter-relationship between social work and the networks of informal resources for providing care, forming a partnership with, stimulating and supporting resources of informal support, families, neighbours, friends, volunteers and voluntary organisations (Barclay, 1982: 209). But such expectations denied the distinctions in definitions of community between descriptions of a locality as a basis for social organisation, and the concentration of relationships rather than the geographical locality as the major organising factor. In doing so they point to the need for some clearer understanding of community, and of women's and men's role within it which are all part of the politics of community.

Political understandings of community

The discussion so far has focused on understandings of community and work within it, as gleaned from sociological and social work literature. In matters to do with welfare, of which community care is a part, the provisions made by the state reflect political ideologies. While it is beyond the scope of this book to give a commentary on the complex interaction between state and community, it is important to be alert to commentaries which either by default or by active consideration signify the gendered nature of community involvement in welfare debates. To illustrate what is meant, three different perspectives, and the way that they impact on constructions of gendered activity, are discussed. The three perspectives are state provision, communitarianism and community as the site of action.

State provision

The impact on individuals of the operation of the welfare state has been seen to be one of its weaknesses. The tension is between the universalising tendencies of welfare provision and the denial of the individuality of the welfare recipient. A further complexity is that as an institution or organisation of services the welfare state is seen to be an expression of reciprocity, moral community and welfarism while at the same time presupposing and reinforcing mutual indifference by expecting individuals to provide for themselves (Skillen, 1995). Where self-help is not possible the state provides, and in doing so has, to date, employed specialised personnel to carry out the necessary activity. This arrangement allows certain individuals, those who are neither in need nor providing for that need, to get on with their own lives. In this way provision of state care by professionals may be accused of taking away the opportunity for freely given 'caring' responses to need which are seen to be indicators of the existence of a community:

> Even though the welfare state exists as an expression and index of community, it is trapped in a dialectic of self destruction: it depends for support precisely on the communal attitudes and values it undermines both through its mode of accumulation and through its mode of delivery. For both occlude the community that the whole edifice presupposes. (Skillen, 1995: 88)

Here is the nub of the community care debate. There is a borderland in which the individual is expected to provide for themselves, but also express their concern for others by being prepared to provide for them. But there are those for whom care is not readily available and the state, acting on behalf of the collectivity, will provide through the agency of others. In the ideology of the mixed economy of welfare that agency might be through volunteering, being paid for informal service or being employed by a providing organisation.

But here is also the nub of the gender debate. This use of 'community' within political debates and policy initiatives has largely ignored, deliberately or otherwise, the differential experience of community from the perspective of, among others, race, class and gender. There is the anonymous, undetermined individual set in opposition to community, which is, in some senses, equally undifferentiated, but includes those who might require care. Community comprises those who can, will or should contribute. It also assumes that all have the means to be independent and self-sufficient. There is little or no discussion of those who are, by a variety of processes, denied the possibility of contributing or have to be maintained in some supplicatory role in order to provide the opportunities for others to make their contributions.

This tension is not constrained to any one political perspective. The cross party report of the Commission for Social Justice in espousing 'reciprocal responsibility and social well-being' (1994: 307) gave support to the notion of 'social capital' which consists of the institutions and relationships of a thriving civil society, the aim of which is to build among local people the capacities and institutions which enable them to take more responsibility for shaping their own future. In attempting a definition, or redefinition, of community as a plank of urban renewal the Commission struggled with the notion of rights for the individual, tempered by responsibilities to others and attempts to be all inclusive:

> [f]rom networks of neighbours to extended families, community groups to religious organisations, local business to local public services, youth clubs to parent-teacher associations, playgroups to police on the beat. Where you live, who else lives there, and how they live their lives – co-operatively or selfishly, responsibly or destructively. (Commission for Social Justice, 1994: 308)

For women, the significance of this plank of urban renewal is that social capital is seen to begin at home, the family is the site of the first activities, and the unit for engaging with the community.

Closer examination of these political understandings of community reveals a desire for wholeness, and denial of difference within the search for community. The very process of setting community in opposition to individualism exhibits a totalising impulse, and denies diversity by not recognising the difference between subjects. It thereby ignores the process of social change needed to avoid the exclusion of alienated groups and individuals. The assumed homogeneity of a community (geographical or relational) not only denies differences between groups but it also fails to recognise the heterogeneity of each individual's identity and lived experience by virtue of their membership of those groups. Iris Marion Young (1990a) questions both the feasibility of an ideal of a shared subjectivity and the desirability of it. She argues that reciprocal recognition and identification with others denies difference, and makes it difficult for people to respect those with whom they do not identify.

Young suggests that the individual, not the community, should be the means of empowerment: that community as the normative idea of political emancipation should be replaced by a politics of difference. This would recognise that while at any one time an individual might wish to describe themselves in a particular way (e.g. Black or female) at others they may wish to identify with a different group (e.g. disabled people or older people). That the state defines individual identity by providing for them in terms of groups is one of the ways in which state intervention as been experienced as oppressive.

This notion of a differentiated community might support Bulmer's 'community liberated' approach, which takes account of the wider framework of networks where ties of kin, work and residence are not necessarily combined (Mayo, 1994). Gender, religion and racial identity are equally important as competing distinctions within any community, or, more positively, they exist simultaneously. Networks do not always recognise or allow for difference, they have overtones of a given collectivity, and resulting community representation may, for example, assume that the interests of women, Black people, and disabled people are inherently nonconflictual and intrinsically the same, because they are all categories of disadvantage (Anthias and Yuval-Davis, 1992).

Two important strands emerge from this analysis. One is the supplanting of 'community' with the notion of network which has been explored already. The second is a focus on a community–individual dualism. This focus can be problematic, not least because of the way in which different political discourses have adopted it for their own ideological position, one of which is communitarianism.

Communitariansim

The invocation of 'community' in policy and legislation of the 1990s was to allow for the introduction of the machinery of the market into the welfare state. However, the introduction of community care with its emphasis on family values, moral and civil education also echoed the emphasis on communitarianism which had emerged in North America (Etzioni, 1993). This movement seeks to engage in a process of re-examining national values and priorities, to rebuild social and political institutions to support healthy and safe communities. Drawing on interested individuals from left and right, it claims to provide a third perspective which includes individualism, justice, participatory democracy and empowerment. In this it has echoes in the policies of the Labour government in Britain elected in 1997.

In an analysis which makes no concession to difference and diversity, Etzioni identifies the problems of the United States as being caused by the breakdown of community, individualism and the proliferation of individual rights, and the imbalance between rights and duties. He argues that reciprocity must exist between the individual and the community, and that it must be the primary principle of social justice:

> beyond self support, individuals have a responsibility for the material and moral well-being of others. The community, on the other hand, is responsible for protecting each member against catastrophe, natural or man-made; for insuring basic needs of all who genuinely cannot provide for themselves, for appropriately recognizing the distinctive contribution of individuals to the community; and for safe-guarding a zone within which individuals may define their own lives through free exchange and choice (Etzioni, 1993: 264)

While social insurances for basic need, and the opportunities for free exchange and choice might be perceived as positive, they may also be seen to be in conflict with each other. More important are the definitions of those who 'cannot' provide for themselves. The distinctive contribution which women may make to the community is to its regeneration through childbirth and child care, but this sometimes means they are not able to provide for themselves. This comes about because of state laws and fiscal policies making it impossible for women to define their own lives. Similarly, the arguments of the disability rights groups are that disabled people would choose to define their own lives, if they were given the means (both economic and environmental) to do so.

In communitarianism, therefore, notions of identity emphasise the boundaries between individuals, as well as asserting commonality with others. This creates a 'community-constituted self', reflecting what individuals have and do in common. The danger is that the common features not only define, they also differentiate and exclude (Skillen, 1995).

In this defining communitarian politics can also essentialise along definitions which are based on a single category, for example, race: 'what might be tenuous, fragile and subject to erosion becomes frozen as a more or less permanent and all encompassing "community identity"' (Skillen, 1995: 82). But community identity is not always positive. Communities identified by nationality, for example, might be seen to have positive qualities which unite them, but may also invite hostility, especially racist practices at individual levels.

Understandings of communitarianism also include notions of responsibilities and 'active citizenship' which are implicit in organisation for the provision of community care, a notion of community service in community activity which Skillen (1995) sees as a matter of spending time, working and caring and describes as part of 'our' lives. In this there is the notion of community as the site of action.

Community as the site of action

In this assumption of some homogeneous notion of citizenship, in an undifferentiated 'our', Skillen contradicts his own arguments and repeats the errors of many social and political commentators on community. His notion of community service, which includes work on the environment, is an expansion of the social capital described in the Commission for Social Justice Report (1994) which he criticises for soft-pedalling on community in favour of individualism. However, his model of community service, with an infrastructure of choice, sanctions, payments, flexibility and democratic citizenship, is implicitly a set of expectations of those who are not already involved in providing services to individuals and groups within the community, namely employed men. It fails to recognise that women and retired men, are already providing unrecognised community service, or that disabled people may be denied the right to participate in such service because they are deemed to be in need of the care that others might provide as part of their commitment to the community.

Such a position is overt in a classic liberal notion of 'community without politics' (Green, 1996), which demands that the majority of the population assumes responsibility for fostering 'a public but not political domain' of duties to care for all those who are not able to support themselves for one reason or another. Community is no less important, but mainly at the level of individual conscience: 'it does not imply a political obligation, rather it suggests a personal duty to set an example in the continuing struggle to uphold the moral and legal principles consistent with liberty' (Green, 1996: vii). In propounding community without politics, Green advocates maintaining an official minimum provision, but that the state should withdraw from some activities and champions of liberty should establish 'voluntary associations for assisting the less fortunate and run them in a spirit compatible with liberty' (Green, 1996: 137). However, his categorisation of groups such as 'frail elderly and mentally handicapped' which, he argues, should continue to receive unconditional assistance sets them apart from those who engage in self-damaging and self-defeating attitudes. Such distinctions, echoing notions of deserving and undeserving, judge the latter group and maintain the former in some form of victim status.

The political arguments from left and right centre around the responsibility of the state, and the extent to which the interventions of the state either uphold or undermine individual freedom liberty. Ironically, Green's claim that there is a great deal that can be done without political power has been exemplified by the feminist movement, which for decades has campaigned and challenged male political institutions to address issues of women's inequality, discrimination and oppression.

This highlights that within the attempts so far to define community within understandings of community care, there has been an emergent tension between the definitions and assumptions about what, or who, constitutes community. The contribution that is expected or assumed of members of communities is implicitly gendered in that it ignores or denies the contribution that women have made in the form of networking and providing care, and it carries with it notions of active membership of communities, of citizenship which excludes those individuals who are sick, disabled or have mental health problems. The Citizen's Charter promoted active citizenship and user and community rights based on individualised concepts of citizenship (Mayo, 1994), and the development of community care planning offered opportunities for increased community involvement of some user groups, mainly through community organisations. Early arrangements for community care planning and commissioning services paid scant attention to the involvement of current service users, and those citizens who might become users of community care services (Waldman *et al.*, 1996).

Repeatedly, therefore, the themes of individuality, identity and community participation are explored in the political literature with little or no attention paid to the politics of gender. These tensions are apparent not only in the ideologies underpinning the policies of community care but are played out in the practices.

Services in the community

Arrangements for both assessment of need and provision of services in community care, while giving emphasis to some notion of choice to, and involvement of, users and carers in decision making may also perpetuate an individualised approach to interactions which pays lip-service to consultation and participation. Significantly criticised as being paternalistic, such an approach denies service users rights or respect as citizens. It also challenges the notion of community as collective.

However, some commentators are less pessimistic and have argued that the process of care management has the potential to introduce a radical set of values into social care practice based on citizenship, participation, community presence, equality, anti-oppressive practice, empowerment and user control (Braye and Preston-Shoot, 1995). To achieve this, the way that the relationship between service providers and service users operates has to be reviewed in order to counteract a notion of user which carries with it implications of 'clienthood' which is in opposition to conceptions of citizenship. In the past the status of 'client' has restricted users' rights to be actively involved in decisions which impact upon the way their own care is provided or from influencing the services for others (Hugman, 1991). Community care implementation promised the means to counteract this. The guidance accompanying the legislation (SSI, 1994) encouraged notions of partnership and advocacy which have led to discourses of empowerment (Payne, 1995).

However, the legislation and subsequent practice guidelines for community care present social workers and/or care managers on one side of a negotiation, with users and carers on the other. The model of care management which involves negotiating contracts for the care to be provided is simplistic. It ignores the complexity of the negotiations between workers and those who use, require or provide services. It also denies the wealth of private negotiations which take place which do not come to the attention of health and social service departments. Finally, it ignores diversity, the potential within users and carers to be both carers and cared for, presenting both in ways which question their status as citizens, as active members of communities.

Limitations to accepting users of social work and health services as citizens are brought about because they are traditionally defined by needs which bring them to the attention of such services and not by their rights to services. On the contrary, being in receipt of services limits their rights in a variety of ways. Assessment and provision of services deny freedom from intervention; personal details not directly relevant to their immediate needs are part of assessment schedules, and, as the previous chapter outlined, there is continuing surveillance of the services provided, and their impact. Users are investigated and monitored in ways in which other citizens are not.

Recognising that those who require community care services are individuals in their own right has implications for notions of citizenship and the politics of the individual. However, the consequences are wider than just focusing on individual need and experience, or recognising difference and diversity when allocating services. Some understanding of citizenship, carry meanings of process and outcome with expectations of individual involvement in communities. However, by involvement in that process individuals acquire agency, they take responsibility for the outcomes for themselves and for others. They also have the opportunity to bring about change. By virtue of being recipients of care, service users are often ignored in discussions about citizen involvement in the community which is assumed to provide that care. Hence the concept of community represented in the community care legislation is flawed in that it not only assumes a neutral notion of citizenship, but also depends on a model of community care provision which takes as given that there are individuals to be cared for, and individuals available to do the caring.

It is because of this individualised approach to the role of the citizen in community care planning, and the definition of citizen which is implicit in the processes of community care which will emerge from the detailed discussions of particular groups in the following chapters, that it is important to look at how a gendered perspective assists understandings of citizenship.

Citizenship

In the early nineteenth century the exclusion of women and most working people from the vote meant that the notion of citizen participation was alien to them. This did not mean that they did not have a sense of 'community', of belonging to a certain set of networks and relationships, but that participation was based on mutuality. The socialist participatory approach to citizenship which emerged at the beginning of the twentieth century conferred both rights and obligations, and Marshall's three elements of citizenship – civil, political and social (Marshall, 1950), have been held as a yardstick and coconut shy by social and political thinkers to develop their understandings of, and make their own contributions to notions of citizenship. Prior to the debates highlighted above about the ways in which community involvement confers citizenship, or more accurately is a legitimate expectation of being 'good citizens', emphasis was predominantly on the relationship between the individual and the state, and the capacity of the individual to participate in decision making processes. In his threefold categorisation, Marshall widened the definition and linked citizenship to membership of a community. His notion of social citizenship involved the right to live the life of a civilised being according to the standards prevailing in the society. The moral basis for the welfare state lies in the resources for what Marshall called social rights of democratic citizenship (Rees, 1996).

Users as citizens

Ironically, with the development of social services, the involvement of people as clients and the stigma that accompanies being the recipient of services denigrates such individuals in ways which have been counter to any notion of citizenship. Also, some groups, by virtue of the conditions which have brought them into the ambit of social services, because they are disabled, old, have a mental illness, or all of these, are denied social rights. More accurately, the degree to which social rights actually extend to ensure that they have the right to standards of living of a civilised society is subject to debate (Plant, 1992).

Notions of citizenship can therefore be used to explore the complex relationships between individuals, collectivities and the state. Recognising that there are many people who might share the myth of common origin of 'the community' but do not share important hegemonic value systems, Yuval-Davis concludes that if attention is paid to dimensions of social divisions and social positioning, such as gender, international ethnicity, class, sexuality, ability, stage in life cycle (all of which include women and men), there is the potential for an inherently contradictory nature of citizenship as individual/communal, inclusionary/exclusionary (Yuval-Davis, 1997: 7), which is not acknowledged in Marshall's work.

Finally, both as users of the services and in the domestic and informal sphere by which they contribute to the work of supporting and providing for those in receipt of social services, the concept of citizenship has operated differently for women and men.

Women as citizens

Marshall himself paid scant attention to the particular situation of women. Limitations of social security, social insurance and the lack of services of importance for women highlight a lack of attention to their position, and 'any conception of "domestic citizenship" poses a sharp question about the continuance of gender ascribed roles in the provision of goods and services for and within the household' (Rees, 1996: 11).

Even though women now have the means for political participation, the development of citizen participation remains gendered. For some liberal theories of citizenship this is necessarily so – that the construction of citizens as political equals can only be achieved by either ignoring the many differences between them, or denying the relevance of these differences to politics. Differences of gender, race ethnicity or class are seen as merely of private significance; individual identities and differences are denied, and the properties of citizens are those of men. Defined as the 'normative justification' of democratic citizenship, this denies that because women have been perceived as dependent on men, they have not been required to make the same contribution, through taxation and insurance contributions deducted from income, to the welfare state as men (Pateman, 1989: 195ff).

Hence denial of social rights of citizenship to women on the basis that they have not made a 'contribution' rests on this assumption of dependency, the contribution being seen in terms of the financial contribution from paid employees. To date women's contribution in the main has been significantly different in that it was in the form of welfare, which remains set apart from political citizenship. For Pateman the connection between employment and citizenship in what she calls the 'patriarchal welfare state' is the way in which 'women' have been opposed to the 'worker' and the 'citizen' – thereby creating a central paradox surrounding women, welfare and citizenship.

The situation is more complex than this in that women have been excluded and included on the very same capacities and attributes. While some definitions of citizenship were achieved by excluding women, a new mode of inclusion which encompassed their formal entry into citizenship actually depended on a notion of difference:

> Women were incorporated differently from men, the 'individuals' and 'citizens' of political theory; women were included as subordinates, as the 'different' sex, as 'women'. They were included as men's subordinates into their own private sphere, and so were excluded from the 'civil' society in the sense of the public sphere of the economy and citizenship of the state. But this does not mean that women had no political contribution to make and no political duty to perform. Their political duty (like their exclusion from citizenship) derives from their difference from men, notably their capacity for motherhood. (Pateman, 1992: 19)

It is those differences associated with motherhood, and the caring capacities which are assumed to accompany it, that are central to community care debates, as is explored in the next chapter. For definitions of citizenship, however, the values and activities which have been traditionally attributed to women are considered to be outside the political world, and largely irrelevant to democratic participation. That this is so involves a particular interpretation of liberal theory built around a set of complementary dichotomies (James, 1992). These dichotomies, these pairs of characteristics, see political life as male and defined in opposition to the private domestic sphere of women, meaning that women lack full membership and are not full citizens.

To create a properly democratic society which includes women as full citizens means either deconstructing and reassembling understandings of the body politic, or reassessing the roles of women and men, or the interpretation of those roles. Either way it produces dilemmas. Pateman argues that Hegel's social order (public/private civil; society/state) is based on both class division and patriarchal separation. For Hegel women naturally lacked the attributes and capacities of individuals who can enter civil society, sell their labour power and become citizens. He incorporates them into the state as members of the family, a sphere separate from (or in social exile from) civil society and the state. Women were incorporated as citizens, according to Hegel, not like men, but as members of a separate sphere – the family. This is echoed in what is known as 'Woolstonecraft's dilemma', that at one and the same time women want their 'difference' to be acknowledged but not in the way that disadvantages them (Pateman, 1992: 20). Put another way, should maternal and related qualities and capacities be accepted as different but valorised and brought into the political arena, or should a universal undifferentiated yardstick of equality be accepted as the aim for women, thus denying any difference?

This dilemma is not restricted to women, it has been a source of debate for Black people and, as is explored in Chapter 7, it has resonance for disabled people. In the case of women, James argues that liberal theory aims to construct citizens who are politically equal, but in doing so recognises differences in so far as they are obstacles to citizenship. Hence the allocation of child benefit is seen as a way of compensating mothers for the loss of economic independence while they are bringing up children (James, 1992). However, to look for single-focus solutions to overcome women's barriers to citizenship simplifies the situation. The barriers are not there merely because some women do not participate fully in the waged economy. Nor are they removed by offering state benefit. Women in the workplace have not necessarily achieved recognition as full citizens, and men who are unemployed, old, disabled and/or Black or of other ethnic minority origin, are also in a variety of ways denied recognition as full citizens.

The emphasis in the policies of New Labour on work for lone parents, unemployed youth and disabled people reflects, as has been said, a communitarian approach and emphasises the connection between citizenship and the capacity, in current policy terms, not necessarily to contribute financially to a welfare state, but to be able to provide for oneself in a form of social investment. It is the contention of New Labour policies that the demands of disabled people for rights, to be treated as equals and to become citizens, can only be met if they participate in the labour force. To argue this is to deny the contributions, other than economic, that can be made by citizens, and it also ignores the complexity of the lived experience of disabled people, and the formal and informal barriers to their involvement in the workforce.

Caring and citizenship

For women, there are other disadvantages inherent in their gender which operate at the level of the private and interpersonal, the formal and informal. But these differences are not clear-cut. The notion of dependence/independence is problematic in a culture which wants to foster independence, self-reliance and personal responsibility. Often in discussions about the position of women, the distinction is on the public/private. Women are seen to depend on men economically (public) while the dependence of men upon women is in the domestic and emotional interchanges (private). It is the ideology of dependency that governs the lives of all women, even those who are not directly dependent on a man (Lister, 1990). But, as is discussed in the next chapter, male dependence rests on the perception and self-perception of women as carers, and by definition caring for someone. Women's informal caring activities are not recognised as making a contribution to society, and involvement in caring can deny women citizenship. The individual and private nature of the activity so defined can disqualify them because it is seen to be an inappropriate quality.

Similarly if one of the bases for citizenship is impartiality, becoming involved in democratic processes and demonstrating objectivity, women are again excluded because of their assumed qualities: 'womanly woman is caring or partial, that is to say, she thinks and behaves in ways which are antithetical to the norms of impartiality valued by legislators' (James, 1992: 55). If women make claims that they can judge impartially they do so at the price of compromising their femininity, of being deemed to be not women.

Here is yet another dilemma in a critique of citizenship which wishes to explore and explain the differences experienced by women and men. As described in Chapter 1, and discussed further in the next chapter, cultural feminism suggests there are differences between maleness/femaleness which include sets of characteristics which set women and men apart. The reasons for these differences are variously described including that they are biological or 'natural' or that women and men are socialised into different ways of behaving. Whatever the reasons for the differences, what is significant is that it is the male characteristics which are privileged, which are seen to be the norm and the desirable. Male characteristics enable men to achieve the qualifications created by liberal democracies for citizenship, women if they continue to demonstrate femaleness will be disqualified.

If the process of constructing differences by ascribing characteristics, and positively recognising some as valid, is seen to be a social process of use and abuse of power then it is possible to challenge it. The challenge is either that the qualifications for citizenship can be changed to privilege qualities which are deemed to be female, or that the very duality of male/female is false. The ascription of characteristics does not have to be according to sex. The very notion of challenging the 'maleness' of the criteria for citizenship would arrive at different understandings of the contributions that can be made by different individuals. In doing this, opportunities are presented to recognise that others who have been excluded from, or denied, the status of citizenship can have their contributions recognised.

James's conclusion is that independence and dependence are reconciled through notions of self-esteem in which there is no assumption that any one characteristic should cause an individual to feel disqualified from participation, and that true self-esteem can only be created in practices which are sensitive to and respectful of difference. Here again the balance of recognising individual identity and valuing difference while recognising common experiences is paramount. This theme is discussed in Chapter 8 where the consequences for social work and social care practice are explored.

Community citizenship

In the light of the above analysis of caring as an activity and as a set of qualities which appears to disqualify women, there is an irony that the emerging view of citizenship and community participation provided by Skillen and Green above rests on personal responsibility and participation:

> much of what makes for a good and fulfilled life is voluntary and unrewarded, and the desire for equalisation has promoted the tendency for the total worth of individuals to be reckoned only in terms of the services for which they receive cash payment. (Green, 1996: 72)

Citing the Charity Organisation Society and the Settlement Movement as examples of ways of fulfilling notions of morally responsible citizen, Green significantly argues that equality derives some of its moral force from utopian theories which advocate *brotherly love*. But, this notion of brotherly love is no more, and perhaps less, than the labour of love that women have been performing for the welfare state, and which is ignored by theorists such as Green. Thus from the right, the argument is to replace the notion of entitlements with that of obligation, an obligation which can be discharged not just through taxes, but through neighbourliness, voluntary action and charity (Lister, 1990). Significantly these are activities which women have performed in the private realm, but for Green it is discharging these duties in the public realm that counts. His failure to think of the citizen as anything other than employed, undisabled and male limits his arguments.

Workfare

But such limitations are not the preserve of the right. In policy articulations from the left, the confusion of workfare with welfare highlights the double standard operating in the area of 'service'. Citizen's service performed by young people immediately on leaving school is identified as a positive contribution to care in the community, but more cynically it is a way of removing young people from the employment statistics. This programme of action while not gendered as such, has the potential to be so and needs to be carefully monitored. Evidence of simplistic constructions of gender might be evidenced by entry into, and participation rates in, the scheme reflecting either that young men have to be prepared for the workforce in a way which young women do not, or that the work taken up is gendered in that young women undertake the personal care work with vulnerable people and young men have more technical opportunities.

More significant is that the introduction of such schemes reinforces a sense that qualification for citizenship is only open to those who can in some way compete for involvement in schemes of public action and thus is closed to many who themselves are in need of care services. The provision of such services through community care emphasises the recognition of public contributions as a qualification of citizenship, for some, and sets up notions of competing rights. For example, the needs of young people for preparation for full citizenship set against the rights of disabled and older people to have some say in their care. Given the nature of the care, the private and personal nature of some of the interactions, the involvement of young people in such activities is open to question. Also, young people's involvement in caring which has largely gone unnoticed and unrecognised when it is in the private and personal realm of the family (SSI, 1995b), is to be introduced, managed and valorised by the state when part of a set of policy initiatives which are directly related to managing the economy.

Feminism, citizenship and community care

The exposure by feminist writers of the limitations of some of the main theoretical positions provides an opportunity to explore notions of citizenship for those who are users of community care services. A major feminist critique of concepts of citizenship is that dependent upon the legacy of liberal democratic understandings, in which to vote is the political act, and citizenship is a status of formal civil or public equality (Pateman, 1987). The campaigns for suffrage as a representation of citizenship were not accompanied by a recognition of women's involvement in, and contribution to the private sphere. Also while some groups, such as older men, had suffrage, they did not necessarily have recognition as citizens if they were dependent upon state welfare.

For women the consequences were that either the qualifications for citizenship had to be changed, or women had to become more actively involved and visible in the public sphere. However, even with a redefinition of citizenship, to be seen to be active in the public realm, as good neighbours, volunteers, or in the political life of the community, takes time, and time becomes a crucial factor in the public/private debate. The unequal and unrecognised distribution of work in the home impacts on all women's capacity to be seen to be active citizens, but also denies citizenship to older people and disabled people who contribute to households, extended families and communities in a number of unrecognised and unvalorised ways. Equally, because of their lack of participation in, or exclusion from, the workforce these groups share the consequences of poverty: 'Citizens thrown into poverty lack both the means for self respect and the means to be recognised by fellow citizens as of equal worth to themselves, a recognition basic to democracy' (Pateman, 1989: 182).

The conclusions of feminist critiques are manifold and have implications not just for women, but for other groups who are excluded by virtue of their assumed lack of contribution to the public good. To address poverty as a disqualifier requires radical changes to arrangements for paid employment and state provisions: 'Different benefits can constitute either a badge of poverty or a badge of citizenship' (Lister, 1990: 453). Alternatively, new theories of citizenship need to dismantle the identification of the private with the family domain and the public with the political domain, and to construct citizenship as a multi-tier concept severed from its exclusive relationship to the state (Yuval-Davis, 1997).

For Pateman it is the divisions between public/private, male/ female dichotomies which have to be eradicated: 'If women are to participate fully, as equals, in social life, men have to share equally in child rearing and other domestic tasks. While women are identified with this "private" work, their public status is always undermined' (Pateman, 1987: 121). Her notion of 'differentiated social order' within which the various dimensions are distinct but not separated or opposed, and which rests on a social conception of individuality, may assist not just women, but also disabled people, older people and those with mental health problems, and within these groups Black and ethnic minority people who are further ostracised and alienated from involvement in civic activities which pertain to their own material and personal conditions.

Citizen participation

This inclusiveness is seen by some as an argument for new forms of citizen participation which will enable people to be involved in decision making. The suggestion is that it is not poverty or difference per se which excludes people but rather that this difference prevents them from taking part in decisions about themselves and others: 'The disadvantaged suffer not because they *have* less than others but because they can *participate* less, it is their impaired agency rather than their inequality as such which should be the focus of moral concern' (Doyal and Gough, 1991: 96). However, participation in a way which allows for active agency is not easy to achieve, and the reason why people are excluded is often because they are different, they do not conform to the imposed norms of decision making.

The rhetoric of community care planning and needs-led assessment of the community care polices outlined in the previous chapter carried with it claims that user participation conferred new rights, but such an approach has been criticised as having the potential to be tokenistic and patronising (Orme, 1996b), or as using false notions of consumerism which have been driven by market approaches to welfare (Biehal, 1993). The planning process took place, users and carers were asked to comment on the outcomes. Who was asked, and the subjects that they were asked about were predetermined by managers and practitioners.

It is therefore the way that processes of oppression are experienced and resisted which is significant. Lister, taking up the theme of human agency, argues that while rights and participatory approaches to citizenship remain conceptually different, they coalesce in the process of negotiation with welfare institutions which, she points out, mainly falls to women (Lister, 1997). In suggesting that the process and the outcomes of citizenship stand in dialectical relationship to one another, the one influencing the other, she draws a distinction between *being* a citizen and *acting* as a citizen (Lister, 1997: 35). In doing so she recognises that women's experiences are replicated in the experiences of others, who are generally subsumed into categories of community care:

> gendered patterns of exclusion interact with other axes of social divisions such as class, 'race', disability, sexuality and age in ways which can be either multiplicative or contradictory, and which shift over time. (Lister, 1997: 38)

It is these multiplicative or contradictory ways of identity which have either been ignored or become problematic for standpoint groups which have campaigned for single issues. In recognising difference Lister does not fully subscribe to a deconstruction of the category woman: 'if "woman" is simply deconstructed and left in fragments, there is no woman left to be citizen. The fact that the category "woman" is not unitary does not render it meaningless' (Lister, 1997: 39). Equality does not mean treating everyone the same, or assuming universal characteristics: 'for citizenship to be equal the substance of equality must differ according to the diverse circumstances and capacities of citizens, men and women' (Pateman, 1992: 29). Hence Lister suggests a 'differentiated universalism' which, while acknowledging that rights can be particularised to take account of the situation of specific groups, also recognises that citizenship rights have to be anchored in a notion of need, on the basis that that need can be seen as dynamic and differentiated.

Such a stance echoes Plant's notion of a 'right to welfare' which challenges the idea that citizenship is only a civil and political status: 'citizenship confers a right to a central set of resources which can provide economic security, health and education – and this person's right exists, irrespective of a person's standing in the market' (Plant, 1992: 16). Concern has been expressed in community care debates that a rights approach is not sustainable if there are no economic resources to meet all levels of need (Means and Smith, 1994), Plant's argument is that while social rights might establish the right to have procedures followed and rights to certain resources, they do not dictate the level of resources, thus making a distinction between needs and wants. Put another way, the right to minimum level of need satisfaction does not necessarily assume the corresponding duty to directly provide it (Doyal and Gough, 1991). It is here that the process of citizenship for users of community care becomes paramount, that as equal partners users should, where possible, be actively involved in the fora which undertake decisions about how resources are to be allocated.

In the second part of this text categories within community care which previously have been seen to be unproblematic are explored in terms of the way that gender has impacted differentially not only on users' experiences of services, but on their capacity to have active agency, to be involved as citizens. Within this exploration the dilemmas for social and health care workers who have to work both at the individual level and at the organisational and structural level are recognised. They have to be able to respond to the diversity of human need and at the same time be gatekeepers of resources; they have to manage community care in the light of a differentiated universalism in a way that is seen to be fair and just, and does not discriminate or oppress.

Conclusion

This chapter has drawn on social policy and political theory to give only a brief overview of the way that understandings of community, and the role of citizens within communities and, in particular, community care, have to be viewed from the perspective of gender. In doing so it has argued that configurations of citizenship impact on many of the participants in community care, from those who are perceived as care providers to those who have identified needs which are in some part met by the care provided by others, and that in mainstream theorising there have been clear distinctions between criteria for women's and men's involvement in the community and recognition as citizens. It is argued that feminist theorising has paved the way for a different analysis of citizenship, different theoretical constructions, which also informs the situation of some men. Such an analysis supports the call that 'diversity' and 'difference' need to be brought into the political order. In extending this analysis to users of community care services, traditional categories, and their assumed homogeneity, have to be challenged, and recognising and valorising differences in definitions of citizenship is important for all groups who have been oppressed by the way services have been delivered and identities constructed in the organisation of welfare services.

Throughout, in discussions both of community and of citizenship the relationship of care provision to those who are in need of services is crucial, because the public/private discrepancy between the provision of care is at the heart of notions of community care policies and understandings of citizenship. The next chapter therefore explores the caring relationship as it is manifest in current arrangements for community care.

4

Women, Men and Caring

Introduction

In the previous chapter care as an activity in the community was seen to have implications for citizenship. Providing care, if it was in the public domain, was a qualification for citizenship. Receiving care was often a disqualification. The politics of care are therefore significant. In this chapter the politics of care are explored from a different perspective. While continuing to set the context for the second part of the text, the chapter draws on a wealth of literature, both theoretical and empirical research, to provide definitions of caring. Within these definitions it is apparent that there is much written about who provides care, the nature of the care provided and the differences in that care. These themes are considered in the first section, providing care. The differences which emerge between women and men in care provision are addressed in the second section on gender and care. What is revealed is that the focus of the literature on care provision has been influenced by, and has contributed to, discussions about gender differences, but that consideration of those who receive care has not been systematically informed by these discussions. In looking at the connections between gender and the receipt of care, the final section of this chapter is a preparation for the second part of the book which looks at the experiences of specific user groups.

Context

Community care policies and legislation raise substantive questions about both the nature of caring and, as was discussed in the previous chapter, the meaning of care. While feminists in social policy have theorised the links between caring and women's status as citizens, other feminist debates have focused on the different definitions, understandings and conceptualisations of caring and their gendered implications (Graham, 1993).

At a simple level it is assumed that women do care work and that therefore caring is 'women's work'. However, this false logic has to be challenged, not only on the basis that men do care work but because equating caring as women's work has had negative consequences for both women and men. For example, assumptions that care is women's work have led to the downgrading of such work in the formal sphere in terms of both status and remuneration, and have impacted on the organisation of services which deliver care. In the informal sphere, the involvement of men in caring has led to challenges to the very association of caring and women's work. More significantly, associating caring with virtue becomes contestable.

Deconstructing concepts of care reveals inconsistencies in understandings of care, with variables including who undertakes the care, who receives it, the relationship between the two and the social domain within which the caring takes place (Thomas, 1993). Just as narrow definitions of care work based on the gender of the carer have to be challenged, so do representations of those who receive care which have been formalised by bureaucratic categories of service providers. In later chapters of this text these categories, older people, disabled people and those with mental health problems, are used to argue that the construction of user groups within policy and practice denies their complex identities. In this chapter the focus is on the provision of care and the starting point is that definitions of care which include only that which is undertaken within the home by family members are inadequate. Various forms of 'care work' take place within the formal and informal sector, and there is a significant interplay between gender and care in each. Discussions about the nature of care therefore have to be set in wider debates about constructions of femininity and masculinity, within discourses about caring and within feminist theory.

The relationship between gender and caring in social work and social care has focused on women's capacity to undertake care work, to care. It is either assumed to be natural or innate, or women are seen to have been socialised into such roles. Men's capacity to care has been discussed more by default. In the light of the discussions of feminist theory in Chapter 1, a more useful approach to understanding the complexities of tasks and functions subsumed under the heading 'caring' may be one which challenges dualities implicit in both terminologies of caring (e.g. carers and those who are cared for), and constructions of gender differences. Such a challenge will have implications for service delivery and practice methodology, but also for understandings of caring as positive. The changes brought about in arrangements for community care highlight that to provide care can involve the use of surveillance with overtones of control and power and the passivity of those who require care, who are 'cared for'. It is significant that in child care policy and practice the terminology has changed. Children are no longer described as being 'in care' they are 'looked after'. However, to suggest that disabled adults and older people should be 'looked after' might be seen to be infantilising them, although as will be discussed in the next four chapters such connotations may well reflect the dilemmas experienced by practitioners and others involved in supporting people in the community.

Hence as part of contextualising care it is necessary to look at definitions and to explore how these are influenced by policy shifts and competing theoretical frameworks.

Meanings of care

Distinctions made between notions of care are often subject specific. Within social and public policy researchers deal with the activity of 'caring' in the sense of providing facilities and carrying out tasks for those no longer able to do so for themselves; carers are, in the main, people who are paid to do this task. Philosophers and theorists, particularly feminists, see the project as more complex than this and deal with 'the association of and disjuncture between the meanings of "care"' (Evans, 1995: 100). Social work and social care have to deal with both. They draw on theoretical and empirical explanations and explorations and utilises them in working with those who provide the care, and those who require it. While the emphasis in both community care policy and feminist literature has been on the impact of 'informal' caring on women, that is unpaid care undertaken in private homes usually by a relative, a comprehensive understanding of gender issues has to consider all aspects of care provision within community care policies. This includes both the organisational structures which provide social work and social care, and the specific interpersonal interactions which are the core of social work and social care tasks. However, the very distinction between on the one hand 'work' and 'care', and on the other 'organisational' and 'interpersonal', begs clarification of what caring involves, how it is further distinguished from 'service', and how all these distinctions impact on different groups.

For example, concentration on informal and familial care has ignored the contribution of women, predominantly working class and Black and other ethnic minority women, to low-paid caring which has often been classified as domestic service (Graham, 1993). Definitions therefore have to be inclusive. Criticising others for only partial understandings, Thomas's attempt at a 'unified' concept of care incorporates all the constituent elements of care:

> Care is both the paid and unpaid provision of support involving work activities and feeling states. It is provided mainly, but not exclusively, by women to both able-bodied and dependent adults and children in either the public or the domestic spheres, and in a variety of institutional settings. All types of relationships fall within the boundaries of such a concept: family care of different forms; child care in different contexts; many social service, health service and voluntary activities; and services which are commercially run as well as those within the state sector. (Thomas, 1993: 665)

While the search for a comprehensive definition, a single concept of care, is welcomed, the focus in this text on the policies of community care as discussed in Chapter 2 means that the extension of the 'care' to child care is not explored. However, the interrelationship between women's involvement in child and family care and constructions of femininity cannot, and will not be, ignored. The construction of motherhood is intrinsic to notions of the family as the site of caring. It carries with it essentialist expectations, based on a biological determinism that assumes women undertake child care through a set of innate skills, and that these skills are then transferable to caring for adults. Where motherhood is not assumed to be innate or natural, it is suggested that through the experience of motherhood, and their preparation for it, women become socialised into caring alongside other aspects of feminine behaviour. Both these perspectives ignore that many women who care have foregone the opportunity, or chosen not, to have children because of their caring responsibilities (Lewis and Meredith, 1988). Such evidence would suggest either that care is socially constructed, or that care is a facet of the social construction of femininity which permeates all discussions about the provision of care, and impacts upon men who provide care, women who do not and those who require care.

The extension of Thomas's definition to include the formal, voluntary and private or independent sector is particularly pertinent to the organisation of care provision arising out of the NHS&CC Act. The involvement of women in voluntary sector employment and as paid volunteers is complex, reinforcing gender, race and class stereotypes which impact on definitions of care. The argument that tasks associated with community care are undertaken *by* the community rather than *in* the community is predicated on assumptions about the ready availability of female kin who will care both for family and other members of the community, and thus provide informal care. But such assumptions concentrate on the experiences of middle-class white women (Finch and Groves, 1983; Ungerson, 1987). As has already been said, Black and working-class women are frequently recruited into the workforce as domestic and care staff in community based projects, or within the homes of others, but this is not always recognised as 'proper' care (Graham, 1983).

There is a circularity in the arguments about caring. All involvement of women in caring reveals underlying assumptions about their limited role in the paid workforce, and notions of sexuality and femininity. It is these which lead to expectations that women will undertake the personal, private and unpaid care of women and men. But when they undertake that care their capacity to take an active role in the paid workforce is limited in ways which fulfil the stereotypical expectations. This spiral has been interrupted by the growing evidence that men are involved in caring, both formal and informal, and by changing patterns in the involvement of women and men in the paid workforce (Hewitt, 1993). It is therefore important to look at the different participation of women and men in caring and to identify what this contributes to gendered understandings of care.

Providing care

Formal care

That social work and social care female professions is evident from the structure of the paid workforce, which is predominantly

female. However, with women employed at lower organisational
levels while men hold managerial positions, being part of a care
workforce obviously does not empower women. The issues are
complicated, involving divisions based on race and class as well as
function.

The distinctions between unskilled, common sense approaches to
care work and a set of professional tasks and skills has been reinforced in formal care by the terminology. In the report of the
Barclay Committee (Barclay, 1982), for example, the distinctions
between social work and social care planning were drawn and
'social care' emerged as the hands-on physical caring provided by
large numbers of unqualified women. Social work was seen to be
struggling to establish a professional identity which required specialist knowledge and drew on a specific body of theory. This
distinction between functions has had an impact on arrangements
for provision of social care and social work and the different involvement of women and men.

Social care

In a study reported just before the changes in the community care
legislation, 86.5 per cent of the workforce in social services departments in England and Wales was female, and women were
employed predominantly as home helps, care assistants in elderly
persons' homes, day nurseries or as occupational therapists (Nottage, 1991). The majority of this female workforce was part-time,
often employed at mealtimes and bedtimes in residential homes
when the workload was heaviest, or as day centre staff. Domiciliary
staff including home helps and home care staff constituted 30 per
cent of the social services workforce. Such women generally had no
formal qualifications, few training opportunities, no prospects and
low pay. It was assumed that these workers would use abilities
developed in domestic situation such as 'caring attitude' and 'experience in performing the full range of household tasks'. The fact that
they provided functions that might otherwise be provided by the
family affected their status, they were low-paid and graded as
manual workers (Nottage, 1991: 19). From the outset, women's
involvement in social work has been associated with domestic skills
and those associated with being a wife and mother which were
deemed little more than commonsense (Brook and Davis, 1985),
an attitude reinforced by the fact that there were few training

opportunities. This denied the role of front-line workers in dealing with interpersonal communications in difficult situations and in assessment involving reporting significant changes in behaviour or circumstances, all of which require complex skills. This lack of recognition of the skill involved in caring has meant that women who work in the formal system are confronted by a contradiction between the expectation of their altruism on the one hand, and the harsh realities of overwork and underpay on the other (Dalley, 1996).

This distinction based on function became apparent when training was introduced for social work. It was initially not available for residential workers who in many ways provided the most direct care work. In the 1940s and 1950s direct care work was held in low regard and therefore thought suitable for women, predominantly working class and Black and ethnic minority women. Such a view is perpetuated by the association of care work with domestic work: 'A commonly held view of care work is that it is unskilled and consists of little more than domestic chores. It is seen as particularly suitable for women, consistent with their traditional roles in the home and as carers' (Wagner, 1988). Ironically the very qualities which were being identified as necessary for performing the tasks were said to hold back the career progression of the women holding the posts. Many of those who argued that this form of work (residential care) suffered from a poor image laid the blame on those women who had been the mainstay of residential services. It was suggested that it was their personal attributes, rather than any structural causes, that had held back the professionalisation of this work (Younghusband, 1947).

This led to a growing distinction between social care and social work in the 1970s and 1980s, but, as is discussed below, there is no evidence to suggest that those women who had entered the profession as social workers fared any better. However, it was women in residential and day care who were most affected by the changes in community care legislation. The purchaser/provider split introduced by the NHS&CC Act enforced a transition of the provision of services into the voluntary and independent sector, with private agencies contracting for the domiciliary services. To ensure 'economic' contracts wages were kept low, labour was casualised and the employment condition of women who provide the services worsened but at the same time expectations of their role increased.

Social work

With the development of social work tensions arose about the skills
needed: 'there was a contradiction between the idea on the one hand
that all that was required for social work were the natural caring
attributes of women, and on the other that it needed something in
the nature of specialist knowledge that could be taught' (Brook and
Davis, 1985: 10). Increasing emphasis on training, promotions and
management structures in an attempt to gain recognition highlighted the distinctions between skills and knowledge which had
significant impact on the workforce.

For example, the Younghusband Reports (1947; 1951) were
commissioned to address issues of the status of social work and
recruitment. The conclusions of the reports created a change of
emphasis in the relationship between women and social work
(Brook and Davis, 1985), and in male attitudes towards social
work as a profession. The emphasis which Younghusband placed
on attracting men into the profession was due to the diminishing
number of women, both married and unmarried, available and
prepared to be involved. Attracting men into the profession had
consequences for the position of women within it, but also understandings of the culture of organisations and the way that services
were delivered.

One way in which differentiation between characteristics of men
and women emerged was in the development of a more managerialist approach to social work. While the naturalness of women as
carers had not been questioned, but was seen as an expression of
their 'emotional' feminine selves, there were suggestions that these
qualities needed were at odds with 'rational' man, and therefore
unnatural if they were performed by men. One response was to
argue that the qualities that men brought to social work had specific
functions within the organisation and management of care work,
rather than participating in service provision.

For example, with the identification of child abuse, the higher
status of child care and the 'technicalisation' of intervention and
management which is deemed to require specialist knowledge and
training more males have become expert social workers and managers in this area, while women continue to provide the day-to-day
caring in nurseries. The notion of 'care' in this context has taken on
a more controlling meaning, involving protecting and providing for,
and it is therefore a legitimate activity for men. There may be an

irony in arrangements which mean that male social workers are thought more capable than women of managing situations which have been precipitated by men's incapacity to express caring, or more frequently abuse of the power inherent in situations of caring for children. Such complexities are part of the intricate relationship between gender and caring which is explored below.

To return to community care, the upgrading of social work because of male infiltration is particularly pertinent when reviewing the changes brought about by the NHS&CC Act. The politicisation of social work has been brought about in part by the challenges to the profession by the market philosophies of the new right which sought both to replace welfare and to introduce managerialist approaches (Griffiths, 1988; Audit Commission, 1986). The culmination of the review of the social work task described in Chapter 2 is the notion of care *management*, where the role of the worker is transformed into rational processes of identification, organisation and acquisition of services on behalf of those in need of care, and the oversight and monitoring of such services provided by a variety of paid and unpaid carers. Care has become a commodity, to be provided by some and acquired, purchased or obtained by other means by others.

What emerged was a widening distinction between and within social work and social care. As has been said, social work as a profession was influenced both by policy initiatives and by an increase in theorising around the social work task. In this context the reformulation of care was seen to reflect a rational 'masculinist' approach required to give the task of caring technical status, thus distinguishing it from the caring skills more often linked to a set of 'essential' feminine qualities.

The pervasiveness of these assumptions, that women naturally possess caring capacities, has locked women into informal caring. Equally powerful are the expectations that women will be available to care. Men do provide informal care but their involvement is by dint of accident or familial circumstances, while for women the expectations that they will be available for informal care are taken as given. It is important to examine the evidence to understand the different contributions of women and men to informal care, and the implications of those contributions for understanding constructions of masculinity and femininity.

Informal care

Since the early 1980s in British social policy there has been a consistent analysis of who does the informal and unpaid caring (Finch and Groves, 1983 ; Ungerson, 1987; Dalley, 1996), providing a rich stream of scholarship illustrating the complexity of discussions about gender and caring.

The gendered notion of caring has many explanations and consequences. At one level the discriminatory effects of informal caring are clear. That married women and cohabiting women who stayed at home were at one stage not allowed to claim the invalid care allowance available to men and single women performing the same role (Equal Opportunities Commission, 1981) supports a simple, if unacceptable, explanation – that community care is resourced by unpaid labour, which is readily available from women who are not in the period labour force because of other caring responsibilities. Thus, at this level, community care both assumes and reinforces the economic dependence of women.

More recent statistics from the General Household Survey 1985 (Green, 1988) illustrate that the situation is more complex than this. While carers of working age were less likely to be in full-time work than their peers who did not have caring responsibilities, there was little difference in relation to part-time work. This was true of both male and female carers in terms of part-time work, but male carers were less likely than their peers to be in full-time work, and were more likely to be seeking work or keeping house. Women were classified as being permanently unable to work (Parker and Lawton, 1994). Recognising that such statistics tell little about the effects of caring, or the characteristics of those who become carers, Parker and Lawton, in what Fisher (1994) sees as a reluctance to accept that men do care, suggest that men 'fill in' as carers when unemployed: 'Unexpectedly, and contrary to what is found in existing literature, women's overall level of labour market participation does not appear to be affected by caring to the same extent as is men's' (Parker and Lawton, 1994: 32). This seemingly surprising finding may occur because women are expected to be at home and therefore did not describe themselves, or are not described, as seeking work.

This analysis of the statistics is important because it highlights how particular ideologies can influence assumptions and interpretations which impact on the identification of who provides care. For example, narrow definitions of care may deny the contribution of

Black women to informal care. Similarly familial ideologies, that is sets of assumptions of the quality and worth of care provided by family members, produces a hierarchy of caring which has ignored or marginalised lesbian women and gay men seeking and providing care. It also denies the diversity of support structures that Black and ethnic minority groups experience, sometimes constrained by lack of family networks (Atkin and Rollings, 1996).

Men providing care

With that proviso, the conclusion that women care and are cared for is not disputed: 'Caring is generally considered a woman's issue, even an older woman's issue, because more women than men are carers and more women than men are cared for, given their long-evity and dependency at all ages, and this situation is likely to continue for the foreseeable future' (Clarke, 1995: 20). However, the evidence from both Britain and the United States is that men do undertake informal caring (Arber and Gilbert, 1989; Fisher, 1994; Kaye and Applegate, 1994), although the extent of their involve-ment, and differences in the way that care is provided by women and men, are subject to much debate. For example, there are neg-ligible differences in carers who support elderly spouses, but a consistent gender difference in co-resident and extra resident carers (that is caring for someone in another household), with women providing considerably more care (Arber and Ginn, 1991).

However, gender is not the only variable in the provision of care. There are class and age differences. Co-resident care, for example, is provided more frequently by working-class men and women than by the middle class (Arber and Ginn, 1992), while middle-aged unmar-ried men and women have a much higher chance of becoming carers than any other group. Although men as a group are much less likely to be expected to provide informal care, young single men and older never-married men are just as likely to have to be involved as their female peers (Parker, 1992). This is primarily by default in that they leave home later, or are less likely to leave at all and therefore become co-resident carers for the older relatives with whom they live.

Similarly, different housing patterns, age structures, and cultural traditions all influence the statistics. For example, that sons in Asian families take a lead role in caring for their mothers reflects the availability of long-term co-resident care among minority ethnic group and challenges the Western notion that men are known to provide care for their partners, but very rarely provide care for other relatives or friends. Therefore, rather than argue that 'spouse care' led to the discovery of male carers, it is suggested that co-residency caring throws greater light on a gendered understanding of caring. The argument that marriage and age play a part in determining receipt of public sector services is a powerful claim and changes the whole debate about gender and community care in a white majority culture (Fisher, 1994). However, the distinctions between co-resident and spouse care again highlight the exclusionary power of such labels. The contribution that gay men make to caring for their partners experiencing the symptoms of HIV and AIDS, and the involvement of male volunteers in buddying schemes, serves to challenge the very distinctions and categories which are being used in the discussions.

With all these caveats the careful analysis of the statistics about male caring has been part of a complicated debate about the impact of caring on women's lives (as opposed to the lives of men), rather than an exploration of understandings of masculinity and femininity. So, for example, the high proportion of men in the statistics for caring are explained by some as a function of the survey method, or of gender differences in the responses. If women regard caring as part of their normal 'duties' they are unlikely to define themselves as carers, whereas men who see caring as something extra, would be more likely to respond positively to the general screening question used in the General Household Survey (Clarke, 1995). Alternatively, there may well be under-reporting of caring by men because, as in formal care work, the perception of caring as 'women's work' or family responsibility has brought about a reluctance on the part of men to be associated with such feminine activities because it challenges their masculinity. Or, in the case of gay men they may not want to be part of official statistics because acknowledging their homosexuality risks discrimination and oppression because of the very stereotypes of masculinity which would be challenged by notions of men caring.

If gender as a variable in the provision of informal care is contentious, does an analysis of differences in the nature of care provided give some insight into constructions of masculinity and femininity? Early studies argued that while women provide constant care and perform the intimate personal caring required of those with greatest need, men are rarely involved in such 'heavy end' caring, having access to domiciliary care such as support at night and daily help with personal care (Charlesworth *et al.* 1984; Arber and Gilbert, 1989). The findings in the Kaye and Applegate (1994) study, that men did provide hands-on personal care but less often than other categories of care, are in line with UK statistics where the majority of personal care, either with or without physical care, is provided by women (Parker and Lawton, 1994).

There have been contradictory findings about the emotional involvement of male carers, with some suggesting that men are less emotionally involved than women and therefore less stressed by caring (Gilhooly, 1984), while others argue that among men there is a lower willingness to report emotional problems. These differences are ascribed to gender rather than age, class or familial relationship, thus affirming a view of masculinity as 'uncaring' or unwilling to own feelings. Some studies, however, report men as experiencing care giving as physically and emotionally demanding, with, for some, an element of sacrifice: 'forfeited dreams of freedom in older age' associated with restricted freedom (Kaye and Applegate, 1994: 227). Male carers also reported the isolating and insulating nature of care giving. That this may be related to their different experiences of friendship (Jerrome, 1990) resonates with gendered assumptions about male and female 'connectedness' which have been at the heart of feminist theorising about gender and caring.

Gender and caring

Having described how differences in the amount of care and the kind of care provided by women and men have been presented, it is necessary to explore in greater detail how these findings both influence and are influenced by the interplay of gender and care. In this discussion becomes clear that the accepted distinctions between sex as a biological category and gender as a set of constructions of behaviour and attitudes play a significant part in the expectations of who provides care. That these distinctions also influence the perceptions and expectations of those who receive care is the subject of the final section of this chapter, and the rest of the book.

The impact of caring on understandings of gender are dealt with under two themes. The first is that the economic arguments for the predominance of women in all forms of care work cannot be separated from a consideration of the impact of men moving into 'non-traditional' occupations, the paid workforce which provides care. However, the reason why care work is low-paid and considered to be non-traditional for men is that underpinning the economic arguments are gendered assumptions about the nature of care and its association with expressions of femininity. This is the second theme.

Women in the care workforce

A glance at the history of social work and of women's employment since the First World War indicates that caring, in its many forms, was the medium through which women were accepted into the social world (Graham, 1993). Through this particular track of the labour market (which includes catering, cleaners, nurses, secretaries, social workers and teachers) women enter and occupy their place in society. These routes are influenced by economics but also reveal of a set of assumptions, beliefs, ideologies and hegemonies.

The economic arguments for why men did not enter the paid care workforce are interestingly complex in that they reflect a rather circuitous chicken and egg conundrum. Care work was low-paid because it was assumed to be unskilled and commonsense. It may have been thought to have such low status because it was performed by women, but it is difficult to unpack whether it was undertaken by women because it was low-paid or because it was an extension of their femininity, of the roles they played in the home.

If it was low-paid because it was unskilled then while male employment was buoyant there was little need for men to be interested in low-paid employment. While women were used to low-paid employment, or their involvement in the labour force was transitory because of lack of resources for child care support etc., they were willing to accept the status quo. As a female dominated profession women social workers were accused of not advocating for themselves (Younghusband, 1947). Male dominated trade unions, arguing for a 'family wage' for men which enabled them to support women and children, did not advocate for women's wages.

This notion of a 'family wage' for men not only served to keep female employment low-skilled and poorly paid so that it did not challenge men's place in the labour force, but was also symbolic of male ways of caring, represented by the provision of goods and financial security. The impact of such a model on men was to lock them into the workplace, and to assume that they did not possess this commonsense or caring capacity.

The economics of formal care provision was therefore dependent on models of family organisation where women would be dependent upon men financially and, if they entered the workplace, would not require an economic wage. Formal care also emulated family care in its organisation and made presumptions about models of care and the motivation and commitment of those offering it.

Men in the care workforce

Such an analysis means that those men who move into female dominated jobs, those developed for women on the basis of cultural assumptions of women's nature and their place in society, upset the gender assumptions embedded in the work. They are open to challenge for not being a 'real men' (Williams, 1993). To cope, they may emphasise their masculinity and distance themselves from women, to some extent resisting the perceived risk to heterosexual identity in a society where stigmatisation of homosexuality is still rife. They do this by constructing different roles for themselves, or redefining the way the work is undertaken.

Such a pattern has been clearly identified in social work with a number of consequences. First, when training for social work became more widespread men were more likely than women to enter the profession as trained workers. They quickly moved through the promotion levels to become managers and controllers of the profession (Nottage, 1991). Those who continued to perform the actual caring functions remained unqualified and female. Second, the whole profession changed in nature and became upgraded. Third, as has been said, the nature of the task changed and social work which was the area of formal care that men signed up to became more technical and scientific, while social care continued to be hands-on and expressive.

Such separation of male/female attributes in the workforce is not specific to social work. Studies of sex-role segregated jobs illustrate that positions in the workforce are not gender-neutral but have built-in assumptions about the kind of workers likely to be employed (Williams, 1993). In part this reflects the economic arguments outlined above, but this single explanation does not seem to be enough. Therefore dual systems theory argues that both capitalism and patriarchy contribute to the devaluing of jobs traditionally performed by women. Male social dominance ensures that whatever jobs are undertaken by men receive high social evaluation reinforced by assumed technical skills which require training while female jobs are assumed to be 'natural' (Bradley, 1993). Hence when men move into female jobs their motivation is questioned, especially if they are likely to experience few rewards – low status, lower pay and challenges to their masculinity. Often such movements are precipitated by economic recession, when unemployment and lack of opportunities may drive men to consider taking up 'female jobs'. It may be this which, according to the Labour Force Survey, has caused a 45 per cent increase in the number of men in the social work industry between 1994/5 and 1998/9 (quoted in Workforce Audit of the Personal Social Services, 1999).

In Bradley's typology of men moving into female jobs the process is seen to be that of invasion, where men enter a profession anticipating they will make rapid career moves. This has certainly been demonstrated in the care workforce where, in an occupation in which the majority of staff are women, the higher management levels (e.g. directors and assistant directors) are men (Nottage, 1991).

In the case of the 'care' workplace the implications of male 'invasion' are more complex because they not only perform tasks which are assumed to be the domain of women, but in doing so they disrupt and challenge assumptions about masculinity. Hence they call into question what it means to be female and male, especially 'meanings which are embedded in the habitual authority, technical expertise, sexual assertiveness and economic advantage of men in the day to day functioning of institutions like the workplace and trade unions as well as the family' (Segal, 1990: 97). They thus destabilise the very structures that have been at the heart of theorising about care work and challenge the distinctions made between men and women on the basis of assumed characteristics.

The nature of caring

So far it has been demonstrated that, while it is taken as given that women care, the involvement of men in caring has either been denied or has been constructed as a different kind of care from that provided by women. In both informal and formal care men have been seen to have different attitudes towards their task or have been observed as wanting to change the nature of the task. For some feminists these distinctions reflect the different moral characteristics of women and men. Women are deemed to be imbued with an 'ethic of care' and men with an 'ethic of justice' (Gilligan, 1993).

In these constructions of femininity and masculinity, differences are seen to be more complex than those which are based on bio-logical determinism, where it is postulated that girls are born with innate characteristics such as non-violence, maternal instincts and the capacity to care. Equally, they provide a more complex explana-tion than theories of socialisation which argue that girls, for a variety of reasons including their reproductive capacities, are encouraged to behave in passive and caring ways, and are rewarded for doing so. Differences are related to sex in that male and female children are said to experience their social environment differently because the main carer is female and this impacts differentially on male and female identity formation (Chodorow, 1974). The con-sequence is the importance for women of attachment in the human life cycle which makes them more motivated to care, bound as they are to emotional and affective behaviour by an 'ethic of care'.

Ethic of care

The assumed similarities between female children and their mothers is said to define feminine personality. Women are said to make connection to other people in a way that men do not, because they have remained connected to their main carer whom they experience as being like them. This connectivity is related to caring because girls: 'emerge with a stronger basis for experiencing another's needs or feelings as one's own (or of thinking that one is so experiencing another's needs and feelings)' (Chodorow, 1974: 167). This is per-ceived as women being 'stuck' at the third stage of moral develop-ment (Gilligan, 1993) which joins the need for approval with the wish to care for and help others – capturing women between the passivity of dependence and the activity of care.

The notion of care in this construction of femininity includes both a paralysing injunction not to hurt others and an injunction to act positively toward self and others, and thus to sustain connection (Gilligan, 1993), a set of characteristics captured by Virginia Woolf's description of woman as the 'angel in the house': 'She was intensely sympathetic. She was immensely charming. She was utterly unselfish. She excelled in the arts of difficult family life. She sacrificed herself daily . . . Above all she was pure' (Woolf, 1931: 3). Here connectivity and caring are construed as in some ways positive, although the impact on both the women who gave and those who received such attentions will be discussed in the third section of this chapter.

For men, the consequences of being separated from the femaleness of their mothers means that they are detached: 'Since masculinity is defined through separation while feminine identity is defined through attachment, male gender is threatened by intimacy while female gender is threatened by separation' (Gilligan, 1993: 8). Thus women's ability to be connected influences both their capacity to care and their motivation to care because it is from this that they get their sense of self. Men, it is argued, because they do not get any sense of self from caring have devalued it:

> Women not only define themselves in a context of human relationship but also judge themselves in terms of their ability to care. Women's place in man's life cycle has been that of nurturer caretaker, and helpmate, the weaver of those networks of relationships on which she in turn relies. But while women have thus taken care of men, men have, in their theories of psychological development, as in their economic arrangements, tended to assume or devalue that care. (Gilligan, 1993: 17)

This analysis has been criticised from a number of perspectives. First, it assumes that femininity is fixed, since women's mothering is universal. Motherhood is not universal. While it is only women who give birth, not all women give birth (or even have the propensity to do so), nor does giving birth assume a set of skills and inclinations which are required for the physical and emotional caring for children. Indeed some have identified that universal conceptions of motherhood have contributed to the subordination of all women, but that they are culturally and historically specific, emerging from industrial capitalism and scientific progress of the eighteenth century where nature was separated out from humanity (Ramazanoglu, 1989: 61).

Second, it romanticises female values such as empathy, mothering and caring, all of which have contributed to the subjugation of women, to their oppression by association with emotion and nature. Ironically, as Gilligan acknowledges in the above quotation, the qualities which differentiate women from men are not recognised, or more accurately are not validated, by men. This lack of validation or recognition has contributed to, or as has been illustrated by, the devaluing of social care as an occupation or profession, and has been linked more generally to poor self-esteem and associated with female oppression and depression (Miles, 1987).

Gilligan's approach has therefore been identified as a 'weak' form of cultural feminism (Evans, 1995). Cultural is used in a dual sense, in that it comprises beliefs and character in its own right, but that the contexts from which they spring are culturally specific, that is they reflect organisation in Western industrialised societies with particular models of child rearing. However, the 'weakness' is that while she appears to be a proponent of difference, Gilligan believes that these differences, which arise between men and women not because of biological traits but because of different responses to experiences, are surmountable especially if women's voice is privileged over that of men.

In contrast to Gilligan, some theories argue that men have always had the capacity to care, but are only allowed to do so in later life because they become 'naturally' more nurturant and concerned for others around them as they grow older (Gutmann, 1987). Others suggest that men have the capacity to care and that the women's movement has granted cultural permission to be nurturant and to care for others, enabling men to display more affective than instrumental qualities. Interestingly, this is again illustrated from a study of older male care givers:

> Overall these men, all engaged in elder family care-giving to a significant degree, saw themselves as possessing substantial measures of affective, nurturant and expressive personality traits usually associated with femininity, but they tempered this personality orientation with a high valuation for autonomy and self sufficiency. (Kaye and Applegate, 1994: 222)

This combination of 'masculine' and 'feminine' traits might be seen to challenge the notion that men operate from a set of rules rather than a sense of duty, arguing that men are driven by love and affection as well as by duty and obligation. Such a stance is not incompatible with those feminist writers who, focusing on filial care, recognised a distinction between 'caring about', in the sense of feelings of affection, spontaneous feelings of affinity, and 'caring for' in the sense of servicing needs, or tending, caring out of a sense of duty (Ungerson, 1983a; Finch and Groves, 1983), and seeing such distinctions as gendered. However, no assumptions can be made about whether one approach to caring is better than another. The 'caring about' represented as male caring has been described as 'rationality with feeling', where instrumental approaches are adopted in the performance of a variety of social and support related functions (Kaye and Applegate, 1994: 230). 'Caring for' carries negative overtones of objectivity and distance which are celebrated in professional care but are deemed to be inappropriate in informal care. However, unless the reciprocity of the informal caring relationship is recognised, there may be an instrumentality which rewards the carer, and depends on the passivity and the gratitude of the cared for. Seeing care as positive may deny the oppressive potential of caring, whether it is provided by males or females, by family or volunteers. Another set of assumptions in the community care policies is that family care is positive. In terms of gender and caring this has implications for women and men who provide care, and for the choice of care by those who require it.

Care as duty

Framed within a familial ideology (Allan, 1983; Dalley, 1988), certain household and kinship structures are experienced as natural, normal and desirable and carry with them expectations of patterns of behaviour. However, constructing them as such legitimises specific forms of family and household forms as normal and right, and has negative implications for those who by virtue of culture, class or any other reason do not conform. The hegemonic nature of familialism is that it is the standard by which all non-family living is judged, as well as the standard by which all other family organisation is assessed. As was discussed above, familial ideology also legitimises the social location of women in the domestic sphere, but in doing so it encourages women to give loyalty to their family and kinship, and not to other women or to public and political organisations (Ramazanoglu, 1989: 148).

Familial obligations operate for men, but influence their involvement in care in different ways. On the one hand, there is an alleged rationale for male carers who are reported to have a desire to 'pay back' the care they have received from their wives (Fisher, 1994). On the other, spouse relationships may operate more for men on a model of fixed obligations, both because of the legal contractual nature of the relationship, which was taken as a deliberate step and that it involves a shared household (Finch, 1995). As such this might be seen to reflect the operation of the ethic of justice, a rational male way of constructing relationships and their own behaviour within them. So for example, that men and women are equally likely to be caring for a disabled spouse (Qureshi and Walker, 1989) may be part of men's sense of duty, but this is a duty to the marital relationship and not a generalised duty to others. The duty arises out of the loving relationship, but their dependence on wives for social networks (Wenger, 1987) might reflect other motivations operating within the marital relationship. The differences and impacts of the assumed connectivity of older men are explored in Chapter 6, but in terms of their commitment to caring Wenger suggests that men may get their satisfaction from their marital relationships in later life because of their lack of connectivity more generally, whereas women are less dependent upon their husbands for friendship and companionship.

Finch and Mason's findings that there was clearly an expectation that adult children should do something to help elderly parents, if this is needed, might seem to suggest notions of duty. However, that there is little agreement at the public normative level of what should be done leads to the conclusion that there are no 'fixed obligations', but 'commitments' which are developed over time on the basis of reciprocity, which are individually negotiated rather than a response to a particular role or genealogical line (Finch, 1995). This questions both the notion of care as duty, and the expectation that female family members would provide it. Similarly, Bytheway's (1987) study of working-class men, which reveals that the moral motives of male carers and the expressive content of their care are similar to those of women carers, suggests the need to re-examine the theoretical framework of the role of gender in evoking the care response (Fisher, 1994).

So far there has been repeated reference to the feminine qualities which are positively associated with caring. Male caring, when it is identified, is explained away as a statistical artefact or is theorised in ways that suggest it is an anomaly. All of which highlights that just as before feminist theory provided a challenge there was a tendency to universalise and homogenise women's experience, so too there are assumptions about masculine ways of behaving and feeling.

Masculinity and caring

In attempting to challenge both the biological essentialism of some explanations of the differences between women and men, and the emphasis on socialisation in others, discourse theorists emphasise that masculinity and femininity refer neither to any collection of traits nor to some set of stereotypical roles, but rather to the effect of discursive practices (Segal, 1990). So as we have seen the discourses, the writing from policy and the analysis of practice, have led to assumptions about differences between male and female ways. While some discourses portray the male position as generally dominant, active, authoritative with the female as the object (Wetherall, 1984), the literature on caring presents some interestingly complex challenges. In parallel to the seemingly positive descriptions of women as selfless and meeting the needs of others, masculinity is patterned in the social institutions of middle-class life in the 1970s with competitiveness, personal ambition, social responsibility and emotional restraint. This was matched by the 'culture of work' of the working-class father (Tolson, 1977). These assumed characteristics were thought to more highly valued in society, certainly in the economic labour market.

Connell (1987) however has posited that the maintenance of men's power over women and the related understandings of masculinity are not reducible to a single and primary cause, but that different patterns of dominant masculinities and subordinate femininities are produced in different spheres of life – family, workplace, state and so on. In this analysis he is supported by Segal who suggests social power is at the heart of the difference:

> Masculinity is best understood as transcending the personal, as a heterogeneous set of ideas, constructed around assumptions of social *power*, which are lived out and reinforced, or perhaps denied and challenged in multiple and diverse ways within a whole social system in which relations of authority, work and domestic life are organised, in the main, along hierarchical gender lines. (Segal, 1990: 288)

Part of this power has been gained from male roles in the workforce and, as was noted above, it was this lack of power which acted as a disincentive to men joining the social work workforce. However, the operation of power, as Segal suggests, is more complicated than this. In caring it is possible to have power over others, to control their lives. Also women's assumed capacity to care, while devalued economically, does have positive overtones it is seen to be a 'good thing'. So part of the invasion which Bradley (1993) refers to could be seen in terms of Freier's anti-dialogical action, a stage of which is cultural invasion (Freire, 1972: 121) Such invasion may be covert or overt and occur in a variety of different forms. Successful invasion leads to the oppressed responding to the values, standards and goals of the invaders – the more the invaders are mimicked the more stable their position becomes. More significantly, those invaded become convinced of their intrinsic inferiority. In identifying the male as the oppressor, this appears to privilege the position of the male, and validate the maleness of certain ways of behaving and organising.

The movement of men into certain aspects of domestic labour, the delivery room or into caring is part of the phenomenon of the 'new man'. Men recognise the benefits of, for example, having a closer relationship with their children or by expressing their commitment to others by caring. It is suggested that they attempt to achieve this by being involved in the more pleasant aspects of care, rather than the heavy end of washing soiled clothes, cleaning soiled bodies or assisiting with toileting. However, to suggest that men should be involved in personal care work leads to other aspects of maculinity and power, including sexuality.

Sexuality and limits to caring

While the economic barrier to men being involved in formal caring may be removed, or more accurately the economic incentive increased, continuing accounts of male abuse within areas of care work will make other barriers, such as reducing risk, challenging stereotypes and ultimately changing male behaviour, more difficult to surmount.

Concerns about the risks which masculinity presents in care work arise out of an approach to the behaviour of men which assumes that the sexuality of men is influenced by, and in turn influences, 'non-sexual' activity; it confirms a sense of power over women, and affirms 'true masculinity' (Segal, 1987). This 'true masculinity' can lead to assumptions that the quality of male care is different, and that part of this difference is linked to sexuality. Men are not assumed to have the 'technical expertise' of caring and 'sexual assertiveness' is seen to be a disqualification for formal care. A frequent reaction to the involvement of men in all aspects of personal care of fellow adults is to raise questions about the rights to privacy and protection of the person requiring care. But to argue this in connection with male carers and not with female carers suggests that there is an essential difference between all men and all women. As such, it reinforces notions of femininity and masculinity which reflect more than the socialisation of girls into specific gender roles of mothering and caring. Males are defined by a masculinity which is socially constructed and presents them as aggressive, sexual beings at best incapable of care and at worst as dangerous entities in care settings. The increasing evidence of child sexual abuse by men, and the involvement of male care staff in sexual and physical abuse, reinforce understandings of this hegemonic masculinity, a way of male behaving which is designed to maintain their power and control, and which influences reactions to their involvement in formal and informal care.

Focusing on economic disincentives to men being involved in caring fails to address debates about male perpetrators of abuse in families which may impact on arrangements for care, and has implications for constructions of masculinity. Abuse in caring is discussed in more detail in the following chapters, but the point at issue here is whether men are assumed to be not capable of gentle, non-abusive caring activities either because of the known extent of violent and abusive behaviour by some men, or because the construction of masculinity deems all men capable of abuse.

For example, Ungerson argues that there are cultural rights which proscribe men from, or allow them to avoid, dealing with human excrement or forms of nakedness, and these effectively preclude men from being involved in personal or 'heavy end' caring which involves both. To be involved in such hands-on caring would impact on men because it would 'threaten their own sense of personal order and that of the people they care for' (Ungerson, 1983b: 74). Ungerson further identifies taboos, which include beliefs about incest, as powerful 'background noise' which, she argues, is peculiarly silent, not articulated by those doing the caring, those receiving care or those responsible for ensuring care is provided (Ungerson, 1983a). These taboos operate for men only, reinforcing not only assumptions about male sexuality but the asexuality of female caring.

Some theorists (Connell, 1987; Segal, 1990) have argued that through a variety of mechanisms a hegemonic masculinity, a dominant heterosexual masculinity, operates which emphasises the power relations between women and men based on sexuality: 'defined through difference from, and desire for, women, sexually driven and relentless in its pursuit of women – in perpetual contrast to the depiction of the passive and restrained sexuality of the "gentle sex"' (Segal, 1990: 99). Constructions of masculinity and femininity seem unable to avoid the implicit and explicit assumptions about sexuality. Chodorow's distinction between 'being' and 'doing' (Chodorow, 1974), for example, has been seen to reflect masculine activity within sexual relations, a definition that is reflected in other understandings of masculinity being actively achieved: 'the mechanics of sex and reproduction demands that "the man has to *do* something in order to fulfil himself"' (Horney 1932, quoted in Graham, 1983: 19).

Caring by women is seen to be passive and is therefore trivialised by men because it does not provide the level of activity necessary to affirm men's identity. Alternatively, it has been suggested that women's caring role gives them simple sureness in their sexual identity, but masculinity has to be kept and re-earned every day and boys live in fear of becoming unsexed by failure (Graham, 1983: 19). Caring therefore is a positive activity for women, but a threat to men's sexuality.

The assumption that women will undertake the intimate personal care of adults, whatever their relationship to them, is not always seen as giving them a sureness in their sexual identity. Implicit in many studies are suppositions about the asexuality of women as carers. Women do not constitute a sexual threat to those for whom they are caring, in the way that men would if they were undertaking intimate and personal care. However, the picture is more confused than this in that accounts, both real and fictional, of nurses (and other carers) being the subject and object of sexual and romantic male fantasies suggest that this asexuality is bounded, operating only when tasks are being performed, but waived when the focus is on day-to-day interactions. More significantly, the expectation that women will be prepared to undertake the intimate personal care of, for example, fathers who may have abused them as children makes significant emotional demands of them, and requires them to deny or suppress their revulsion. Such requirements are associated with notions of filial duty which do not extend to sons.

Sex, gender and providing care

Hence debates about the construction of femininity and masculinity impact on understandings of care, and knowledge of the patterns of care undertaken inform understandings of masculinity and femininity in a way that destabilises some of the stereotypical understandings that have informed social work and social care debates. As Fisher observes, theories of women's involvement in caring highlight an unresolved problem of whether women's greater capacity to care is something to celebrate or regret:

> Every time a man finds some aspect of hands-on care difficult to undertake is confirmation of the contradiction between caring and men's inherent 'nature'. It allows service providers to cite the carer's masculine gender as evidence of the need for service. It allows the myth of the incompetent man to be reproduced, and to be imposed on male carers and on care receivers. (Fisher, 1994: 673)

If such a situation continues, women will be consigned to caring, and if care work is not validated they will continue to be oppressed. It could be argued that what is needed is not for men to 'invade' care work but for the work undertaken by women to be celebrated, and properly remunerated, or recognised as a contribution to the community and as such as a qualification for citizenship. However, if this is the only change that occurs, then with increasing emphasis on care in the community women will continue to have little choice about their professional careers, or how to spend their time. More importantly, if notions of innate and natural characteristics are rejected, then there is no reason why men should not care, and both women and men should have active choice.

However, as Fisher's quote highlights, assumptions about who can or should provide care also have implications for the those who receive services, and it is this notion of how gender and caring impacts on users which is the focus of the next section, and indeed the rest of the book.

Receiving care

In the early analyses the views of care receivers were seen to be significant for the recruitment of carers. Hence Finch argues against the recruitment of men as carers on the basis of women's choice:

'partly because one would want to defend the right of women who need care to be cared for by another woman, not by men' (Finch, 1990: 54), but in doing so she may be accused of ignoring the voice of those men who require care. Morris, in contrast, quotes research indicating that spouses/partners are the preferred carers of both men and women (Qureshi and Walker, 1989), thus indicating it is not the sex of the carer that is important but the nature of the relationship between the giver and recipient of care.

In the light of this conclusion it is important to review the way that issues of gender influence the arrangements for care and the delivery of care services.

Arrangements for care

Discussions about the gendered nature of caring have emanated predominantly from the perspective of carers, emphasising the burden of responsibility, especially for women. This has been seen to be one of the negative effects of feminist analysis, framing, for example, disabled women as a burden, and denying their role in caring (Morris, 1993b). Similarly, prioritising filial care marginalised care given to older people by older people, especially spouse care ignored, and in doing so the huge amount of care given by older women, and made male care invisible (Fisher, 1997). Finally, conclusions that residential care for older and disabled people is the only way to prevent the exploitation of women as informal carers (Finch, 1984; Dalley, 1988), was seen to deny choice for those who require care:

> the only way to ensure that the assumption of the responsibility by women, against their own interests, can be broken is the physical removal of people who cannot manage without extensive care. Institutional care is the only effective way women have effectively to say no. (Baldwin and Twigg, 1991: 127)

This emphasis on the needs of women carers reinforces the lack of citizenship afforded to users of community care services, male or female, and denigrates them as inessential. To make this point is not to set women against women but to recognise that the arrangements for community care which depend on care by the community, by those who have other responsibilities and demands, will constantly lead to conflict.

A second consideration in arrangements for care is that, just as assumptions about masculinity and femininity influence who undertakes the caring, and the way that care is offered, such assumptions also influence the way that services are received. As an illustration of the latter point, studies which document the way care is experienced have concluded that men were more likely to be receiving personal not physical care, while women were likely to be receiving practical help only (Parker and Lawton, 1994). In populations of older people significant gender differences were highlighted in the response to the need for certain services. Men were more likely to get help with heavy laundry, housework, cooking, shopping and decorating. For some this was seen as confirmation of assumed sex role differences: that older men 'are not expected to do housework, and that women are expected to do housework for men as well as themselves' (Qureshi and Walker, 1989: 81). Others have argued there was little evidence to suggest the systematic discrimination against female carers per se, but a firm conclusion that, all other things being equal, service provision is biased against those who have resident carers, and those whose carers are related to them irrespective of their gender.

As has been discussed, the sex–gender constructions within caring relationships operate at the level of the emotional and the practical or economic. For women and men, receiving care is a dependant status, but for women it is often conditional upon their being simultaneously depended on by others. As Morris argues, many disabled women undertake caring for their partners and for others within households. For many women, disabled and undisabled, being dependent is synonymous not with receiving care, but with giving it. For men the cost of being cared for is experienced as economic dependency and poverty, but for women economic dependency and poverty is the cost of caring (Graham, 1983).

One response to the inequalities or oppression said to be brought about by the expectation of women to provide unpaid care has been to recommend that the state provides wages for informal caring. The concern of some feminist commentators was that such a wage was unlikely to be an economic one, and its provision might enshrine women within a caring role, and change the nature of the caring relationship (Finch and Groves, 1983). If wages were available, however small, this would negate women's argument to become part of the paid labour force, where women's wages were traditionally low. However, if women were paid to care, then the tasks to be performed would be seen to be duties, and expectations of what should be done, and with what regularity, would be part of a caring contract. The person requiring the care may benefit by feeling less emotionally dependent, the care provided becomes a right rather than an act of charity, loyalty or love. In terms of user empowerment, this is no bad thing, and the introduction of the facility to provide direct payments for users of services to purchase their own care needs provides choice and contributes to a sense of self. But the right to choose, and to purchase, who provides the care may be in direct conflict with the rights of women who might provide care to choose to organise their lives differently. For both users and providers of care, payment may remove the emotional dimensions of care which are said to enshrine women into caring, and those receiving care into dependence and gratitude. It is this set of expectations which emphasises what Morris calls the 'custodial nature' of care (Morris, 1993a). As was said on page 110 the seemingly selfless nature of female care, the assumed intrinsic goodness of the act of caring, is challengeable. Just as the definitions of care are constantly changing so the concept of care is contestable.

Care as discipline

Understandings of 'care' have changed significantly and they are now not always positive. It is not just that harm can come to those who are being cared for because of the actions of a particular carer, but the actual process of care can be seen as the exercise of power, whatever the gender of the carer:

> [t]he codification of caring practices and the formulation of a body of knowledge create disciplines of caring which supply the basis for authority and power for those who practice care. (Fox, 1995: 111)

Fox, while seeing these processes as in one sense ungendered, in that female carers such as nurses and social workers are having to undertake the managerialist surveillance tasks of care, does relate them to concepts of masculine and feminine. More significantly, in exploring the distinction between care as a vigil, which is disciplining and controlling, and care as a gift, which enables and empowers, he highlights that community care discourse is not explicitly a discourse on liberation or emancipation. As was discussed in the previous chapter, the organisation of welfare assumed a supplicatory role of those requiring care was necessary in order for the state or the community to be seen to be providing, to be meeting need. These dynamics also operate at the level of the interpersonal relationships of those providing and receiving care.

It would appear to be difficult to avoid domination within a caring relationship; even notions of empowerment *by* agents of the state (social and care workers) may be prescriptive, determining the identity of the cared for person by the expectations of the formal, professional, disciplining care. Assumptions about how those requiring care will behave, even to the extent of assuming they will want to participate or want to advocate on their own behalf, are no more empowering than acting on behalf of someone. In contrast, a more emancipatory discourse of caring acknowledges the right of the cared for person to be different: 'This *gift* enables and empowers, it allows the recipient of the gift to "become other", to establish a new subjectivity' (Fox, 1995: 117). But there is a danger that this may be understood simplistically with a failure to recognise how difficult it is to give unconditional care. In social work literature, for example, the one-to-one relationship has been derided as being oppressive and capable of pathologising individuals. In community care literature, identified differences in male and female attitudes to care giving are contentious. That men are said to take pride in the cared for (their spouse) as a keeper takes pride in a pet rabbit (Rose and Bruce, 1995) is seen to suggest an instrumentality which is demeaning to both the male carers and those for whom they care (Fisher, 1997). What Fox argues is that public giving is underpinned with notions of reciprocity, and the implications of the caring relationship can impact negatively on those who require care. Speaking primarily of nurse/patient relationship, he argues:

> [it] might be managed through compliance and docility on the part of patients, or by the gratefulness for the expertise of the carer. But if patients come to see that the efforts at reciprocity – to return something of what they are given – are inadequate, they are humiliated degraded and stigmatised. (Fox, 1995: 118)

With the rhetoric of user choice and user involvement, community care policies would seem to provide the means to reciprocity between carer and cared for, to redefine the relationship. However, Fox suggests that quite the opposite has occurred. Informal care has become 'professionalised' and, as has been noted already, moved into the realms of disciplining and surveillance. Examples of this are evident in discussions in the following chapters of the impact of the statutory requirement for annual assessment of people aged over 75-years, the influence of informal carers in systems for mental health assessment and review, and unqualified staff receiving training in risk assessment.

Interestingly the notion of gift employed by Fox in opposition to this surveillance is not uncomplicated. To be able to give assumes a recipient and gratitude What is being contested by disability rights groups and mental health advocacy services is that if community care is a right, they should be able to make decisions for themselves about the nature and amount of care they require and not be passive recipients.

Rights to care

The right of those requiring care to choose what kind of care they receive, and from whom, may restrict the rights of others to choose not to have to care. Alternatively, if a person who requires care opts for residential care, s/he should not be prevented from that choice because of guilt generated in the family, by concern about the opinions of others, or notions of familial duty.

This notion of choice is fundamental to the gendered organisation of care. If it is assumed that a person requiring care will want female care, then this severely restricts the rights of women to choose to be involved in other activities and other employments. If, however, those requiring care want to be able to choose a male carer then revisions to the recruitment of carers and the expectations of men in the organisation and delivery of care will be necessary. In that the role of men in informal care seems to be circumscribed by assumptions of masculinity, this will require some review of the received understandings of masculinity and femininity.

Decisions about who should provide assistance may well be made in accordance with a consistent hierarchy of preferences among available familial and kinship network members, but the actual experience of the caring relationship is related to the meanings defined by the actors involved. The existence of intrinsic rewards from particular relationships is one feature of social exchange which distinguishes it from economic exchange (Blau, 1968). However, that does not deter those who require care from wanting to maintain some dignity, and independence. This is achieved in a variety of ways. Some provide by informal remuneration for the care received (Baldock and Ungerson, 1994) and more formal arrangements are reflected in legislation to move towards direct payment for care to be administered by those requiring care, rather than being dependent upon services commissioned by statutory sector organisations. However, whether services are provided, or are purchased directly using income or payments calculated as part of a care package, focus on the arrangements of care to be provided is still necessary. The relationship between those who provide care and those requiring it is susceptible to conflict of needs, and misuse and abuse of power will occur within caring relationships whatever the gender of those involved.

The conclusions of Baldwin and Twigg, that community care provided on a non-sexist basis requires: attention both to the conditions of women, and to the conditions of men; that sexist assumptions which are present in the delivery of care are challenged; and that attention is given at the point that the decisions are made (Baldwin and Twigg, 1991: 133) while a starting point do little to challenge the potential for the caring process itself to be experienced as oppressive. Oppressive understandings of both gender and care have to be challenged within users groups as well as within service providers, but in that many of the arrangements are made in the private domain of either family relationships or the interaction between professionals and users, then attention has to be given to processes for ensuring just outcomes for those who require care, and those who provide it.

Conclusion

This analysis of the affects of gender on arrangements for care has raised a number of themes which are examined in the rest of this text. The first is that understandings and constructions of masculinity and femininity permeate arrangements for the provision of care both explicitly and implicitly. Despite earlier assumptions by feminists and others, there is evidence to show that caring capacities are not necessarily organised along such dichotomous lines of, for example, caring and being cared for, women care and men do not.

Second, and just as important, the concept of care as a necessarily positive activity is challenged. Seeing an ethic of justice as being in opposition to an ethic of care suggests that female caring is positive, and that justice, as a male rational activity, has negative connotations. Examining the changes brought about by the marketisation of the welfare state, and the arrangements for community care which ensued that have reduced care to a commodity, has highlighted that care can be reduced to a form of technical oppressive surveillance, whoever provides it. Finally, care can be oppressive because of the denial of the reciprocity of the caring relationship, whoever provides it. At its worst caring requires a passive subject, someone who is prepared to be cared for, and in this sense the feminine ethic of care can be as oppressive as the rational ethic of justice.

To explore further how gender influences community care it is necessary to explore in greater detail the ways in which it is implicated in the experiences of those receiving care.

5

Mental Health: Assessment and Planning

Introduction

The development of community care for those with mental health difficulties has attracted public attention because of concerns about the potential for error in the diagnosis of people as mentally ill or disordered. These concerns come from two perspectives. The first is that misdiagnosis may lead to unnecessary treatment interventions and detention of individuals whose behaviour deviates from some assumed norm. The second is that failure to diagnose acute mental health problems can create unnecessary risks both to the individual and to others. Debates about the criteria used for mental health and ill health assessment are therefore crucial. They provide the starting point for this chapter, which argues that the diagnosis, assessment and treatment of women and men as mentally ill and the criteria used to discharge them into, or maintain them in, the community are imbued with notions of femininity, masculinity and gendered roles within society.

In arguing this position the chapter provides an introduction to the following three chapters which focus on groups commonly referred to as the recipients of adult community care services. Each chapter will focus on a particular group of service users and will examine the policy and practice literature to explore how gender is, or is not, alluded to. This examination will explore how references to gender contribute to an understanding of how gender is constructed within the particular user group. What becomes clear is that understandings of gender within specific groups both reflect and expand constructions of women and men in wider society. A further interesting finding is that attention to gender draws attention to significant aspects of practice. As has been said, this chapter focuses on diagnosis and assessment, but Chapters 6 and 7 provide insight into methods of intervention.

Context

Feminist scholarship has been influential both in ideas about constructions of mental illness and in policies and practices in community care for those with mental health problems. Focusing on women, it provides necessary questioning of medical processes which define people as mentally ill. However, there is not necessarily agreement in the conclusions drawn.

A simple analysis suggests that the description of mental disorder as a 'female malady' (Showalter, 1987) is supported by statistics which show, for example, that women are more likely than men to be defined as mentally disordered. Not only are women diagnosed more often as having psychiatric disorder than men, but they also identify themselves as having related symptoms. For example, in a self-report survey in Britain in 1993 women between the ages of 16 and 64 were almost twice as likely to be suffering from some form of neurotic disorder (Whitmarsh, 1995). However, such statistics rarely give definitive explanations; they raise questions. In the area of gender and mental health diagnosis these questions have focused on the lived experience of women. Does the high incidence of women with neurotic disorder mean that women's biology necessarily constitutes them as in some ways mentally inferior? Or do other factors emphasise the negative experiences of women's biology, framing their behaviour as neurotic while validating men's as 'normal'.

One response is to examine the pattern of reporting mental health problems. The differential responses to mental illness in men and women might serve to highlight both women's socialisation into a passive feminine role and men's reluctance to admit to illness behaviour, or to interpret symptoms in a psychiatric framework (Miles, 1987). It has been suggested that men have been excluded from some studies and discourses about mental health, or that feminist discourse has selectively represented women's experience and women's treatment (Miles, 1987; Pilgrim and Rogers, 1993), but to see this as misrepresenting gender differences is too simplistic. The inclusion or exclusion of particular groups from research and enquiries in the field of mental health in itself reflects how gender operates at all levels and can be seen as actively misogynist:

> Within feminist analysis, the labelling process is seen to serve the function of maintaining women's position as outsiders within patriarchal society: of dismissing women's anger as illness – and so exonerating the male oppressors; and of dismissing women's misery as being a result of some internal flaw – and thus protecting the misogynistic structures from any critical gaze. (Ussher, 1991: 167)

The emphasis on women's experience of mental health by some feminists has therefore been a direct response to the male domination of psychiatric services which have ignored gender, or dealt with it as an unproblematic given, a set of essentialist differences which do not warrant consideration or exploration. The position held by others is that the mental disorder of women is a social construct or that mental disorder itself is a social product. From this perspective, simplistic, dichotomous distinctions of male and female influence the way that mental health services, both medical and social, respond to the needs of women and men, but do not necessarily assist in understanding the experiences of women and men within those services.

Gender and mental health

As has been said, early feminist analysis of mental health explored the treatment of women by psychiatrists. Gendered constructions influenced these encounters in that clinicians treated 'female misery' according to biological definitions (Chesler, 1974). The very biological symptoms which are acknowledged by, for example, de Beauvoir, as characteristic of women, have been interpreted by some psychiatric schools as the reasons for, and the cause of, women's mental instability:

> This lack in [biological] stability and control underlies woman's emotionalism, which is bound up with circulatory fluctuations – palpitation of the heart, blushing, and so forth – and on this account women are subject to such display of agitation as tears, hysterical laughter and nervous crises. (De Beauvoir, 1972: 64)

Labelling these experiences as 'abnormal' in terms of emotional well-being, but 'normal' in terms of women's experience, has created tensions for feminism. The choice has been to deny their validity in an attempt to refute biological essentialism, or see them as part of women's experience and therefore a testimony to women's suffering. While some see these constructions of femininity as both inaccurate and unnecessary (Allen, 1986), others have emphasised the impact of women's social position and the way that it has contributed to their diagnosis as being mentally well or ill (Brown and Harris, 1978; Miller, 1988). Such debates focus on the experiences of women, but by default they are exploring constructions of gender. The acceptance of the 'abnormality' of behaviour associated with mental illness assumes a norm against which women and men should be assessed. Early studies (Broverman *et al.*, 1970) indicated that clinicians privileged male behaviour as normative of adult mental health whereas women's behaviour, even when not diagnosed as mental illness, was seen to depart from the general conception of mental health. Normative adult mental health poses rationality in opposition to emotion and situates women on the side of irrationality, men on the side of reason. Attributions of irrationality, passivity and dependence constitute one of the mechanisms through which power can be maintained and enhanced (Busfield, 1996). Linkages between gender and assumptions of rationality and agency are therefore significant in mental health assessment and intervention.

Role performance

Studies which postulate that male and female behaviours differ in the way that they cope with emotional issues often relate this to women's capacity to nurture, drawing on the literature of caring outlined in the previous chapter. It is suggested that the maternal and domestic roles associated with caring lead to pressures which cause differential experiences of mental health and illness, differential diagnosis by professionals and different treatment (Miles, 1987). This position argues that the diagnosis of women is therefore not do to with biology and suggests that if men were exposed to, or endured, the impact of these roles they would respond in ways similar to women. If this is so, it is not the condition of femininity but the impact of the social conditions which disproportionately fall on women which is the significant factor.

However, it is important not to universalise experiences. Not all women who perform these roles experience or display mental health symptoms; and not all women who are treated within the mental health system have been expected to fulfil these roles. Finally, as was explored in the previous chapter, some men do perform these roles, but there is no evidence of higher levels of mental health problems in older male carers. This could be seen to support the argument that the tendency to mental ill health is associated with some notion of femininity. This does not mean that there is some biological propensity to mental ill health in women, but, as was discussed in the previous chapter, that assumptions about the different roles performed by women and men lead to them being validated and acquiring status by performing these roles. Role performance is therefore significant in discussions of mental health either because of the stress caused by performing certain roles, or because of a failure to perform them.

Chesler, for example, argued that gender is intimately linked to (what she calls) madness, because madness embraces the total or partial rejection of one's sex role stereotype. However, she also saw an association between madness and the sex role stereotype of women: 'the acting out of the devalued female role' (Chesler, 1974: 6). This suggests an impasse for women who either accept their femininity, perform their allotted roles and suffer in that performance, or are deemed to be disturbed if they act as not feminine, i.e. masculine. Such distinctions are supported by Miles's (1987) analysis of both the different experiences of women and men in society and the way that male and female behaviour is viewed and reacted to differently. The consequences of this are that not only are the causal factors for women being involved in psychiatric services the source of debate within feminism, but the extent of gender differentiation by psychiatric services is also contested.

Diagnosis, for example, is said to operate differentially and gender differences are found to be far more clear-cut in the cases of neuroses and behaviour disorders than of psychoses and the organic mental disorders (Busfield, 1996). This precipitates different outcomes for women and men; what is typically problematic amongst men is to be assigned to the category of wrongdoing, amongst women to the category of mental disorder.

It is for this reason that Busfield (1996) sees limitations in focusing solely on women. She argues for discussions of how gender is linked to constructs of mental disorder for both men and women and an examination of the factors that cause women and men to feel and act in ways which place them within the boundaries of mental disorder as currently constituted. She cites the use of case studies which lead to typification of symptom and diagnosis and interweave categories of disorder with masculinity and femininity. The association of gender with particular disorders is 'verified' by statements about the gender balance, but also by explanations of gender-specific causes and circumstances. However, equally influential is the association of disorder with performance of duties and responsibilities. This is particularly evident in case notes where woman's inability to 'do normal household chores' is cited as a symptom of mental illness and male cases are defined by their inability to manage paid work properly. Mental illness is not therefore defined only in terms of gendered tasks and roles, these are sustained by attributions of irrationality that are not independent of task performance (Busfield, 1996: 112). In this way not only are the distinctions between sex and gender socially constructed, but the diagnosis, or construction of mental illness is linked to these distinctions.

Masculinity and mental health

Such an analysis has implications for constructions of both femininity and masculinity. While assumptions that male behaviour, whether deemed normal or abnormal, is taken as given, and it is women's behaviour which requires analysing and explaining, could be seen to contribute to the problematising of women's behaviour, there is a more positive outcome which involves deconstructing the relationship between the two.

The oppressive construction of gender into male and female as consisting of specific and oppositional characteristics which go beyond role performance affects both women and men. Masculine attributes are only associated with more positive mental health when displayed by men, thus causing women who present behaviour which is seen as 'male' to be seen as psychiatrically ill (Ussher, 1991). Men who do not demonstrate these typically male behaviours, or more significantly demonstrate symptoms which are 'feminine', have different experiences. For example, those men who returned from the First World War displaying classic signs of 'hysteria' could not be deemed to be suffering 'disturbances of the womb' (the literal meaning of the term), and were therefore dismissed. In some instances they were deemed effeminate, if not homosexual, by psychiatrists for such unmanly behaviour (Barnes and Maple, 1992). Equally, gay men freely expressing emotions when diagnosed as being infected with the HIV virus were diagnosed as hysterical and referred for psychological treatment because of this 'inappropriate affect' (Ussher, 1991: 169).

Why focus on gender?

To turn the spotlight away from women might be seen to be devaluing their experience, particularly so when understandings of mental disorder are linked to resources and to policies and practices for providing services. If there is no understanding of why women are diagnosed as having mental health problems more frequently than men, then there will be no change to the labelling and stereotyping which are seen to be part of that process of diagnosis. These concerns have led to discussion of male mental health being set up as oppositional to the experiences of women. However, there is a consistent link between the perceptions and expectations of male behaviour and women's experience. For example, studies which have looked at the connection between masculine self-image and social expectations of male behaviour have labelled all men as potentially dangerous and interested in sexuality (Pilgrim and Rogers, 1993). If this norm of male behaviour is to be aspired to by all men then it has implications for all women who are the potential objects and victims of men's sexuality and dangerousness. Hence, to unpack constructions of masculinity as represented by the diagnostic and assessment processes in mental health services is as important for women as challenging the constructions of femininity.

For men, the implications are that the concept of danger influences the way their behaviour is interpreted or diagnosed, and may lead to their being dealt with in the criminal justice system rather than the psychiatric system. They are deemed to be bad not mad (Ussher, 1991). While there may be advantages (prison sentences are fixed-term while hospital orders may be indeterminate, subject to review and extension), the notion of danger and risk can impact negatively on men who offend and are subsequently referred to forensic psychiatry provisions (Allen, 1986). Alternatively, it could be argued that men are dealt with more 'harshly' by being subject to restraint (both legal and physical) because of gender stereotyping of male behaviour as violent.

This is not to deny that men are more likely to commit acts of violence and sexual abuse, but some men are negatively affected by a combination of both demonstrated behaviour and intervention on the basis of stereotypical assumptions. For example, there a disproportionate number of young men Black men diagnosed as schizophrenic and detained on the basis of this diagnosis. It may well be that they present as distressed or different but then make a physical response to attempts to detain them, and this in turn induces coercive behaviour from the professionals which exacerbates the situation (Pilgrim and Rogers, 1993). Hence they may not be essentially violent, but the interplay of assumptions, expectations and behaviour precipitates a violent reaction. For women, the association of violence with masculinity can also impact negatively. If women are violent, they are deemed to demonstrate behaviour which is not feminine and can be dealt with more harshly because of this, even when the violence is an understandable reaction to their circumstances (Orme, 1994).

This introduction to the gender dimensions of mental health has drawn on the contribution that feminism has brought to the construction of knowledge about mental illness and the processes of labelling. The questions that feminism asks about the assumptions of science, and within that medicine, are important both in privileging women's experiences and influencing the way theory and knowledge about gender can positively influence for the good of both women and men. Assumptions inherent in constructions of femininity and masculinity are germane to the diagnosis of individuals experiencing symptoms associated with mental health problems and are significant within assessments for community care which influence treatment decisions and resource allocation.

Assessment

The process of assessment and diagnosis for the purposes of community care is paramount both in determining the entry of the person to the system, and their treatment within it (Orme and Glastonbury, 1993). It is for this reason that a focus on the assessment in the area of mental health provides significant insight into

the gender implications of community care from the perspective of
mental health service users.

The complex underpinning of gender in patient populations in
mental health is influenced on the one hand by the institutions
developed to cater for mental health problems, and the professionals
within them who provide intellectual categories for understandings
of mental health problems, and the flow of patients. On the other
hand, lay judgements of what is problematic mental functioning are
becoming increasingly influential, and involve attributions of behaviour which are affected by factors such as gender, class, ethnicity,
by the distribution of power and by the social and cultural preoccu-
pations of a society at a given moment (Busfield, 1996).

While assessment in mental health has been dominated by clinical
diagnosis of psychiatrists and other medical professionals, the
involvement of lay people not only in initial diagnosis but also in
continuous assessment for the purposes of review is becoming an
increasing feature of care in the community. Attention to assessment therefore requires an analysis not only of the extent to which
formal processes are influenced by gendered perceptions, but also
how the involvement of lay people might further confuse or con-
found the influence of gender in mental health services.

Professional assessments

Community care policy documentation suggested that procedures
introduced would counteract the bias in assessment. For example,
cultural differences would be treated positively :

> The emphasis on the responsibility of the social services to assess need,
> and arrange appropriate packages of services for individuals within their
> own situations, should help to ensure the different needs of people with
> different cultural backgrounds are properly considered. (Griffiths, 1988:
> para 26)

However, what is needed to counteract the complexities of stereotyping within assessment and diagnostic processes is more than a
focus on the individual within their situation. The behaviour and
understanding of the professionals involved in assessment also need
review because it is the interplay between the professional, the
sufferer and their situation which influences the outcome of the
diagnosis or assessment.

As an example, the Royal College of Psychiatrists (RCP) was given a remit to set up a commission to develop: 'appropriate instruments for a brief standardised assessment measure in association with users, carers and professional groups to assess symptom state, social disability and quality of life' (DoH, 1993c: 44). This could be seen to be a positive step. But brief standardised assessments inevitably codify and classify behaviour in ways which make it impossible to challenge stereotypical thinking, and may even encourage it. These processes of codification and classification are becoming an increasing part of assessment in many fields including, as was discussed in Chapter 2, care management in community care. Moreover, the need for multi-agency assessment has produced schedules which depend on the technicalisation of the process. Information systems, while focusing on the individual for the necessary data, do not recognise or take into account the ways in which different experiences and circumstances of individual users of community care have to be recognised and validated.

To return to the remit for the RCP, the interpretation of 'symptom state' and 'social disability' are not merely clinical definitions. Research in the area of race and mental health has shown the significance of the role of diagnosis in the differential treatment of particular groups, and particularly lack of positive attention to cultural differences. The over-representation of Afro-Caribbean males in diagnoses of schizophrenia and the frequent characterisation of Asian women as depressed has more to do with the cultural contexts in which diagnosis takes place than the symptoms presented (Fernando, 1988). The diagnostic process depends on sets of interactions, usually between doctor and patient, influenced by society's norms and institutionalised in education, training and so-called common sense. In a study of processes of access to 'voluntary' admission involving referral from GP to psychiatrist to mental health team, cultural factors of those undertaking the diagnosis influenced recommendations for treatment, rather than identifying what services were needed. The long-term consequences were that the community-based services which were subsequently commissioned to meet need were both inappropriate and inaccessible (Watters, 1996).

Cultural factors influence what is perceived as normal behaviour. Differences in perceptions of what might be deemed 'normal behaviour' are overlaid with gendered assumptions, which for both men and women will be culturally defined. The intersection between race

and gender can be powerful, and can act as a negative factor which
denies women access to treatment, as is evidenced by a GP handbook entry which compounds stereotypes of Asian women:

> Asian women whose days are spent in loneliness and social isolation, cut off
> from family and social networks. Many older Asian women speak little or
> no English. Some are confined to their home, by their husbands or their own
> timidity, and are seldom seen; others may become surgery haunters –
> perhaps because a visit to the doctor is one of the few opportunities for a
> culturally sanctioned outing. (Rack, 1990: 290)

The negative consequences of the social situations are crystallised
in the notion of 'surgery haunters', suggesting that the symptoms
are not to be taken seriously even when the conditions in which
women live are recognised. It is not suggested that Asian women
should be accepted into the ambit of mental health services merely
because of their social situation, but that as women their needs
should be taken seriously. This applies to many groups. Afro-
Caribbean men may be inappropriately caught in the system
because they are men; Asian women are ignored, because they are
women.

Social assessments

In social assessments in mental health little or no attention has been
paid to either the differential needs of women, the influence of
gender on their experiences which lead to mental health difficulties,
or to ways of responding to them. For example, the model of
assessment put forward by Butler and Pritchard identifies a *social*
modality to encompass ethnic or cultural dimension, but makes no
mention of gendered perceptions. In fact the criteria for assessment
given could be seen to reinforce assumptions of male rationality in
that they include: disruption of cognitive abilities which are translated as impairment of a person's ability to 'think straight'; disruption of psycho-social defences which 'increase the likelihood of his
[sic] withdrawal from interpersonal contact' and disturbance of
emotions which mean that 'he has difficulties in responding *appropriately* in inter-personal relations, particularly with those with
whom he is most closely involved' (Butler and Pritchard, 1983:
44–6).

Such lack of attention to gender also fails to address the significance of data on men. For example, while discussions of suicide

involve an analysis of statistics by gender, no significance is given to the fact that middle aged, or older men, are more likely to make successful suicide attempts (Butler and Pritchard, 1983: 116ff), thus ignoring specific pressures linked to expectations of masculinity which can impact negatively on men if they are unable to fulfil these expectations.

Such illustrations from both the medical profession and from social work and social care have been supported by research which identifies that at various points of the assessment process a series of filters operates through which patients pass (Goldberg and Huxley, 1980). It is at these points that constructions of gender will impact on the differential careers of women and men through mental health services, and at which decisions will be made about the appropriateness of community care.

Assessment filters

The power of assessment filters in community care decisions is illustrated by statistics that in the 1990s most people with mental illness were not in hospital. Although 230 out of every thousand people attend the family doctor with mental health related symptoms, only 21 are referred to hospital and six times more people attend outpatients than are hospitalised (DoH, 1992). Thus a large number of people are filtered out of the mental health services at an early stage either by not being diagnosed as mentally ill, or because they are diagnosed but dealt with in the community.

The first formal filter, the GP, is the point at which a disproportionate number of women might be identified or labelled as mentally ill and will be precipitated into the next stage of mental health treatment and diagnosis. Statistics which show that women consult their doctors more frequently than men, and that women with psychiatric symptoms are more numerous than men with psychiatric symptoms among primary care attenders, do not necessarily lead to conclusions that this assessment filter is more permeable to women. Goldberg argues that because female rates of mental illness are almost double those of males in community samples the reverse seems to be true. Without addressing reasons why the rates of women with mental health symptoms are so high in community samples, he suggests that having arrived at the surgery women are more likely to have their illness identified, but they are less likely to be referred to psychiatrists, and therefore less likely to be referred to hospital as in-patients: 'The small female excess among in-patients is therefore a reflection of a much larger female excess in the community' (Goldberg and Huxley, 1980: 159).

But filtering women out of the psychiatric system might not always occur for positive reasons. Miles's study (1988) found that while both male and female patients criticised treatment skills and prescribing habits of GPs, women were more likely to complain that doctors minimised their symptoms, labelling their complaints as 'usual women's problems' related to childbirth, menstruation, menopause or childlessness. The GPs were also experienced as lacking sympathy, often giving the impression that prescriptions were given to get rid of them (Miles, 1988: 120). Men's experience may be more positive because they presented their problems differently, in terms of both cause and effect. They were usually perceived as work related, and it may be that doctors were more sympathetic to the concern that neurotic illness in men might disrupt employment, and therefore did not diagnose them as such.

Goldberg's conclusions would also seem to be contradicted by Sheppard's study of referrals within the mental health system (Sheppard, 1991). Women constituted the overwhelming majority of GP referrals, but only half of those referred from other sources. Of greater significance is the finding that the women referred by GPs were less likely to end up sectioned than either the men referred by GPs or women referred from other sources. Sheppard concludes that these outcomes suggest apparent discrimination on the part of GPs against women, a discrimination which was subsequently mediated by Approved Social Workers and Psychiatrists. In the informal admissions which resulted from GP referrals, Sheppard comments that the prevalence of familial disruption, as opposed to the woman's behaviour being a problem in the wider social environment, reflects the social role expectations of women as homemaker, family manager and housewife: 'Informal admissions were characterised by a combination of mental health and transgression of traditional social role expectations' (Sheppard, 1991: 669). He identified a different threshold which triggers GPs to refer women rather than men, with greater emphasis on neurotic problems, fewer psychiatric primary problems and more social problems, which leads him to speculate that : 'GPs were attempting to deal, both medically and compulsorily, and only in the case of women, with problems which at subsequent assessment were considered to be primarily about social relationships' (Sheppard, 1991: 672). The medicalisation of these problems has implications for women's civil liberties, in that GP referral patterns and the subsequent outcomes might represent an extreme form of social control of women, the loss of liberty. This may reflect notions of femininity and female status in society held by GPs in that they may not consider the threat civil liberties if, for the reasons outlined in Chapter 3, they perceive women as 'not citizens'. Alternatively, notions of citizenship for men mean that the impact of their behaviour on the wider social environment was seen as more serious and cause for intervention.

The second level filter could be seen to be operating effectively in Sheppard's study in that the women that GPs referred were less likely to end up sectioned, and psychiatrists and others may be assumed to be more alert to gender implications. However this is not supported in the accounts of women's experiences in Miles's study. While both women and men thought psychiatrists were more helpful than GPs, women had negative experiences throughout, reporting that psychiatrists would reformulate and reinterpret their problems, distorting their original statements:

> Women who thought that their problem was loneliness, or the hardships of life, or female biological processes, had their thoughts directed to their husbands and children, to their own childhood experiences, or to their innermost worries and fears. I wanted to tell him about our flat having no bathroom, and my mother half-paralysed after her stroke and he wanted to talk about my marriage. I could see there was no help there after only two sessions. (Miles, 1988: 125)

Apart from a lack of attention to women's descriptions of their own needs, psychiatrists were also thought by women not to believe what they said. When women explained the hours needed to nurse relatives or clean the house, they were met with disbelief. Miles speculates that because most of the psychiatrists in her study were male, they were more inclined to accept the statements of their male patients especially when they were work related. However, women in the study were no more accepting of female GPs and psychiatrists, but she argues that this may be because the professional responses and diagnostic procedures of women doctors were affected by male dominated training. Psychiatry, in its response to women, is either involved in 'gender role maintenance' (Allen, 1986) or gender regulation (Busfield, 1996) and this permeates both the training for, and practice of the profession.

But the responsibility does not lie solely with professionals. Referral patterns may reflect differences in perceptions of behaviour, but also differential presentation of symptoms. Gender distinctions in the behaviour and attitudes of male patients led Miles to conclude that men were likely to think less deeply about their emotions, and would arrive with clear-cut explanations which would be accepted by the psychiatrist (Miles, 1988). Such an analysis may reflect generalised and essentialist thinking about the differences between women and men, but may also highlight ways in which men are disadvantaged by having been conditioned into presenting themselves in such a way to conform to some notion of masculinity. Either way it illustrates that men who experience depression or other symptoms precipitated by their inability to conform to the gendered stereotypes held by the medical profession, or indeed by society, may suffer further disadvantage within the mental health system.

Informal assessments

While the medical professionals in mental health care are given primacy in influencing the system, the extension of care management to carers, both formal and informal, has implications for assessment. The introduction of the purchaser/provider split for service provision will involve far more lay people in assessment. One consequence of this is that the initial filtering processes will be moved further away from qualified practitioners and the involvement of lay people in assessment and diagnosis will involve informal judgements: 'Much of the pathway to becoming a clinical case depends on informal judgements and a range of other information about intellectual performance' (Busfield, 1996: 116). Ongoing review and assessment will fall to unqualified staff, family and friends, who will contribute information on which decisions will be made about the level of disorder, and appropriateness of intervention. This information will be based on observations of daily activities of those diagnosed as mentally ill. Often the daily activities which are used for such assessment are described in gender neutral terms, but are overlaid by gender stereotypes in their application. So, for example, women who are not performing household responsibilities and maintaining certain levels of personal and domestic hygiene may be assessed as more dysfunctional than older men, who may be assumed not to have the capacity or the commitment to performing such tasks.

While the rigour (or gender neutrality) of psychiatric diagnosis might be open to question, the outcomes of widening involvement in assessment are that the identification of cases, the elaboration of an understanding of normality, will influence the boundaries of mental disorder (Busfield, 1996). There are implications for correlations between normality and gender stereotypes, and work needs to be done with all those working in the field of community care to make transparent understandings of 'normality'.

Thus, the focus on the involvement of a variety of professionals and lay people in the operation of community care highlights the need to understand their constructions of gender. As care managers, social workers and health care workers are the gatekeepers of definitions and understandings, as well as resources. In the processes of case identification, assessment and review they have a primary role in constructing arguments for allocation of services. Hence gendered assumptions may become significant in assessing whether a situation is serious enough (that is, the level of need is great enough) to warrant service, but also what kind of services will be allocated. The decision to offer services may well be influenced by what the recipient is deemed capable of doing, but also what they 'ought' to be able to do. What is significant for professionals and lay people alike is how this 'ought' is interpreted. For the patients or users of mental health services the interpretation of the 'ought' is often associated with risk; either risk of hospitalisation for the individual on the basis of concern about danger to the public or danger to the person themselves or risk to the person or the public as a result of non-intervention or inappropriate intervention.

Assessment of risk

There is a tension between expectations of, and policy imperatives for, community care and concerns about risk. In community care it is only in the area of mental health that this is an explicit concern, although it is likely that it will extend to other user groups as they are given increased choice and autonomy and are expected to take more responsibility for their actions (Parton, 1996). Risk frequently has gender implications in that as the behaviour associated with males and females is interpreted differently, the level of risk is assessed differently.

Risk of hospitalisation

The ultimate assessment in community care for those experiencing mental health problems is admission to hospital-based psychiatric services. Women are less likely to pass through this 'fourth filter' (Goldberg and Huxley, 1980) and this might suggest they are treated more favourably. Although they are in the majority in general practice surveys, they are less likely to be admitted to the ward and more likely to be offered a day place. Significantly, more women might be admitted to the ward via outpatients. This is usually the route for less severely ill patients to gain admission to a hospital bed and the choice to present at outpatients may be because of lack of attention to their symptoms at earlier points in the diagnostic process.

The differential diagnosis and subsequent admission of women and men is illustrated by studies which show that, while referral rates are higher for women (Barnes *et al.*, 1990), males who are compulsorily admitted are younger and more likely to be diagnosed as suffering from schizophrenia (Sheppard, 1991; Hadfield and Mohamad, 1994). Sheppard's study also found that for both men and women an unspecific referral to hospital led to a subsequent assessment of a psychosis, with rather more men being diagnosed schizophrenic and rather more women suffering affective psychosis. Men were more frequently placed on a Section 3, requiring a longer period of hospitalisation (Sheppard, 1991). This may, according to Sheppard, reflect the perceived longer-term treatment needs of men which may be related to risk assessed on their lack of social stability as evidenced by single status and less permanent accommodation. If criteria of unemployment and housing are used as indicators of disadvantage, men in Sheppard's study were more disadvantaged. That women were more likely to be married and have children might be seen to be a source of support rather than being contributory factors to their mental condition, and they were deemed to be less at risk, and less of a risk.

While the possible bias of those responsible for diagnosis and assessment should not be diminished, it is possible that gender differences in hospitalisation rates may come about because men delay seeking help relative to women, so that by the time their mental illness becomes obvious to others they may be more severely ill and more at risk. Ironically, understandings and constructions of masculinity which make it difficult for men to 'own' their emotional problems, or to seek help with them, that is, the very characteristics which influence perceptions of women as irrational, emotional and prone to mental disorder, might well disadvantage men.

The over-representation of single men and women in hospitalised populations is more perplexing. It is difficult to assess whether single status is assumed to mean there is little opportunity for sharing distress and emotional problems, or that there is no one to look after them. If they never had the skills to make and maintain partnerships this may be a causal factor of their illness, or an outcome of it. Older women who were likely to be widowed or living alone having never married, may be assumed to be in situations of social vulnerability in which loss and isolation are features (Hadfield and Mohamad, 1994). It might well be that such women do not have a partner to care for them, but it is possible that interpretations of what is appropriate behaviour bring such women to the attention of the community care services, or deem them to be more at risk and therefore subject them to hospitalisation.

Risk of dangerousness

Episodes involving young males diagnosed schizophrenic in situations which have created risk for members of the public or for the person diagnosed are exemplified by the cases of Christopher Clunis and Ben Silcock. Such cases have increased attention to assessment of risk and dangerousness. One consequence of community care for an increasing number of younger males with schizophrenia is a pattern of repeated assessments for a known population brought about by limited community resources for that particular group: 'Arguably, emergencies arise more often because continuing care resources are not available following discharge, or are reused by the individual' (Hadfield and Mohamad, 1994: 9). One response has been the establishment of supervision registers with criteria including risk of violence to self and others and serious self-neglect. The preoccupation with dangerousness and its association with masculinity leads to a preponderance of young males in the target group. While this response is understandable, focusing on young men in this way might mean that some are inappropriately targeted, and that some women who demonstrate similar behaviour may be ignored, because they are women, with drastic consequences for themselves and for others. Risk assessment has to focus on the behaviour, irrespective of the sex of the patient. That is not to say that gender is ignored, but that there is no automatic assumption that men will be violent, or women non-violent.

Other gendered consequences are evident in the outcomes of registration, which is accompanied by prioritising services under the Care Programme Approach (CPA). More men are being assessed and detained using the more punitive sections of the legislation and it is suggested that women's community-based support needs are likely to be different because of their different social circumstances. To provide community support for men which accommodates an increased emphasis on risk, danger and non-compliance with medication may therefore operate against the delivery of services more tailored to women's needs (Hadfield and Mohamad, 1994).

Mentally disordered offenders

The attention to risk is particularly significant for individuals diagnosed with a mental disorder who offend against the law. The preference for consensual and community-based treatment for offenders who seem least disturbed means that men are seen as 'really mad', or more disturbed and are more likely to get a psychiatric (institutional) disposal:

> The assumption of male intractability often makes them unwelcome to modern 'short-stay' psychiatric units. The expectation of male dangerousness often makes them unsuitable for treatment in open wards or probation. The presumption of 'deliberate badness' often makes them undeserving of the benefits of psychiatry. Even prior to any evidence, and often despite it, these prejudices direct the deliberations about male offenders away from psychiatric disposal, just as the opposite ones direct the assessment of female offenders towards it. (Allen, 1987: 120)

It was her study of the differential treatment of women and men in forensic psychiatry which caused Allen to question the feminist claim that women were more oppressed within psychiatric structures and systems. Her finding that a smaller proportion of diagnosed male cases were subject to psychiatric disposals than of female cases, while the use of psychiatric disposals for non-diagnosed cases is largely restricted to female cases, caused her to question the 'objective existence' (Allen, 1987: 8) and argue that categories of mental disorder and illnesses and abnormalities are socially constructed. The differential treatment of women and men, based on different assumptions about their rationality, becomes a yardstick for their behaviour. From the construction of male cases it became apparent that it is possible to confront even the most extreme or abnormal of human behaviours without suspending the knowledge of a human conscious subject as the agent of that behaviour, without pathologising him, without obscuring the social meanings and consequences of his needs, in the full reality of their harm and threat. Men were culpable of their offences, their behaviour was part of their masculinity. From the construction of female cases, Allen argues that even the most destructive and regulated of criminals may be judged in ways that do not exile them from human feelings or pity; women are dealt with as irrational, in need of pity by paternalistic agencies. Public attitudes towards Myra Hindley and Rosemary West, however, suggest that Allen's conclusions do not hold in the most extreme cases. Also, her suggestion that judicial personnel tend to regard male offenders as more likely than female offenders to be 'really mad', and in male cases were more ready to interpret unruly or emotional behaviour as evidence of 'real mental pathology' (Allen, 1987: 113), is at odds with the perception of male behaviour as bad not mad (Miles, 1987).

Perhaps the strongest conclusions that can be drawn from discussions of risk factors in community care are that at this level obvious perceptions of gender differences are seen to be operating, and in their operation they reflect significant expectations of the behaviour of women and men. What is less clear is the response to those differences by the various actors, agents and organisations involved in providing community care services.

To put this into context it is necessary to explore the way that policy initiatives in the area of community care for mental health services have addressed issues of gender.

Community care and mental health

Opportunities which were presented for positive change by the NHS&CC Act included the possibility of more flexible responses to the needs of users, but particularly women, in the form of self-help groups, women's therapy centres and other women-centred resources (Barnes and Maple, 1992; Orme and Glastonbury, 1993). While resource constraints were always going to be a problem, the principles and policies of user choice and user involvement were seen to be positive developments. In the field of mental health negative factors influenced policy outcomes, but it is difficult to discern whether it was the philosophy behind the policies which was at fault, or lack of resources. Care in the community for mental health patients had been operating at a variety of levels since the 1957 Mental Health Act introduced the concept of the revolving door. However, as was explored in the introductory chapters, the ideologies of policies and legislation do not always achieve their intended outcomes. Care in the community per se is no bad thing, it is the outcomes of the changes which have been less than benign because of the conditions in which many ex-hospital patients find themselves. Speaking about community care generally, Scull presented a depressing picture:

> Many become lost in the interstices of social life, and turn into drifting inhabitants of those traditional resorts of the down and out, Salvation Army hostels, settlement houses and so on. Others are grist for new, privately run, profit-oriented mills for the disposal of the unwanted – old age homes, halfway houses, and the like. (Scull, 1977: 152–3)

Twenty years later, public concern about community care policies was aroused because of the perceived risks to the public of mental health users who were unsupported in the community and lived in conditions not dissimilar to those described by Scull. Lack of resources, inappropriate responses from the social and health care services and stereotypical assumptions based on gender, race and social class all operate in ways that impinge upon (mis)diagnosis and risk assessment which constitutes danger both for the public, and for the users of mental health services.

At a simple level, the preceding discussions illustrate that while women may constitute the majority of those identified in the community as having mental health problems, they are neither hospitalised nor provided for within the community. Homeless provision in communities is available for males, but less so for females. Women are thought to require less provision because it is assumed they are looked after by others, that they are in relationships with men. This set of assumptions can confine women in, or cause them to enter, abusive relationships. When they are provided for by social and health care services, women with mental health problems are seen to be difficult within residential establishments, either because their behaviour does not conform to the feminine norms of submission or passivity, or because they are deemed to be at risk from the sexual attentions of males. In these circumstances it is the women who are removed from, or denied access to the accommodation.

Having said that, for some men the constraints imposed by the qualities which are associated with masculinity mean that they are not able to express their anxieties in ways which might enable them to access support systems. The consequences are that symptoms become acute and they are then more likely to be dealt with by restrictions of their liberty.

It is apparent that if the needs of women and men are to be addressed through effective community care policies then attention to gender has to permeate all aspects of practice. A review of the literature and policy guidance indicates that where references are made to gender, they are usually on the basis of simplistic definitions of people's experiences or problems, which are unidimensional, either seeing them as belonging to one group, or subsuming their problems into one category. So when there is particular emphasis on the needs of women this both ignores the needs of men, and problematises women.

Community care planning

The Department of Health guidance (DoH, 1993c) recommends the application of the process of health needs assessment to mental health to enable purchasing authorities to identify particular needs of different groups of service users. Specific mention is made of different groups, which include women, and within this notion of difference women's particular concerns are said to be:

■ access to child care facilities at day centres or outpatients' clinics;
■ the choice of a female professional including a female keyworker;
■ the choice of single sex ward (or area within a ward) (DoH, 1993c: 35)

Similar considerations are documented in the *Key Area Handbook* for agencies who are purchasers of services and who may wish to take into account specific needs when making purchasing decisions

(DoH, 1993b: 139). Again women are identified as a separate category, as having special needs which include the choice of female worker and availability of single sex area units. However, within other classifications of difference or special need no attention is given to gender. When the needs of homeless people, children and adolescents, elderly people, Black and other minority groups are considered there is no acknowledgement that within each of these categories there will be women and girls. Even when the groups are likely to be predominantly women, e.g. older people, people with eating disorders and people with puerperal disorders, there are no specific gendered requirements identified.

More complex is the implication of setting performance targets. Examples of local targets appropriately include aims to reduce numbers in detention under the Mental Health Act from Black and other minority groups by 50 per cent. What is not made explicit is the gender dimensions of such targets; no one criteria for assessment can be taken in isolation.

But it is not just within the imposed targets that gender is implicated. The processes which have contributed to the outcomes or targets also have to be reviewed. For example, a suggested target 'to increase detection rate of depression in general and social work practice' is not accompanied by an acknowledgement of the need for gender sensitivity in analysing differential causes of depression in women and men, or the differential influences of the diagnosis of depression on women and men.

Despite this seeming lack of attention to gender, training for all staff is deemed to be crucial for a better understanding of the needs of users and carers, and all professional staff groups are thought to benefit from general and specialist skills in:

- appropriate care and treatment of postnatal mental illness, eating disorders and pre-senile dementia;
- equal opportunities – particularly for women and ethnic minority users of services. (DoH, 1993b: 119, 10.9)

Such recommendations raise concerns that sensitivity to women's needs will be confined to traditional areas such as menstruation, childbirth and child care, and that there will be no recognition of the need for staff to understand the way that gender impacts throughout the mental health systems, and that this requires a consideration of male as well as female needs.

Other concerns are that when women's needs are attended to, it is done in a paternalistic way that problematises women or legitimates their needs only by reference to other factors. For example, the Audit Commission Report references women's need for privacy and safety in wards and other treatment environments, but does not acknowledge that in part that need may be constructed by male behaviour. Only religion prevents women from being problematised: 'Women's experiences of mental health services can be particularly harrowing. Living on a mixed ward is unacceptable for many, especially certain religious groups' (Audit Commission, 1994: para 21).

Charters for good practice

Another theme in community care planning for mental health services is user involvement which is deemed to be symbolic of good practice. The identified means of achieving this include equal access and opportunities and appropriate fora and structures for involvement. However, merely asserting this pays little attention to the processes which influence or deny access to the various structures, and how these may be influenced by, for example, gender, race and class.

The invocations for user involvement have been accompanied by a discourse of charters, declarations of rights and statements of good practice. Each statement demarcates a specific population (e.g. women, Black people), and thus suggests that the needs of these groups are relative to each other. This denies that many users experience contradictions by being identified with different sets of demands from different groups. This discourse of rights which assumes a common identity for particular user groups, coupled with the competing claims between specific user groups, is not a phenomenon limited to mental health users. As was discussed in Chapter 3, the recognition of the citizenship status of users of community care is complex and, as Bornat observes, the introduction of charters as a means of recognising that citizenship adds to the complexity: 'This sharing of common forms and language while at the same time fragmenting into a plurality of self determining interest groups mirrors the image of community care practice and policy in the 1990s' (Bornat, 1993: 262).

Charters for community care were constructed by local authorities as a requirement of the Secretary of State, and as such are seen to be tokenistic and not necessarily responsive to complex needs of user groups. Advocacy services have been active in attempting to influence the agenda and in the area of mental health services the focus has been on ensuring a diversity of service provision. Hence the *Women and Mental Health Project* (Harding and Sherlock, 1994) has produced a pack of eight documents of good practice for specific groups of women experiencing mental health difficulties. Attention is paid to differences between the origins and nature of mental distress experienced by women and men and to their differential treatment within the mental health services. The pack also identifies and focuses on the needs of different women, and the responses required. Much of the good practice identified applies equally to men using mental health services: promoting self-esteem, space to talk through feelings, enabling people to take control of their lives; acknowledging the commonality of bad feelings and the 'normality' of mental distress. However, that is not to deny that good practice in attending to aspects of gender also has to acknowledge difference between groups.

Two further examples serve to illustrate how welcome attempts to disseminate good practice fail to address directly the complexities of gender in mental health services. Survivors Speak Out is an organisation for people who use psychiatric services. A fifteen point charter of needs produced in 1987 adopts a gender neutral approach which sees the focus of oppression as the category of mental health problems and includes such principles as requiring an end to discrimination against people who receive, or have received, psychiatric services, with particular regard to housing, employment insurance etc. (Point 15, cited in Bornat, 1993). It therefore assumes that all those who experience mental health problems experience the same oppressions, or experience oppression in the same way.

In contrast, Good Practices in Mental Health (GPMH) is a national charity established to promote and assist the development of good mental health services through information services, consultant and developmental support to mental health agencies and users. They identify five principles of good practice which should underpin all mental health services: participation, respect, information, choice and individuality (cited in Bornat, 1993). Individuality encompasses a recognition of each person's unique individual life experiences and requires that services should not treat users as a homogeneous group with common needs, nor assume that those needs can be elucidated or satisfied by standard approaches.

Within this it is especially important to recognise the individual needs of men and women from different racial and cultural backgrounds.

Here is the complexity for good practice in community care. Political and other activity is focused on the needs of user groups, but if the focus is solely on a set of categories (e.g. users of psychiatric services), then individual identity is lost within these definitions. If a different descriptor or identifying feature is highlighted, such as gender or race, then shared needs might cut across the categories according to illness or user group. Each of these groups is legitimate, the members, however categorised, are differentiated from other groups by identifying features, cultural practices or ways of life. However, what is not clear for those providing community care services is whether they should respond to individuals on the basis of a specific identity. As Young (1990b) argues, the tension is whether the identified groups are aggregates, where the individual is prior to the collective, or whether the group identity is the basis for action. This dilemma in community care planning and consultation can be seen in terms of how representatives of groups can be responded to, and how the needs of the individuals can be met in the provision of services. If, as Young argues, 'our identities are defined in relation to how others identify us, and they do so in terms of the groups which are always associated with specific attributes, stereotypes, and norms' (Young, 1990b: 46), what are the implications for social and health care workers who have to work within categories such a 'mental health user', with all the negative stereotyping that this involves? Just as importantly, how do workers identify whether women users have different needs to men, without invoking further stereotypes?

Just as it is important not to assume homogeneity within user groups so it is not helpful to universalise either the subject or the agent of control. So, although psychiatry as a profession has been criticised, if change is required it is not necessary to abandon a belief in all psychiatry or psychiatric diagnosis (Busfield, 1996: 237). While madness, mental disorder or mental illness do assert the existence of individual pathology that characterises the person's individuality, they do not require that assumptions are made about individual pathology in the causation of the state of mental ill health. That is, they do not hold the individual responsible for their illness. What is required is an awareness of the ways in which factors such as gender, class and race help to set the boundaries of mental disorder, and influence the assessment of, and intervention in, individual cases.

Intervention

Initial assessments frame the combination of services ultimately allocated to the individual. Frameworks developed for community care, and systems of care management and care programming evolving from policy directives, involve targeting and prioritising services which have to be commissioned from the voluntary and independent sector. This commissioning process is designed to improve community facilities and reduce the need for acute psychiatric beds. It is this dual strategy which makes assessment crucial for the development of community care mental health services.

The appropriateness of service delivery, with due attention to gender, will depend on three factors: the alertness of the person undertaking the initial assessment to the ways in which gender affects both the individual's experience and the interpretation of that experience; the opportunities within the commissioning agency to aggregate data on identified need in order to discern patterns of provision required, without depending on stereotypes, custom and practice, and the responsiveness of provider agencies to deliver resources which will both respond to and challenge the influences of gender in mental health. The complexities of these processes are illustrated by examples of mental health practice which include care planning and evaluation of services for users.

Care planning

The Social Services Inspectorate (SSI) introduced standards for a Care Programme Approach (CPA) which included a requirement that particular account is taken of the needs of people from Black and minority ethnic groups, of women, and of needs relating to sexual orientation, culture, religion, language, age and disability (Standard Two SSI, 1995a: 18, section 4.2.2). A further expectation was that of social services development staff of social services departments would demonstrate an understanding of the different needs of the various sections of the community. In their review of the practices in mental health the Inspectorate had found that while most departments had general statements referring to the importance of equal opportunities issues for users in community care plans, only two of the areas inspected had separate equal opportunities statements for service users. Examples of good practice were isolated and were usually the result of the sensitivity of individual workers, rather than proactive policy.

In its review of mental health services the Audit Commission presented *The Care Programme Approach in Practice* at Tameside and Glossop Mental Health Services as an example of good practice (Audit Commission, 1994: 42). In this provision twelve dimensions of need are rated on a five-point scale. These include: the caring network; leisure and social network; emotional support; medication; symptoms and course of illness; employment/vocation; self-care; housekeeping; accommodation; finance; physical health; and safety. In presenting this as good practice it is assumed that these are neutral categories, with little attention given to the ways in which individuals' experience of gender (or race and class) might impinge. However, each of the categories could be overlaid with specific gender and cultural expectations which could influence the scoring.

It becomes apparent that while these approaches represent good intentions, paying attention to issues of gender requires more than codification. What is required are complex responses to the competing demand to recognise the differences between women and men, but not to discriminate unfairly against women because of these differences. For example, a female service user resident in the community was moved from an unstaffed unit in the community because of her tendency to go walking at night. This was deemed to put her 'at risk' in a way that a male user would not be so assessed. Because of the limited provision for women-only accommodation she had to return to a hospital hostel. This is not to say that the worker involved should not attend to matters of safety, but the differential standards combined with the lack of appropriate levels of provision led to unintended consequences. While it is appropriate for service providers to recognise that women are the subjects of violence, the desire to protect, to care, leads to a more restrictive service environment.

Watters argues that the development of care management and CPA for Black people with mental health problems highlights the need for key workers to receive training in the needs of Black people and to identify forms of racial discrimination Black people might suffer in mental health services (Watters, 1996). While the same arguments can be made on the basis of gender, the above examples show that even when key workers are sensitive, when they are working with codifications and procedures which do not facilitate understandings and responsiveness to difference, and if there is a lack of appropriate resources there will be little impact on the overall systems.

The conclusions of the Social Services Inspectorate's review of the CPA identified differing needs of men and women. In particular it recognised the special responsibilities they may have as parents as areas that should be given attention (SSI, 1995a: para 4.2.10). This too might have unintended consequences. While the CPA requires that the needs of the whole family have to be considered, this impacts disproportionately on female users of mental health services. Assumptions about the parenting roles of women often require them to put their needs secondary to the needs of children and others (Webster, 1992; Hugman and Phillips, 1992–93).

Similarly, practical guidance for working with those experiencing mental ill health recommends that social workers should concentrate on the impact of the illness on the individual and his/her family. In focusing on the individual, social workers should 'tease out the specific implications that a particular clinical manifestation might have for that individual and see it within the context of an earlier and ongoing social world' (Butler and Pritchard, 1983: 30). This raises specific challenges for care managers, social workers and others about whether they work with the accepted definitions and stereotypes of the patient's/user's social world or whether they choose to challenge these. For example, studies which reaffirm the importance of employment to the rehabilitation and resettlement of those who have suffered a mental illness identify the loss of paid work as possible triggers for psychiatric disorder and suicidal behaviour (Butler and Pritchard, 1983). But this focuses on male needs in a society where men are given status by their paid employment and denies men attention to their affective or emotional needs. This point is reinforced by Wainwright's study in a northern town of carers of people with mental health problems: 'Users appeared aware that filling in the day was no substitute for the dignity associated with holding down a paid job. This was often more keenly felt by men where tradition expects them to earn a living.' (Wainwright, 1997: 175, emphasis added).

The significance of work and activity in community care programmes reflects different assumptions for women and men.

Women with long-term or recurring mental health problems have programmes characterised by definitions of femininity which include: women being passive, emotional and childlike; women being encouraged towards relatively dependent roles and domestic pursuits; work being seen as less important for women; low programme expectations because women are deemed less capable than men; 'feminine' behaviour being used as an index of recovery; less input being given to female users as compared with males (Perkins, 1994).

The description of a resource provided by a day care development group illustrates how different expectations for men and women can affect the dynamics between staff and user. In a centre for 18–40 year old ex-patients on regular medication who lived in various forms of accommodation, were on fixed incomes and with no good prospects of work, the aim was to make the centre an interesting and enriching place. In doing so workers also had to respect a person's choice to do nothing. The conflict of the staff role between providing for the members, and making sure they provided for themselves was said to be compounded by the fact that the majority of staff were women, and the majority of the members men. In an observation which resonates with the discussions in the previous chapter about care work the report observes: 'This meant that the stereotype of the caring mother figure looking after [feeding] the helpless male has been difficult to overcome' (MIND, 1993: 26).

There is therefore a danger that in attempting to achieve 'normality' in provision for male and female service users oppressions and stereotypes are reinforced. For example, the impetus for mixed wards in secure hospitals came from an assumption that the presence of females would reflect 'normal' life and would have a good socialising effect on males. However, such arrangements put women residents at risk of abuse, or they are held responsible when the male behaviour is disruptive rather than acquiescent. This is particularly significant when women with serious long-term mental health problems experience alarmingly high rates of sexual exploitation and violence, both within and outside residential settings (Perkins, 1994).

Recognising such dilemmas in community practice has led to the publication of examples of good practice in responding to the diverse needs of women with mental health problems (Perkins, 1994). However, apart from specialist groups for perpetrators of sexual and violent abuse, there has been little consideration of the need to challenge assumptions of masculinity. The code of practice for Approved Social Workers requires that discrimination based on assumptions relating to a person's sex should be avoided (DoH, 1993a), but to date there is little guidance on how those involved in decision making in mental health services will be responsive to the complex interplay between constructions of masculinity and femininity in assessment, diagnosis and intervention in mental health services.

Conclusion

This chapter set out to explore the impact of gender on the construction of the category of mental health in community care. It has documented how received understandings of masculinity and femininity have negatively impacted upon women generally, and women and men as users of mental health services. These understandings operate most significantly in the assessment process, which in mental health services involves a complex interplay of reported symptoms by sufferers and those closely associated with them, and the interpretation of these symptoms by a variety of professionals. The latter provide a series of filters or gatekeepers to services, but also reflect a range of understandings of behaviour according to stereotypical categories of maleness and femaleness. The import of these categories in mental health is that they can lead to the restriction of individual rights, ultimately by the detention of the person within an institution, and they are also perceived as being influential in the protection of the public.

Attention to risk factors is seen to reflect and reinforce gendered assumptions of behaviour which, if not challenged, can impact negatively on individuals, and put the public at risk. For no other category of community care user groups is the assessment process so crucial and the need to challenge the assumed neutrality of scientific categories, or the 'normality' of experience, so compelling. Policy and practice guidelines have suggested that the greater involvement of users in decisions about service provision, and the availability of charters and advocacy services will impact upon the way that services are provided, but in mental health the influence of the assessment or diagnosis of the category of mental illness and the way that this is integrally tied to understandings of constructions of gender have been identified as crucial.

However, within these injunctions there is a tension between the need to recognise the oppression and disadvantage experienced by those in a particular group or classification, and the rights of the individual to have their needs recognised and met. The next chapter considers whether these themes emerge in reviewing the provision of community care services for older people, and the extent to which they attend to issues of gender.

6

Older People: Participation and Consultation

Introduction

The category of mental health users draws greatest attention in community care because of perceived risk; older people are a focus because they are likely to be the largest group of users of community care services and the group most likely to increase over time. As such they present a different set of complexities for social work, social care and social policy, drawing negative attention because of the alleged drain on resources and getting little positive regard despite the wealth of experience that the population of older people represents.

The introduction of community care might have offered social and health care workers opportunities to reflect on the impact of gender issues for practice with older people. However, policy and practice literature appears to have been unaware of, or unresponsive to, debates about gender and age (Arber and Ginn, 1991; Hughes and Mtezuka, 1992). In reflecting on the context of community care for older people, this chapter uses a variety of literature to explore how a gendered perspective contributes to an understanding of difference, and, more significantly, how social and health care practice can valorise individual differences while working with and advocating the causes of particular groups.

Context

Although age is an administrative category for the purposes of community care, older people can feature in statistics in a variety of ways, which means that their representation in the debates about community care is unsystematic. For example, only 5 per cent of respondents to the OPCS census reported old age as the reason for care. However, 70 per cent reported their dependant was physically limited (Church and Summerfield, 1995) and it is likely that some physical limitation would be associated with age. The identity of older people in community care is therefore masked by their physical or health needs. On the positive side, older people may have their needs attended to because they are perceived as physically limited; alternatively those limitations may be ignored, primarily because those experiencing them are older people.

The association of age with need is often seen as axiomatic. Despite the fact that it is likely that only a small percentage of the ageing population will actually become dependent upon social work and social care services, attitudes to those who do influence perceptions of the ageing population. Stereotypes about the ageing process permeate reactions to all older people and influence the way that services are delivered.

The association of age with gender and need is more complex. At the simplest level ageing is a gendered phenomenon. Demographic data demonstrates that women outnumber men in the population of the UK, and the ratio of women to men increases with age. For example, women constitute the majority of people over 80 in British society, and among those aged over 85 there are three women to every man. As well as being the majority of the ageing population, older women are more likely to live independent or isolated lives. All age groups include those who have married, separated, widowed or never married, but 9 per cent of women aged 75 and over have never married (Church and Summerfield, 1995). Among women aged 70 and over, 54 per cent lived alone compared with only 24 per cent of males of the same age. Longevity as well as partnered status becomes significant because it influences women's social conditions, especially in relation to pensions, housing and other aspects of health and social care in the community.

Given the differences represented in the statistics, gender and ageing have been the source of controversy. This has usually focused on the way that women have been treated, with very little attention given to the ways in which an analysis of age can contribute to understandings of gender. It has been argued that gender and the ageing process have a commonality in that both can be described by biology or physiology, but for both those descriptions do not have to define or construct understandings and behaviour: 'Gender is more than a biological factor and aging is more than an organic process' (Gonyea, 1994: 237).

Despite this commonality, academic discourses are criticised for not exploring the connections between gender and ageing in more detail. Sociology is said to have failed to address issues of ageism per se. The gerontological literature has been accused of being gender blind, and feminism is said to either ignore older women or portray their experiences negatively. In the light of this analysis the conclusion of masculinity studies that all recent studies feminise old age (Thompson, 1994a) seems perverse. The differential impact of age on the experiences of women and men is an important area of study, but has to be undertaken with caution. Gender differences in the population generally are seen as negative factors which identify women's experience as different from the male norm. The claim that the extension of these processes into later life is frequently ignored needs to be explored and theorised. If gender is relational, and the definitions of masculinity and femininity have historically reinforced men's power relations over women, then an exploration of these power relations in populations which are predominantly female should provide important observations. As Jerrome argues, it is the combination of age and gender that is significant, but not all-encompassing: 'age and gender together produce a distinctive status overriding social class and other achieved statuses in later life, but for both men and women the ascribed status of "old person" takes over' (Jerrome, 1990: 197). The consequence is that old age is genderless.

This may have come about because gerontological literature has failed to address the different experiences of women and men.

Gerontology and gender

Attention to the ageing process and differentiation among older people emerged as a gendered critique out of critical gerontology which identified changes over time in attitudes to retirement (Peace, 1986). The initial dominance of role theory was replaced first by the disengagement hypothesis and then by retirement being seen as socially constructed (Phillipson, 1990).

Role theory

Role theory reflects some of the classic aspects of theorising. Despite the fact that the majority of older people are female it paid little attention to women's experience of old age, describing the crisis of retirement from the perspective of men's experience. Concentrating on roles associated with paid employment meant that it was assumed that retirement and change of status when leaving the workforce was unproblematic for women, because traditionally they had been excluded from the paid workforce. The roles that women did perform, within the family or other caring domains, were not seen as significant as those in the public domain. Alternatively, universalistic criteria such as performance and achievement within the workforce which influenced men's attitude to retirement were not seen to be relevant to women because their low labour force participation meant that the transitions from mid life to late life would be less dramatic, and therefore less traumatic (Jerrome, 1990).

When women's retirement was considered their assumed connections with the home led to speculation that their interests, activities and social participation would continue throughout old age. Their positive sense of self was thought to come from a capacity to achieve productive activity in unpaid activity inside and outside the home. They were therefore deemed to be more able to cope with daily life not bounded by workplace routine, and less emotionally dependent upon being waged. For men status was assumed to be integrally tied to their place in the paid labour market, and loss of status on leaving it precipitated crises.

However, as women took up more active roles in the workplace loss of work could have profound implications for them. The type of work undertake was often disrupted, low-paid and without access to pension schemes, which meant that economically women would be disadvantaged on retirement. More significantly, paid work for women might have provided some independence from domestic duties, including caring. In this context retirement for women might cause significant trauma because it could involve a return to, and in some instances an increase in, responsibilities in the area of informal care. For some the retirement experience itself might be precipitated by demands structured around a range of caring activities (Phillipson, 1990), and as such could precipitate crises for women equal to those which men were described as experiencing.

Disengagement

The OPCS returns identify the peak age for caring as occurring between the ages of 45 and 64 years. This reinforces that patterns of caring impact on the life course of women (Church and Summerfield, 1995). If disengagement means that older people begin to disconnect from the wider world then the relevance of the theory to older women is questionable. The involvement of older women in unpaid caring activities suggests that for some they continue to work, albeit unpaid, while for others they have to 're-engage' with activities from which they had previously detached themselves. Significantly, as was argued in Chapters 3 and 4, caring does not necessarily contribute to the status of citizenship, and disengagement might not be seen to be relevant to those who were assumed not to be connected to the wider, public sphere.

However, just as changing socio-economic circumstances have had an impact on women's participation in the paid labour force, they have also impacted on perceptions of men. As older men's labour market attachment becomes more tenuous and varied because of changing workforce profiles this has precipitated a review of their disengagement which has also recognised other variables which might influence experience. For example, different coping patterns in old age have been related to class differences. Middle-class people are identified as having extensive activities through membership of age-mixed associations, extra-familial ties, voluntary work and other aspects of public life, while working-class people are said to be more attracted to old people's clubs (Jerrome, 1990). However, observations about class differences in the way that groups deal with, and compensate for, the changes associated with retirement, suggest that the behaviour may be an outcome of the circumstances which have been part of 'normal' life experiences influenced by factors such as socio-economic group, race and culture. Hence it might be possible to argue that the gendered understandings of ageing are integrally tied to constructions of gender in early life which contribute to individual life histories.

The concentration on the effects of disengagement from the paid workforce, while valuable in demonstrating the ways in which social gerontology has analysed experiences of age, has also been seen to be counter-productive. Analysing the ageing process as one in which people become economically inactive contributes to the negative construction of old age generally with a concern about the 'burden' of the ageing population. Age, like gender, becomes a social construction, and more complexly, the construction of each is integrally tied to the other:

> Ageism is a matrix of beliefs and attitudes which legitimates the use of age as a means of identifying a particular *social* group which portrays the members of that group in negative stereotypical terms and which consequently generates and reinforces a fear of the ageing process and a denigration of older people. (Hughes, 1995: 42)

It is because of this association of ageing with negative stereotypes that the social construction of age became the focus of gerontology.

Social construction of old age

Critical gerontology recognised that during their life cycle people have access to different resources associated with factors such as social class, gender, race and personal biography which protect them from, or equip them to deal with, challenges. Old age is therefore constructed from the outside by those who perceive or label the experiences of others, and internally by the individuals who might use their resources to interpret their experiences both in the light of what they feel, but also how they respond to the views of others. So, for example, women's friendships are said to be characterised by emotional intensity and self-disclosure, men's are sociable rather than intimate, based on shared activity often workplace or activity based. Women retain a capacity to make new relations throughout life, men are likely to lose friendships with loss of employment or loss of ability to participate in group activities. One consequence of this is that men become reliant on their wives in retirement and experience greater disruption on widowhood (Blieszner, 1993). It is difficult to discern whether this dependence is related to innate characteristics of relationship-making, or is constructed by the lack of meaningful activities available to men on retirement because of limited attention to the social needs of older people in general.

This interlinking of assumed characteristics and social consequences is also highlighted in studies which argue that in old age expressive activities which have been described as 'women's work' come to be valued. Retirement offers little scope for the pursuit of instrumental goals and the use of conventional masculine skills and this is said to contribute to the loss of self-esteem for men (Jerrome, 1990). This loss of self-esteem can contribute to depression in older men and, because they are assumed not to be able to be expressive, they are not expected to, or encouraged to talk about their feelings. This merely compounds the stereotypes.

Attention to the ways in which the experiences of older people are theorised therefore highlights that these are influenced both by constructions of old age, but also constructions of gender which have powerful implications for both women and men.

Feminism and age

From the critique of the gerontology literature it is apparent that attempts to counteract oppression and discrimination have to acknowledge the dual impact of age and gender on the conditions of older women and men, and to pay attention to the specific conditions of each, and the way these resonate with other user groups in community care.

In focusing on the experiences of older women, feminism has been subject to a threefold criticism. The first is that in its attention, or lack of attention, to issues of age feminism has constructed a vision of womanhood which emphasises power and strength, and has failed to address diversity: 'the multiplicity of images of women which would include the frailty and dependency of some older women' (Hughes and Mtezuka, 1992: 221). Similarly, the impact on older women of the valorisation of youth has been criticised for presenting the experiences of older women as predominantly negative:

> Gender discrimination results in a situation where older women are seen as less deserving than other groups. Studies of older women indicate that they are aware of the substance and consequences of ageism, although they do not necessarily talk about it in those terms; rather they refer to instances where their privacy is disregarded, their choices curtailed, their requests ignored, and where they feel others have little regard or few expectations of them. (Ford and Sinclair, 1989: 84)

This negative imagery and experience is compounded by critiques of community care which emphasise the individualistic approaches to welfare based on a familial model which produces negative stereotypes of older women. For example, in arguing for residential care to help free women from the burden of caring Dalley reinforces such a view: 'the dementing old lady being maintained in her home, living alone, perhaps with a few relatives who might be able to visit, or more importantly, perform caring tasks' (Dalley, 1996: 26). Not only does this present a negative view of the requirements of community care by older women, presenting them as at risk or as always requiring care, it also fails to recognise the positive contribution that older women make to community care by providing care for others. When older women are acknowledged it is as needing the care of younger women, thus emphasising competing needs and engendering a sense of worthlessness and dependence for which the disability movement has criticised feminism (Morris, 1993a).

The second criticism is that feminism has failed to address the structured dependence of older people as a whole, and has assumed that the problems facing older women are the same as those facing all women. In this analysis it is possible to claim that age as a powerful agent in processes of inclusion/exclusion of women has been missing from feminist analysis. Just as malestream scholars have difficulty in considering that their system of knowledge excludes female perspectives, so too have feminist scholars, who easily apply divisions such as class and race, resisting the claim that age can function as a selective filter on the social world (Gibson, 1996). This may be a function of the way that feminist understandings have been constructed, in that preoccupation with social problems and the social construction of inequality, which focus on paid productive labour, reproductive labour or sexual services, means that older women, culturally divorced from these indicators, cannot be easily incorporated into any feminist analysis. Hence understandings of the experience of older women 'stall' at the level of theoretical analysis, if such an analysis goes no further than patriarchy and capitalism: 'the underlying ideologies of both patriarchy and capitalism with their emphasis on male power and male domination have culminated in the use of the family and women's traditional role within it as a controlling vehicle for reproducing the status quo and reinforcing sex inequalities' (Peace, 1986: 65).

A third criticism is that when there is a specific commitment to exploring issues of gender in the study of older people, feminists concentrate solely on women's experience, as compared to those of men. This focus redresses the balance of academic research that has privileged the male, or made normative assumptions that descriptions of male experience includes that of the female. However, researchers and theorists, both male and female, have failed to take the opportunity to investigate a situation which is dominated by women's experience and privileging it, not only by description and analysis in its own right, but by using the positive messages to inform the experiences of all.

Even in cogent criticisms of the literature on ageing on the basis of race, that elders are 'frequently lumped together as homogeneous and insignificant group' (Patel, 1990: iv), issues of gender are not addressed. Patel's discussion of social contacts among Black elders is interestingly confused in terms of gender. Illustrating the relative levels of mobility and the potential usage of day centre and other services, she argues that there is no qualitative measure of social contact, and draws attention to the numbers of Black elders who are socially isolated, illustrating this with reference to Bangladeshi men, but not emphasising the large number of, for example, Asian women who do not go out daily (Patel, 1990: 24). The lack of specific attention to issues of age among Black and other ethnic minority communities (see Ahmad and Atkin [1996] for an example of an excellent text on community care which does not deal specifically with age), may be because minority groups are, on average, younger than white populations and/or because there is little research available on resources for, and reactions to, community care within ageing populations of Black and ethnic minority people (Atkin and Rollings, 1996). Gender issues here, as in literature on white populations, are predominantly about the role of older females as informal carers.

The lack of, or limited, attention in feminist literature compounds negative images of older women and denies differences: 'By focusing on issues of disadvantage, feminist analyses of old age have tended to obscure not only the heterogeneity of old women but also the aspects of being old and female that are a source of both celebration and strength' (Gibson, 1996: 435). One consequence of this is that older women are seen as a problem for society, but little attention is given to the problems society creates for older women. Positive factors such as their greater experience of, and investment in, the private sphere, their involvement in the informal economy, and their experience of moving more frequently between formal and informal sectors and public and private spheres over the life course are not commented on.

More significantly, the advantages of older women's lives – their longevity, social networks and coping skills – are often constructed as disadvantages, or problematised because they are framed in terms of men's experience. Solutions to these 'problems' focus not on valorising women, but changing men's experience. Hence Gee and Kimball, in documenting that women live longer therefore may live alone or be institutionalised, suggest that attention has to be given to the question of men's shorter life spans (Gee and Kimbal, 1987). Similarly Bond and Coleman (1990), in commenting that the possibility of women's economic independence in the twenty-first century is unlikely to reduce the physical and emotional isolation of older women, seem to support the notion of not positively discriminating in favour of women, the disadvantaged, but redressing the imbalance of men and women by focusing on men. They argue that women are more likely to adopt the unhealthy lifestyles of men, rather than men being encouraged to emulate women.

This compounds the view that, despite the emphasis of the negative experience of disengagement for men leaving the workplace, ageing as a process for men has been seen to be more positive, or at least lacking some of the negative assumptions associated with the double disadvantage experienced by women. For example, qualities associated with masculinity such as competence, autonomy and self-control are said to withstand the ageing process better than those associated with femininity (Victor, 1987).

Masculinity studies and age

In continuing to privilege and assert the positives of male characteristics, writers in the area of masculinity studies deny the negative portrayal of older women in other discourses. Also they do not accept that feminism and gerontological studies have made women invisible. Arguing against the homogeneity of the older population, those in masculinity studies assert that research in gerontology and family studies have not studied 'men as men', and have therefore failed to recognise that numerous masculinities exist for older men (Thompson, 1994b). In what is seen as the 'feminisation' of the population of older people, men are said to be invisible because of their low numbers, and because of the differential impact of ageing according to gender. The suggestion is that men are ignored in gender literature because of their seeming advantages: 'Failing to acknowledge elderly men as a distinct group of men may have homogenized not only adulthood but also theory on masculinity' (Thompson, 1994a: 9).

In this critique masculinity studies echo post-structural feminism in arguing that conventional discourses describe gender in binary terms of simple categories of men and women. For example, Thompson challenges studies which suggest ageing diminishes men's masculinity, and, by default, heightens femininity over time, arguing that the social construction of old age maintains that old men are not men at all because they are framed in terms of negative constructions of femininity e.g. dependence and passivity (Thompson, 1994a). In this he echoes Jerrome's claim cited above, that it is 'age' as a category that takes over for both women and men.

However, some aspects of masculinity are clearly not negated. For example, in her studies on caring, Wenger found that constraints of modesty and propriety, which were presumably connected with male sexuality and which echo the discussions on caring in Chapter 4, meant that, outside the marital relationship, it is quite inappropriate for adult men to tend adult women whatever their relationship (Wenger, 1987). The ascription of active (hetero) sexuality to older men is therefore still very powerful.

This brief overview of literature suggests that emphasis on constructions of ageing has created confusing and, in some cases, conflicting understandings of gender and age. Emerging theoretical positions of either ageing as the 'continuity' of gender across the lifespan, or the more general 'discontinuous' model; both fail to acknowledge the variety of lived experiences of women and men according to race and class. There are apparent disagreements between theorists who argue a convergence of masculinity and femininity in later life (Gutmann, 1987) and those who propose that there is greater consistency in masculinities over time (Victor, 1987). However, both appear to want to classify and categorise, rather than valorise differences and diversity.

It is this tendency to attend to administrative categories which are assumed to be homogeneous, rather than explore the complexity of identities and needs within those categories, which has permeated writing on community care provision for older people.

Community care and older people

It could be argued that the NHS&CC Act implementation was driven by the particular situation of older people and their need for community care, in that it was the economic costs of residential accommodation for older people which precipitated the early studies for community care (Griffiths, 1988). However, having attended to one set of specific needs, the consequences of community care for older people, in terms both of service provision and of the way that the reforms have impacted on understandings and constructions of old age, have not always been positive.

For example, the requirement introduced with the NHS&CC Act that all people over 75 years of age should have an annual community care assessment, while intended to make effective service provision and to reduce elements of risk to vulnerable older people, encroached upon the rights of all older people. Such statutory observation transforms older people from consumers into objects of consumption with the medical and social gaze observing, investigating and regulating older people as part of the 'vigilant' interpretation of care (Higgs, 1995). In doing so it infantilises all older people, making assumptions about their incapacity to care for themselves, or act appropriately when they recognise their own needs.

Such attitudes are compounded by the initial exclusion of older people from the receipt of funds to purchase their own services which were made available to disabled users of community care services through the Direct Payments (Services) Act 1996. These arrangements failed to recognise that many older people have been responsible for their own financial affairs, and those of others, for most of their adult life.

The consequences of these negative effects of community care policies are that older people attempt to avoid involvement in community care services by managing their own care provision (Baldock and Ungerson, 1994). This means that their situations may become chronic before statutory services intervene, and the necessary interventions by social workers and social care workers are seen to compound the negative perceptions of older people requiring care.

While evidence that policy initiatives were influenced by the gendered nature of the older population is limited, it is possible that the lack of political activism as a reaction to the consequences of the legislation means that the negative impact goes unchallenged. This lack of activism may be related to the assumed passivity of a predominantly female older population. That is not to ascribe essential characteristics but to suggest that older women, by virtue of their limited involvement in the workplace, are more accepting of the status quo, and less likely to assert, demand or have an aware-ness of their rights. For example, in commenting on the early policy reviews which advocated alternative forms of community care, including radically new forms of residential care, Peace suggests that the barriers to innovation are in the attitudes to older people who were predominantly female: 'the problem lies in the socially constructed inferior and dependent status of both women and old people' (Peace, 1986: 84).

This inferior status is compounded by negative attitudes implicit in the emphasis in community care reforms on older people as requiring care. It is an irony that changes in care arrangements for older people (predominantly women) are deemed to impact negat-ively on women as informal carers, and on formal caring services, which are provided mainly by female staff. Commenting on com-munity care policies in a text which is describing positive changes in the service provision Walker observes: 'This development is of profound importance for both families and the providers of home care and other services' (Walker and Warren, 1996: 13). This negative view of community care for older people as a drain on both human and other resources denies the contribution that older people, women and men, make to care provision.

Older people as care providers

While community care services are traditionally predicated on acceptance that there are families and networks of relations who will provide the necessary support and caring (Allan, 1988), 13 per cent of all carers who reported as 'caring' in the OPCS census were aged 65 and over (Church and Summerfield 1995). Many people in relationships who provide caring functions do not describe them-selves as 'carers' in any formal or informal sense and therefore there may be a higher incidence of caring amongst older people. This is particularly so in familial care where care is accepted as part of close personal relationships, or understandings of duty (Finch, 1995). That only one-third of those aged 80 and over require formal care (Walker and Warren, 1996), suggests that there is a great deal of mutual caring occurring. This caring, often seen as reflecting the fierce independence among spouse carers in the older population (Manthorpe, 1994), is integrally tied to the interdependence which may be more related to the nature of the marital relationship than the nature of the illness or the care needs. The implications of this for understandings of men as carers and therefore to assumptions of masculinity has been discussed in detail in Chapter 4.

Older people not only provide care for each other within couple relationships, but there is evidence that they retain long-term caring responsibilities for disabled adult children, particularly those with learning difficulties (Grant, 1986), and the care that older people – women and men – give in all sorts of ways within their own social circle, including child care on either regular or intermittent basis, is hidden, unrecognised and taken for granted. This active caring role is in sharp contrast to negative constructions of older people as requiring demanding, time consuming and emotionally draining terminal care (Wenger, 1992) and, if recognised, has implications for the way that social and health care workers intervene in familial relationships. Also, if unrecognised care reflects interdependence, then male and female behaviour within the private domain is unac-knowledged within the public sphere reflecting the way that care in general, and women care in particular, has been undervalued:

> The positive contribution to the welfare of grandchildren and children of many elderly women is greatly underestimated just as their labour specifi-cally on behalf of their husbands and in general on behalf of the economy throughout adult working life goes largely unrecognised. Capital and state separately or in combination, may have fostered the dependency of women within the family, but paradoxically, has created an independent system of interdependence, occupation, mutual respect and loyalty. The defensive restorative mechanisms of the family temper the dependency created for the state. (Townsend, 1993: 181)

There is an irony here that the analysis of dependency is based on the experiences of men; the restorative function of the family describes the experiences of women. Where do older men achieve their status and mutual respect? Townsend concludes that stereo-types about old age do not hold: 'Empirical studies of capacity and desire for productive occupation, reciprocation of services and familial and social relationships, as well as self-care, challenge the assumptions which prevail' (Townsend, 1993: 183). If this is so then older men will have to participate in the provision of services and familial social relationships, instead of being described as the sub-ject of their wives nurturing tendencies. These changes will come about because of the demands of familial involvement in commun-ity care, and the different patterns of availability of older men to care in the light of changing patterns of paid employment for women and men. They also will have to be accompanied by changes in assessment of the differential requirements of women and men either directly as users, or as carers.

Arrangements for community care

In terms of arrangements for community care it is apparent that these changes have not yet been accepted and differential patterns of demand on, or allocation of, resources reflect gendered paradoxes in community-based services. Early studies showed that women tend to live in the community for longer with more severe health problems than men, but older men were more likely to receive home help, meals on wheels and other domiciliary services either as carers or in their own right (OPCS, 1982; Peace, 1986). One of the paradoxes therefore is that it was the needs of older men which precipitated the policy reviews of the 1980s which led to the community care reforms, and which ultimately impact on the experiences of women who predominate in the population of older people.

A further paradox is that although there are more women in older age groups, that they are more likely to be living independently might suggest that men are assumed to be unable to cope, or that they are more demanding of residential and day care resources. Constructs of masculinity and femininity describe men's autonomy and independence while in the workplace, and women's capacity for self-care whatever their age, but when care is offered it is often patronising and denies the autonomy of older people and their right to self-determination. For this reason it has been suggested that regimes in residential care might impact more negatively on women who may suffer from enforced loss of role activity involved in household management and self-care. The reaction of older women to this 'role reversal' of requiring care rather than providing it has been presented as a failure of older women to conform to the stereotypes of womanhood: 'passage into old age increases the potential for dissonance with social norms of womanhood and femininity' (Hughes and Mtezuka, 1992: 223). Men are said to be used to domestic dependence because of organisation of family households and therefore acquiesce to the care provided. However, such acquiescence would seem to be at odds with the independence valorised within the workplace, and an alternative analysis is that older men have used their skills and assertiveness developed in the workplace to argue for services to meet their expressed needs.

These arrangements are the direct consequence of the interactions between social workers and social care workers and individual older people and/or their carers. It is useful to look in greater detail at aspects of these interpersonal interactions to ascertain how understandings of gender influence or impact on interventions.

Intervention

Community care policies have the potential to bring about positive change. For example, the right to assessment by a care manager could mean that older people will be receive the same skill attention as other groups, especially disabled people and those with mental health problems. This will happen only if care managers are recruited from qualified staff who are not only responsive to the specific needs of user groups, but in that responsivity do not stereotype or inappropriately label older people.

However, specific attention to the needs of older people in the delivery of services is not addressed in general texts on social work or social care intervention when discussing, for example, interviewing and counselling. These are addressed primarily in publications dedicated to old age, suggesting that older people do not require interventions available to other users of social and care services. There has been an absence of radical and innovative social work approaches to working with older people (Finch and Groves, 1985; Bowl, 1986), a problem which has been compounded by the lack of attention to age in feminist literature and masculinity studies.

There is no doubt that some older people will require intense social and medical support whether for acute or chronic physical illness, or for mental health problems such as dementia, but many require minimum levels of support and intervention which will enable them to cope independently. The concern is that the financial restrictions on the construction of care packages will deny people their individuality or provide so little support in the community that older people will not be able to access basic services. This is particularly so when the demands on community care budgets leads to service rationing. An example of this is the changes in arrangements for home care which make it available for personal care only (e.g.

washing and dressing) rather than home help (i.e. house cleaning and shopping). In one study it was documented that several older people 'struggled on' because help with personal care meant loss of dignity and independence (Richards, 1996: 160). The outcome of such changes could have differential consequences for women and men. If stereotypical assumptions lead to men being seen to be less able to undertake housework they may be offered resources. Meanwhile women may be assessed negatively because standards of housekeeping may be used as an assessment criteria for quality of life and become part of risk assessment for older women. The lack of ability to provide what is deemed necessary to perform household chores might lead to unintended and inappropriate consequences, as in the case of an older woman who wanted help with her housework, but in the absence of this ended up with a day centre place, a much greater intervention in her life (Richards, 1996).

However, some of these unintended consequences are not only the result of limited resources, they reflect the lack of expertise in the assessment process, or more particularly an inability or unwillingness to discern differences and diversity. The capacity to see the person as an individual rather than judging them against a set of assumed norms of age and/or gender is a crucial skill in social work with older people.

Age appropriate assessment

That age and gender presents complexities for social work is evidenced by referral patterns and responses based on stereotypical assumptions. For example, in the OPCS statistics (Church and Summerfield, 1995) older people between the ages of 64 and 75 years refer themselves to care services, and these referrals included both men and women. By contrast people over 75 years old were usually referred by a third party, often on the basis that physical health and/or domestic circumstances reached a point where they required help. It is significant that when women begin to predominate in the population expectations and tolerance of family and friends becomes a factor in the referral and assessment: 'designation of elderly person's circumstances as warranting social work intervention are partly dictated by cultural norms about what family, friends and neighbours find acceptable and tolerable' (Finch and Groves, 1985: 98). As was explored in the previous chapter, in lay assessments for community care this tolerance is influenced by assumptions of appropriateness. Expectations that people behave in particular roles or situations are overlaid with both age and gender assumption. Finch, in focusing on older people with mental health problems, argues that certain types of social behaviour which might be tolerated in younger people are not tolerated in older people; or that behaviour which is tolerated in older men is not tolerated in older women. She suggests that the powerful imagery from which nurses derive sets of stereotypes into which they fit older women patients and handle them accordingly (Evers, 1981) are likely to be replicated in social work practice (Finch and Groves, 1985).

That such opinions might be powerful in informal assessments is evidenced by the strong reactions of a group of older people to a video where an active 80-year-old woman is described as being too positive about life at 80 plus, she was: 'intoxicated with the exuberance of her own verbosity' (Tozer and Thornton, 1995: 26). Such responses demonstrate the extent of the internalisation of the negative messages received by older people which become manifest in low self-esteem and the denial of the individual's identity within the social construction old age (Marshall, 1990). That the 80-year-old was a woman may well reflect the expectations of gender as well as age appropriate behaviour. The video was ultimately dismissed by the group as unrepresentative because it was deemed to be subjective and lacking in depth, suggesting that when individuals do not conform their individual identity is deemed invalid. It is significant that this is so when the behaviour is challenging negative perceptions of old age.

This interrelationship between the way individuals present themselves and the perceptions of others is powerful in services for old people because once practical care has been provided the assumption is that some form of group care is important to assist in their social experiences. The choice of being separate and private has to be set against the negative effects of loneliness and isolation. However, participation in groups, and the interventions that social workers and social care workers utilise in groups, may perpetuate the oppressions of both age and gender. Reminiscence, for example, has been seen to give positive support to older people by affording them respect for themselves and their past (Coleman, 1990). However, unless conducted by those alert to issues of gender it may have negative outcomes.

Limitations of reminiscence

Because it is offered in groups reminiscence is thought to provide a relatively simple, structured way of offering effective intervention to older people in day care and residential settings. While some accounts of reminiscence work suggest that it has the potential to counter aspects of ageism, others argue that reminiscence groups are not self-evidently ant-discriminatory, or even anti-ageist (Harris and Hopkins, 1994). The difficulties echo those which have been identified in the assessment process which are to do with the complexities of recognising the shared experience of people who comprise a specific user group but also valorising difference. Reminiscence assumes that to be in touch with past memories will provide positive experiences and that the work involved in accessing the memories gives attention to the individual. However, accessing memories is integrally tied to identity and for each individual the impact of reminiscence will be different.

Concerns about reminiscence expressed in feminist and critical gerontological literature are threefold. First, the terminology is thought to be controversial. That personal biography work is referred to as reminiscence is seen to trivialise older people because it has 'connotations of misty romanticism and sentimentality, while with children it is called life story *work*' (Hughes and Mtezuka, 1992: 236) This is seen to be a reflection of the lack of status of older people among those who provide services.

Second, the proponents of reminiscence who see it as combating ageism are thought to have a simplistic view of the homogeneity of age. This view is assumed to be ideologically neutral, driven by the technical expertise of those running the groups in the selection of materials (Harris and Hopkins, 1994). However the experience of ageing, reflected in people's life histories, is complex and diverse. This is recognised in feminism where the significance of personal biography is celebrated, not as a technical rational exercise but as a personal and political statement. Sharing life stories can be undertaken in ways which do not negate either the common experience of older people or those which individualise them: 'but rather articulates the ways in which the minutiae of experiences throughout life is another context through which different older people interpret, negotiate and respond to old age (Hughes, 1995: 40).

This positive use of reminiscence has to be mindful of the third criticism which emerges from studies which questioned the inadvisability of divorcing the memory of older people from its function. The consequences of such separation are that older people who, for whatever reason, show reluctance to reminisce may be seen as having indications of a pathological condition rather than an expression of individual choice (Harris and Hopkins, 1994). However, if for many older people accessing past memories can be a powerfully negative experience then they may need to continue denying those experiences. For women accessing memories might revive the horrors of childhood abuse, and for men the traumas of involvement in war. Shared experiences of Jewish women and men of the holocaust and separation traumas caused by immigration experienced by other ethnic groups illustrate the potential for negative outcomes of reminiscence.

The potential for positive connotation of reminiscence is the conferring of the role 'sage' to older people (Biggs, 1993). However, even this may either lock them in the past, or the gendered reactions to the notion of sage may impact differentially on women and men. Concepts of life history and personal biography can reveal older women as endowed with resources and experiences which are not sufficiently acknowledged. Their biographies may be about personal and private experiences of home and family which are not acknowledged as important while they are fulfilling these duties. Hence reminiscence might exacerbate feelings of low self-worth, or cause confusion that previously denied experiences are suddenly deemed significant. Alternatively, men's biographies of employment and civic activity are deemed to be in the public domain and are acknowledged. Reminiscence may therefore be seen to be a positive experience for older men. However, the potentially negative consequences are that reminiscence might reinforce the crisis of role transition. Men may be deemed to have succeeded or failed on the basis of this public biography and recalling lack of achievement may be painful. Where there has been achievement this may be in stark contrast to their usefulness as older men not in the workplace, and as such may contribute to low self-esteem and depression.

Therefore the capacity of reminiscence work to address both the range and social divisions and the variety of influences acting on the construction of an individual's life history (Coleman, 1990) has to reflect the diversities of the lived experience of women and men. But to achieve this Harris and Hopkins (1994) argue that older people, rather than be passive recipients of the reminiscence material, should have more involvement in the selection of the reminiscence content and the process. For example, assumptions about mixed groups and other practical matters may well be challenged by those who participate: 'older people might come to radically different conclusions both about which past experiences they regard as important and also about the sense they now make both of their history and their present lives' (Harris and Hopkins, 1994: 82). Some argue that older men may be less likely to have been given access to feminist methods of life history and biography because constructions of masculinity mean they are deemed less likely to want to address the emotional complexities of ageing (Hughes and Mtezuka, 1992). If that is the case, then workers have to ensure that resources are offered in a way that is gender (as well as culturally and ethnically) sensitive and not gender biased.

Using a gendered lens has drawn attention to the way that, for a variety of reasons, women and men may respond differently to interventions which are designed to be positive. In doing so, the differences between women and men have been highlighted and that there is a danger that attention to gender in older people may reinforce stereotypical assumptions about gender divisions. The discussion of care provided by older men in Chapter 4 demonstrated that focusing on older people can also challenge the assumed norms of gendered behaviour. The recent attention to the abuse experienced by older people is equally important in questioning both biological determinism and social construction.

Elder abuse and gender

The concept of elder abuse was slow to be recognised because of the low status of both older people and women. The very term 'granny bashing', as the early identification of the phenomenon was labelled, trivialised what has since been recognised as a significant phenomenon. Despite the use of the feminine term, an early critical overview of the literature (Phillipson and Biggs, 1995) does not identify the gendered nature of elder abuse as a reason for its late recognition. As further analysis of both the incidence and the nature of elder abuse have been undertaken it is apparent that the interrelationship between gender and age in abuse provides interesting insight into constructions of masculinity and femininity.

Early debates about elder abuse concentrate on the negative aspects of the social construction of ageing in which it was assumed that age was the focus of, or precipitating factor for, the abuse. Such limited analyses of violence have been challenged by feminists' attention to family violence as a gendered phenomenon. Even without an explicit feminist analysis, the identification of abuse among a predominantly female population has to be seen to have a gender dimension. The tentative conclusion that there is some evidence that: 'women are more likely than men to be victims of serious domestic elder abuse and the same pattern may exist in nursing homes': (Phillipson and Biggs, 1995: 192), shows cautious acceptance that gender may be significant. Kingston and Penhale (1995) acknowledge the predominance of women in the population of older people. They point out that women are more likely to be subject to abuse and to live in situations where abuse might occur. However, in doing so they conform to a typical process of describing the victims and their conditions negatively: 'Their ability to avoid or resolve such [abusive] situations may be limited by poverty which faces many people in later life and thus restricts available choices about where and how to live and with whom' (Kingston and Penhale, 1995: 239). But avoiding abuse involves more than making choices about with whom older people should live, and limitations are not just to do with poverty.

The reluctance to accept that gender might be a significant variable in elder abuse may be because of a tendency, already discussed, to deny the continuities of gender into later life. More importantly, elder abuse highlights that the interplay of gender, intimacy and violence is complex. In domestic violence and abuse the predominance is of males abusing female partners and there is no reason to assume that abusive relationships will cease in later life. Indeed added stress might precipitate problematic relationships into abusive ones, especially if spouses are thrust into caring roles for which they are not prepared (Kingston and Penhale, 1995).

However, a significant factor in abuse of older people is that the abuse may be perpetrated by carers who are family members other than partners, or formal and informal carers who have no familial relationship. These carers will be predominantly, but not universally, female and the situational explanations could be seen to be woman-blaming. More significantly they challenge assumptions about femininity as being non-violent.

In what might be an attempt to maintain distinctions between masculinity and femininity studies have charted differences in the nature of elder abuse. Miller and Dodder (1989), for example, concluded that men were more likely to use physical violence and women neglectful acts. They argue that it is the incidence of reporting which is significant and that because the reporting of neglect is higher than that of physical violence the perpetrators are identified as predominantly female.

Other studies also focus on the reporting of abuse. In one, nearly three-quarters of the abuse victims of care staff were women, and in 18 per cent of households of women living alone or with someone else there were reports of abuse. The rates for men were much lower (Wilson, 1994). This study argues that the subjects in the research, who were older women who suffered from mental illness or dementia, had reduced citizenship entitlements and the abuse of older people can therefore be seen as an extreme manifestation of ageism in a society which devalues old people, as well as a consequence of it (Wilson, 1994: 692). As the study showed that the abuse was of women, by men, it is presented as evidence that power relations between men and women remain in old age. Significantly this is seen as more acceptable than early research evidence which was characterised as being abuse by mainly overstressed caring daughters. This reflects the confusions brought about by gendered stereotypes of women as naturally caring which led to: 'fear that female carers of the old and frail were going against their nature and resorting to violence' (Wilson, 1994: 692). However, to normalise male violence even into old age means that little is done to challenge it, and men are removed from situations where they may abuse their power, for example, in formal caring relationships. Another consequence is that women's capacity for violence is denied and abuse by female carers is unrecognised. This puts older people, women and men, at risk and demonises those women who, for whatever reason, resort to abuse of older people.

However, even acknowledging abuse of older people might focus on ageing in ways which contribute to, or perpetuate, negative perceptions of old age. This may lead to the reduction of all older people into victims or potential victims who therefore have to be infantilised in the process of receiving care. It is this very infantililising, and assumptions about lack of power, which may contribute to the abusive situations. What is required is a positive recognition of the status of older people in their own right and as a growing sector of society:

> Ageism cannot be challenged by itself, what has to be understood, revealed and rolled back are the processes of exploitation and hegemony by which

not only ageism but sexism and racism are perpetuated and expanded. What is required is a weakening of the power of the processes of domination, people gaining a sense of themselves as having a continuity of human history, elderly people can be valued as symbols of the continuity of generations. (Vincent, 1995: 196)

As the next chapter discusses, disability rights groups, and feminists within these, have highlighted a need to challenge the welfarism which has trapped users of community care services into being passive and dependent recipients of care. For older people the gendered life histories of the participants creates both challenges and opportunities.

Positive practice

From an early date, the emphasis on practical help in assessment served to detract from the status of care for the older people in social work (Brearley, 1975; Rowlings, 1981). With community care reforms social workers are required to work with policies that aggregate information about user groups, but to recognise that the individual older person has both needs and resources (Ford and Sinclair, 1989; Challis *et al.*, 1993). Acknowledging older people as a resource could enable them to continue as active citizens, recognising the wealth of knowledge and experience, and indeed skills which older people can contribute. In this way older people can be regarded as experts in the assessment process (Smale *et al.*, 1993), but can also draw on these resources in specific interventions. Such an approach could be used to radically change approaches to service provision which would allow for greater participation.

For older people therefore what is required is a change of perception on behalf of those involved in service provision, but perhaps also those who receive services:

> To break away from the notion that compensatory services should be seen as altruism, a gesture from a benign and generous society for which each old person should be grateful and uncomplaining. This can best be done by viewing old people as a group with a set of rights. (Bowl, 1986: 138).

This recognition of rights has been developed in some of the community care initiatives which have fostered participation and partnership.

For many user groups rights have been concomitant with notions of citizenship. However, merely to ascribe the status of citizenship which attempts to achieve full integration of older people into society, rather than an acceptance of their disengagement or separateness, ends up homogenising older people into an undifferentiated group who have to be made equal, and denies the complexity of notions of equality and the differentiation within the group labelled 'older people'.

Citizen participation

This emphasis on the involvement of older people is a recurring theme in the writing about community care and older people. Arguing for participation of older people as service users in the identification, provision and monitoring of services raises many issues which are pertinent to the development of notions of citizenship.

As was discussed in Chapter 3 notions of citizenship, while powerful, are complex when considering users of community care. The positives of Marshallian definitions, with their emphasis on rights for the individual and reciprocal responsibilities for both the individual and society, are more relevant to an anti-ageist base, since it gives positive status to older people: 'it postulates the validity of the older person not only as a person but also as an equally important and valid *member of society*' (Hughes, 1995: 46). The argument is that economic dependency has denied some older people the right to participate as full citizens, and that what is required to combat ageism is the extension of citizenship so that the simple fact of exclusion from the wage economy does not lead older people into an inferior social category. This echo of the feminist criticism of economic definitions of citizenship falls into the trap of universalising older people, of failing to recognise difference. Exclusion from the wage economy is a phenomenon which impacts particularly on older men, because women who have had diverse careers have in the main been excluded from regular participation in the wage economy. The juxtaposition of gender and age, therefore, is that men will become non-citizen as they get older, experiencing the assumptions of non-contribution, either present or future that women have carried. Valorising other aspects of citizenship to include older men would give status to the activities and qualities which women have traditionally demonstrated. While this may be an extension of feminist arguments for women's citizenship, it is ironic that it is used to respond to the negative experiences of older men. More positively, it is an example of how the political campaigns of feminism can impact positively on women and others in oppressed groups.

Hence Lister's notion of a 'differentiated universalism' (1997: 39) explored in Chapter 3 becomes significant in debates about older people as citizens. Age becomes one of the differences between people, one of the aspects of identity which have to be acknowledged when seeking to change notions of citizenship. Reformed notions of citizenship, however, will not just evolve, they require public activism and advocacy on behalf of the group in order to achieve the necessary status.

Within the category 'older people' there are further levels of differentiation. One is gender, another is reflected within representations of old age which negatively compare those who are physically frail and those who are active and healthy. Changes in citizenship impact differentially on both these representations, with the physically frail being particularly disadvantaged:

> Ironically, the new rights of citizenship provided by the reforms to health and social services relate to the first while only being meaningful to the second. The ability to exercise choice depends on there being an active consumer who is able to make informed and real decisions. Frailty and dependence are not ideal circumstances from which to exercise consumer sovereignty. Power imbalances and real physical limitations are just two impediments. (Higgs, 1995: 547)

There is evidence that the active and healthy older citizens have been influenced by a rights-based approach and have recognised the need for campaigning work to challenge material condition (Phillipson, 1992). The formation in the United States of the Gray Panthers in the 1970s and the Older Women's League in the 1980s were not mirrored in Britain, although the formation of the Pensioners' Union indicates that there was some political will. Women's capacity to make social bonds is thought to protect them from isolation from the social collectivity (Gibson, 1996). Movements such as the Older Feminists' Network have sought to build on this notion of collectivity, but they present a particular perspective which might have been too narrow and too exclusionary to be meaningful to all women. The Older Women's Network is gathering more ground, and utilises the networking skills of women to involve women of all classes, racial backgrounds and level of need. It is within this notion of networking that the strong positive qualities of women can be validated and privileged and used in social care and social work interventions, but for the benefit of all.

However, such political and social activity is not appropriate or attractive to all older people, and may present problems for those older people with significant health problems, the frail and dependent. Also, while campaigning work is important, the struggle for recognition is necessary also at the level of direct intervention, thus highlighting the tension of the individual and the structural, which feminist analysis and practice offers (Hughes and Mtezuka, 1992). Positive interventions therefore require a mix of the individual focus which provides support and guidance in periods of crisis for individual older people and their carers. However, in mobilising practical support it is necessary to avoid reinforcing negative notions of dependency, and to beware dangers of alleviating adjustments to old age which legitimate ways in which society restricts life chances and opportunities of old people (Bowl, 1986), and reinforces gender stereotypes.

Consultation in community care planning

The need for older people to network, to participate in social movements to confront ageism and campaign for whatever changes are thought necessary by the older people themselves could be facilitated by the notion of partnership in community care planning. The necessary consultation required by partnership could be a significant development for both older men and older women. Community care legislation requires statutory organisations to consult with organised user and carer groups, but these consultations have been constrained by who becomes a member of organised groups and which members emerge as spokespeople or advocates. Individuals who are in need of community care service but who are not involved in organised groups often do not have a direct voice in the consultation processes.

In formal bureaucratised arrangements for community care, participation can be invoked in a limited way. Modes of delivery of services involve social workers and care managers as the gatekeepers of resources, making difficult and informed choices about which individuals should receive services, and about the level of services to be offered. Described as 'marketing' services or limited two-way communication (Goss and Miller, 1995), options or plans are put out for consultation, and users and carers decide on the best option, without any facility to reject all of them, or suggest an alternative model. A responsive approach, by contrast, feeds users' and carers' views into the process, thus influencing the agenda that is set, not constructing it (Tozer and Thornton, 1995; Waldman *et al.*, 1996). To be consulted, users join fora where commissioners of services have set the primary agenda and where methodological expertise and access to resources are privileged. Users may have the franchise on the language to be used, and the subjects to be covered in consultative processes, but the point at which this expertise is invoked will be controlled by the commissioners.

Tozer and Thornton's Older People's Advisory Group recruited a cross-section of older people in terms of age, sex and personal circumstances, and how much use they made of services. However, they were not selected to be 'representative'; the notion of representing other groups, being in touch with networks with whom they might consult, was not relevant. It was the knowledge and the views that they held which were thought to be typical or 'representative'. Significantly, those who had been users of services were elevated in status because of knowledge which they could share (Tozer and Thornton, 1995). There may be gender dimensions to involvement. Older women might be reluctant to be involved because asserting their opinions is not their way. Also, to involve older women in some tokenistic way is counteractive to notions of partnership: 'the legitimate aim of raising the consciousness and expectations of older women must not be used to deny older women the right to determine their own future and lifestyles' (Hughes and Mtezuka, 1992: 237).

Although Tozer and Thornton (1995) make no observations about the gender dynamics of their group they do record concerns that large meetings were inhibiting to older people. They also acknowledged the need to pace the group to the needs of the older people. However, their caution about the dangers of tokenism and ageism are strangely ungendered. Their conclusions are that the barriers to participation were to do with living alone, and not being used to formulating ideas, responding quickly or developing ideas by discussion with others. Were these observations more pertinent to women than men, in that the group consisted of more women? It may be that gender was seen to be irrelevant, or that workers failed to take into account the complexities of gender because of stereotypical assumptions which led to identification of assumed characteristics.

It is the interplay between these stereotypical assumptions and the differentiated experiences of individuals which is significant. Participation of older people was important because, as well as producing important information for service provision, it impacted on those involved. Membership of the group led to increased self-esteem of individuals, widened their horizons and introduced them to new activities. The approach also helped to dispel some of the negative stereotypes which even those working regularly with older people held: 'The diversity of membership in the group reminded the researchers of the range of circumstances that exist under the grouping "older people" ' (Tozer and Thornton, 1995: 36), and the researchers had their assumptions about what mattered to older people challenged.

In this way the right to participation influenced worker perceptions and gave older people active agency, and opportunities to influence the nature of service provision. It moves away from an individualistic rights approach where empowerment in community care is framed as either invoking 'voice' as advocacy or choice in terms of 'exit' (Means and Smith, 1994), and draws upon Rees's (1991) notion of 'cause' advocacy which involves arguing for reform of a system, based on knowledge of relevant cases. Importantly, this approach offers a synthesis of collective action and individual need and is illustrative of Plant's (1992) notion of social rights which was discussed in detail in Chapter 3. There the discussion explored the different citizen status of women and men. Here the argument is that such an analysis is not only pertinent because the majority of older people are women, but also that in assuming passivity of older people, and denying them status because they are not contributing to the paid workforce, there is a feminisation of all older people.

Involvement and participation require that older people in general, and older women in particular, are perceived as having active agency, and are not viewed as passive recipients of services, or consultation about choices defined by others. It also recognises that within any provision of community care there is a tension between the needs of the individual and the needs of the collective, be that the wider group of older people or the common interests of others with needs. As Jordan (1990) argues this implies cooperation, sharing and collective action, not individual moral duties and contracts. However, this does not mean that individual identity and diversity have to be ignored or denied.

Conclusion

This chapter has continued the process of looking at an identified user group of community care services through a gendered lens. In recognising that the population of older people is predominantly female, it has highlighted that gender differentiation has operated in a negative way, consigning women to assumed passive roles and denying them services. This assumed passivity of older people has had negative impact on older men too, in that services which involve increased surveillance and risk assessment infantilise all older people.

More significantly, experiences of older people of, on the one hand, therapeutic interventions and, on the other, abuse from carers has confounded dichotomous characteristics of maleness and femaleness. The effects of negatively separating experiences highlight the tensions for social workers and social care workers in working at the borderland between individuals and their identified group or collectivity. The diversity of membership of user groups has to be validated by responses of social work and social care staff which involve more than a mere recognition of differences and similarities between women's and men's experience. What is required is a change in the nature of the relationship to strive for partnerships in care provision which acknowledge the citizen status of older people.

Many of the claims of older people for recognition of diversity and status are shared with disabled people as users of community care services, and the next chapter describes how disabled people have taken the arguments for recognition and rights even further than the tentative suggestions made in this chapter on behalf of older people.

7

Disability: Identity and Difference

Introduction

The final group to be covered in the overview of categories of users is that which is generically referred to as disability. This group, perhaps more than any other, highlights the inadequacy of attempting to categorise users of social services. The term disability can refer to a number of impairments, all of which have different implications for the individuals experiencing them and all of which impact on the individual's identity in different ways. What is shared is that being labelled as disabled has led to individuals and groups being discriminated against, disadvantaged and dismissed as non-citizens.

It is because of the negative impact of the generic category that disability rights groups have taken up the term as part of a political campaign to challenge negative perceptions and discrimination. More significantly, they have questioned the response to the needs of disabled people which frames them as clients or patients of the health and welfare services. In their critique of welfare provision for disabled people activists have fought for participation in decision making about service provision, but more significantly have sought to remove categories of disabled people from the umbrella of welfare, arguing for their rights as citizens.

In this the disability movement could be seen to be pathbreaking for other groups of service users. The demand for a shared, fixed and universal category has been the basis for much political activism. However, in analysing the progress made it is necessary to consider the complexities and challenges associated with collective action. These are particularly pertinent when examining the

186

relationship between disability and gender. For example, feminism's contribution to the community care debate has, at times, alienated disabled women by concentrating on the needs of women who provide care, by both ignoring disabled women's contribution to caring and failing to recognise and advocate for the different needs of disabled women.

These omissions have been compounded by developments in the disability movement. The challenge to the oppressiveness of a welfare approach to disability and championing a rights approach to service provision, while positively influencing debates in social work and social care, has failed to recognise the differences in experiences of disabled women and men. In doing so, not only have the needs of disabled women been disregarded but also the complex interplay between disability, masculinity and femininity has been ignored.

These omissions illustrate the difficulties of claiming a shared identity which has been created or constructed by others as a cause for action. To do so may require a denial of difference. Strands of feminism which advocate for category 'woman', deny or ignore both the differences within that category and that these differences can themselves be a source of oppression. Similarly, those working for disability rights do so on the basis of a shared identity of being disabled, not recognising that age, gender, class, race, sexual orientation and the nature of the disability might lead to different experiences, and to sources of oppression within the disability movement.

This is not to deny that in championing the rights of a specific and assumed homogeneous group, disabled people, the disability movement has provided theoretical and political understandings which benefit all users of community care services. This chapter seeks to explore the positive aspects that such an approach has brought to the redefining of community care, recognising that this is the logical consequence of the arguments for citizenship in earlier chapters. It will demonstrate how the debates have been influenced by the contribution of disabled women both within feminism and within the disability movement. They have demanded that both differences within groups and commonalities of experiences between groups be acknowledged and responded to in any activity, be that political activism, welfare provision or academic research (Begum *et al.*, 1994; Morris, 1996a).

The chapter also highlights the multiplicity of shared identities that each user of community care experiences and explores how notions of difference can become problematic in movements which seek recognition on the basis of assumed norms.

Context

Women make up the greater proportion of the population of disabled people. This is in part due to women's longevity, but there are more disabled women in all age categories. The nature of the impairment differs between men and women which influences the construction of 'disability', including differences of perception of visible and invisible impairment and between causes of impairment. All contribute to the experiences of the disabled person. However, terms such as 'dis-ability' or 'differently able' carry with them assumptions of 'ability' which certain groups do not achieve, or are constructed as being unable to achieve, or even aspire to. Within this notion of ability social constructions of age, gender, race and class influence perceptions which in turn affect expectations of lifestyle and responses to impairment by health and social services professionals.

Therefore categories used for the purposes of community care policy and provision are not just inadequate, they perpetuate divisions based on assumed differences which are counter-productive. There may be, for example, an overlap between the experiences of disabled people and those of older people as recipients of welfare services. Through illness or accident older people constitute a growing proportion of those who experience impairment and in doing so may become users of, or may be assumed to be in need of, community care services. However, because the illness or accident is seen to be a function of growing older, a separate category of user is created. This is not to deny that older people have specific and different needs within service provision, as is evidenced in the previous chapter, but to recognise that the political activism of the 'disabled lobby' is equally pertinent to the needs of older people.

Alternatively, people with learning disabilities are often discussed, as in this text, as part of the group of users labelled 'disabled', but because of manifestations of their impairment, assumptions about their ability to communicate and the unpredictability of what is usually called challenging behaviour, they are more likely to be labelled by the general public as being significantly different, more disabled, or mentally ill. It is therefore assumed that they are in greater need of intervention.

Therefore, while there are points of shared experience between the bureaucratic categories of community care, within each category there are differences. It is possible to create descriptors which can be applied to people who require some form of welfare intervention because of their impairment which recognise experiences of gender, race, ethnicity and/or class and thus reflect the multiple identities of users categorised in any one group. What is problematic is recognising how interventions can be organised in ways which do not privilege certain groups, and which do not perpetuate hierarchies of disadvantage or oppression.

But even this starting point can represent negative stereotyping. It could be argued that merely seeking to encourage those who work in social work and social care to recognise difference within categories does not go far enough. It perpetuates assumptions that being identified as part of a particular group, being differently abled, carries with it assumptions and preconceptions that welfare intervention will be necessary at some point, and that the consequences of impairment through illness or accident are that the person cannot take responsibility for themselves.

This is clearly not the case. Social services intervene in the lives of only a small percentage of disabled people. For example, of the 26,000 households surveyed in the 1993/94 Family Resource Survey 7 per cent had at least one long-term sick/disabled person in them, and more than three-quarters of these had not requested assistance with personal care or other practical things. Local authority social services departments were reported to be the source of help in only 2 per cent of all sick/disabled households (Morgan, 1995: 42). This puts into sharp relief the notion that social services are a primary source of care for disabled people. Those households which call upon social services for support do so for a variety of reasons which may be to do with the severity of the impairment, but it is more likely to be to do with the nature of the familial relationships. The 'household' may be a single person no longer able to live independently and with few support systems to provide the necessary services. In other situations, something will have occurred in support arrangements that has precipitated the need for statutory intervention. This does not mean that all disabled people will be dependent upon the state, nor does it mean that those who present to social services are any less competent to be involved in decisions about the services they require.

Tensions arise because once statutory services are involved legislative requirements have to be met. These requirements exist to ensure minimum provision for service users, but they are also a means of gatekeeping resources. More significantly, those disabled people who do require services are assumed to be in need of more than just the financial and physical means to their own independence. The umbrella notion of care is often used to describe the services offered but, as Chapter 4 described, the concept of care is complex. Challenging the negative connotations of care provision and the way that assumptions about care have permeated attitudes towards all disabled people has contributed to the politics of disability.

Politics of disability

The challenge to stereotypical assumptions about disabled people and their ensnarement in the 'welfare' net has been at the heart of political activism and research in the area of disability and has brought about significant legislative changes. In its treatment of disabled people the welfare state has been criticised for creating passive rather than active citizenship through welfare legislation (Oliver and Barnes, 1996). For example, the Chronically Sick and Disabled Person's Act 1970 made rights to services dependent upon a right to assessment by a social worker employed by local authority personal social services. The very nature of social work intervention was predicated on an individualist and medical model of disability. This meant that disabled people were perceived as clients who required treatment, and who were assumed to be deficient in some way simply because, by illness or accident, they had specific needs. The implications of this were that disabled people were assumed to be in need of care, and that the professional was the expert in defining what form of care was needed and controlling resources for that care. It is because of this imbalance of power, and because disabled people have needs which are not necessarily subsumed under a concept of care, that the disability movement has been at the forefront of those highlighting how the language of community care legislation, with overt references to 'caring for' people or 'managing' care, denies people who are users of services the right to be treated as fully competent autonomous individuals, as full citizens.

This is not to say that the intentions of the early legislation were deliberately negative. In recognising the deprivation that disabled people experienced, welfare legislation attempted to 'provide for' them, albeit in a very limited way, in terms of both goods and services. But this very provision emphasised negative assumptions of difference and inferiority. People were labelled by their disability based on an individual and medical model, assumptions were made about their capacities, and in this labelling process there appeared to be no distinctions made on the basis of ability, age, gender, race and/or class.

Services developed to provide care by that very provision contributed to processes of oppression by adhering to an individual or medical model of disability. Disabled people in receipt of care were made to be dependent, and this marginalised them, excluding them from equal citizenship rights (Young, 1990b). At the most extreme severely disabled people, including people with learning difficulties, were confined by care arrangements to the private world of the family and excluded from participation in the public domain. Their dependency meant that any notion of citizenship is mediated through someone else and as such they were perceived by some as restricting the rights of others to citizenship, namely those who fulfil the unpaid care (Walmsley, 1996). The alternative, institutional care, often denies all citizen rights.

Even those who were not entirely dependent on others, but had to go through welfare agencies for the means for independence, were often denied the positive rights to participate simply because they were deemed to be recipients of welfare. Moreover, as with all service users, they gave up their right to freedom from interference and their right not to reveal details of their personal life.

In this way disabled people could be seen to be experiencing the five aspects of oppression: exploitaion, marginalisation, powerlessness, cultural imperialism and violence (Young, 1990b). The response was not merely to challenge those providing services, but to change from a welfare approach to a rights-based approach. Drawing on the experiences of other groups who had been discriminated against, namely Black and ethnic minority people and women, the disability lobby looked to equal opportunities policies and anti-discrimination legislation to bring about change.

Equal opportunities and disability

The challenge to this welfarist approach came from the now widely accepted analysis that it was based on an individual or medical model which focuses on the limitations of impaired people (Oliver, 1990). The alternative view, the social model, locates the physical and social environment as disabling of people who experience impairment, and was an attempt to challenge assumptions of dependence and illness inherent in welfare provision. The outcome of campaigning, the Disability Discrimination Act 1995, (DDA), while not as radical as some would have wished, marks the recognition that disabled people are not always in need of welfare, and are not satisfied at being labelled 'sick'. The legislation reflects the United Nations Standard Rules on the Equalisation of Opportunities for Disabled Persons with Disabilities (Standard Rules) 1993, thereby locating disability in the discourse of rights and equal opportunities. In this way it mirrored the sex and race discrimination legislation which had been introduced in Britain some two decades before.

The rights afforded, while framed in terms of rights to equality, are essentially negative rights, rights not to be discriminated against in the workplace and in the provision of goods and services. There is some guidance in the legislation about how changes in practice and attitudes can remove disabling barriers (Swain *et al.*, 1993), highlighting the complexities of understandings of equality of opportunity. In particular the distinction between equal access, equal outcomes and equality of opportunity (Forbes, 1991) is significant in ensuring that there were not unintended consequences. For example, the right to equal treatment is particularly problematic for disabled people. If they are be treated like everyone else, as in a starting gate approach to equality, this may not recognise the barriers, physical, social and economic, that they experience. If they are treated differently in recognition of the particular disadvantages they experience because of their impairment (Michailakis, 1997) this may perpetuate negative associations of difference. On the one hand, recognising the barriers that individual impairments create could be associated with an individual-centred approach which de-contextualises and therefore de-politicises social processes. On the other hand, the individual-centred approach to equal opportunities recognises differences but questions the social processes which interpret and evaluate functional limitations or impairment.

The individual's specific needs are acknowledged without the individual being held responsible for the cause of those needs, or the means to alleviate them.

The social processes which contribute to the evaluation of the individual depend on prevailing conceptions of normality and often include cultural and gender assumptions. As such they are problematic; for example, recognising that using white, middle-class norms as a standard to be strived for would disadvantage assessment of Black disabled people. Using some standard of normality based on the experiences of undisabled males disadvantages disabled women. This is particulalry relevant when considering the complexity of policies designed to remove barriers to the workplace.

Welfare to work

This is problematic as illustrated by policy developments of New Labour where the alternative to welfare, the recognition of equality, is to enable or require disabled people to take up paid employment. The welfare-to-work policies reflect a notion of active citizenship which requires that individuals contribute economically to society. This will impact negatively on those who are differently abled, and whose impairments mean that they cannot, or do not want to, seek access to the paid workplace. Linking assessments of fitness to work with threats to benefits highlights that policies which espouse inclusion into society can create a greater divide for some people, making them further excluded. Just as it should not be assumed that all disabled people are incapable of physical and mental tasks, neither should it be assumed that all disabled people want to, or indeed are able to, function to any particular level or in particular work environments. Undisabled people have some notion of choice in the employment they undertake, albeit limited by skills aptitude and availability. The limitations on workplaces which provide appropriate resources and technology will mean that disabled people's choice will be curtailed even further. If full citizen's rights are to be afforded to disabled people the agencies required to find employment and place the unemployed need to be active in ensuring that work bases are made accessible, rather than focusing on slotting disabled people into inappropriate employment and holding them responsible if this is not acceptable.

More significantly, such policies espouse a notion of rights which is limited to economic rights and as such represents a narrow view of citizenship which has been challenged by feminism (Pateman, 1992; Lister, 1997). The politics of disability become more complicated when the social construction of disability is overlaid by the social construction of gender.

Women and disability

The emphasis on the workplace as a means of affording disabled people recognition and rights has come from both the disability lobby and government policy. But to argue, as disability rights movements have, that to recognise the rights of disabled people will facilitate access to the workplace and improve their economic position denies the experiences of women, both disabled and undisabled, who are consistently denied equal access to the workplace, and when they do gain access are not necessarily freed from discrimination and oppression. Rights to work therefore have not only to address the additional barriers experienced by disabled women but also the limitations of the policy in achieving equality. This is not to argue against a rights approach to disability, but to highlight that there may be different outcomes for different individuals. Moving away from an individual-centred approach may therefore reinforce an assumed and false homogeneity of those who are disabled by the social, structural or economic environment, and as such contribute to a collective notion of 'the disabled', where the overriding factor is the disability.

A simple difference might therefore be seen to be between disabled women and men. The forceful disability lobby is said by some to be led by 'young' or 'active' disabled men striving to eschew negative attributions of disability. One such attribution is the association of disability with the assumed passivity of femininity. Striving to challenge such assumptions, however, impacts on all disabled people and can deny individuals the right to choose to describe or present themselves, and their experiences of disability as they wish (French, 1993).

The differences, however, are not just between disabled women and men. While the medical model of disability was initially criticised for seeing the responsibility, problem or fault as resting with the individual, a more positive outcome was that it precipitated an understanding of the individualised nature of the oppression of disabled people. Each person with her/his unique social and physical circumstances faced different barriers and different challenges.

However, the overwhelming argument against a medical model is not only that it holds the individual responsible for the causes and the solutions to her/his problems, it further oppresses by assuming a specific set of responses. The tragedy model, which expects disabled people passively to accept their disadvantages and gratefully receive care, has been associated with the passivity of femininity alluded to above. As we have seen in relation to women, if an individual does not conform to such a role they are perceived as deviant. Such a model denies disabled people their rights, and if they choose to assert them this is often interpreted as a refusal to accept the 'reality' of their disability, a psychological defence which often led to further medicalisation of the individual.

For women, the assumption of passivity meant that any resistance to the limitations created by barriers was perceived as a double deviance. They also experienced a double disadvantage because neither policy makers nor disability activists attended to their rights.

However, the notion of double disadvantage, whether that be Black and disabled or female and disabled, is seen to be problematic because focusing on those who experience the disability shifts attention from undisabled people and social institutions as the cause of the oppression. Some argue that political action requires that oppression caused by disability is dealt with or responded to first, and that other oppressions will be attended to in the process:

> The first step is to acknowledge that disability is socially created and that action committed to reducing the efforts of a disabling social economic and physical environment will also reduce the need for anyone, man or woman, to provide informal care. (Parker, 1996: 254)

Others argue that the aim of retaining the oppressor–oppressed dichotomy, as signified by the split between disabled and undisabled, while acknowledging difference, may reflect a longing to hold on to homogeneity which is reinforced by simplistic, inappropriate and divisive social policy initiatives which ignore difference and fail to help those for whom they are designed (Stuart, 1996). Stuart's support for the notion of simultaneous oppression is based on a belief that the recognition of a distinct and separate Black disabled identity would help to obtain a better understanding of how the development of particular identities includes or excludes people from mainstream life (Stuart, 1996: 94). But asserting that there is a simple and essential Black disabled identity ignores intra-racial differences based on class, ideology, gender etc., and renders the position and experience of Black women as both marginal and invisible (Carby, 1982). It could be argued that a category 'disabled woman' could draw attention to their specific and unique experiences.

It is for these reasons that Michailakis finds formal equality on the basis of unidimensional groups limited. What is required is the elimination of the social conditions which may adversely affect the lives of certain groups, which he calls disabled minorities (Michailakis, 1997: 27). These minorities may include Black and other minority ethnic groups, and would allow for multi-descriptors such as Black disabled woman, or Black disabled older person. Such an approach recognises that while particular groups may be seen to be disadvantaged and oppressed, the practices operate through less formal social processes and individual acts of oppression which impact on the way that each person constructs their own understanding of their condition.

This conundrum of individual experience versus collective political action has been at the heart of criticism of the welfare state. Parallel to the developments in anti-discrimination legislation the changes brought about by community care legislation moved the focus away from the individual to provision of services, but in doing so continued to ignore or deny differences in the experiences of disabled women and men.

Community care and disability

While the rights approach enshrined in anti-discrimination legislation may bring about change for many disabled people it is difficult to assess what the impact will be on service provision in community care. The DDA reflects the dilemmas of policy makers in recognising difference, and ensuring that oppression and discrimination do not occur on the basis of that difference. As was discussed in Chapter 2, the anti-discrimination legislation of the 1970s (Sex Discrimination Act 1975 and Race Relations Act 1976) did not automatically bring about necessary changes in the provision of welfare. The response in social work was to emphasise the need for anti-discriminatory and anti-oppressive practice, to argue that users of health and welfare services were women and men of different class, race, religious and ethnic background. Although they did not come to the attention of those services because of their different backgrounds, they may be treated differently because of them.

Disabled people come to the attention of welfare services through a variety of routes and a multitude of precipitating factors, but the initial focus for attention is that they are deemed to be disabled. Health and social care workers therefore have to respond to that focus, but in doing so have to be mindful of the differences. While it is apparent that notions of citizenship and human rights resonate with the values and principles on which good social work and social care is predicated, including the principle of individualisation, it is difficult for social workers to mediate the legislation and policy of the welfare state without seeming to marginalise and oppress on the basis of having to offer services to disabled people. What is unclear is to what extent services offered further oppress, because they fail to recognise differences within particular user groups.

From the outset community care legislation challenged the notion of choice, predicated as it is on assumptions that care in the community is a preferred option over residential care. In policy terms the right to residential care has been replaced by the requirement that to receive services an assessment will be made by a care manager and, if it is deemed appropriate, provision will be made from a variety of sources in a 'package of care'. In this way services are provided or identified to 'maintain' disabled people in the community (Morris, 1993b). However, because of resource constraints it is likely that such maintenance is not necessarily independent living, but an existence which involves dependence on others, mainly family and friends, or less frequently volunteer and paid carers. As was discussed in Chapter 5, the assessment process is crucial in determining the services to be provided, and it is at the point of assessment and commissioning of services that distinctions on the basis of gender will influence both the perception of need, and decisions about how that need will be met.

Care management in community care requires that the needs of the individual are assessed, and resources to meet these needs are commissioned. This change in focus was designed to involve service users in decisions about their care, but ultimately care is provided from a range of provider agencies who have been recruited or are promoted by the statutory services. If due attention is not taken of the different needs and requirements of individuals, if stereotypical assumptions are made about the needs of individuals on the basis of their gender, or if, in some form of cultural imperialism, all services are based on white Eurocentric norms, then it could be argued that needs will be met at one level but in meeting these needs other oppressions will be perpetuated, and in some cases exacerbated, by the organisation and delivery of the services.

This creates tensions for social work and social care practitioners who are part of a system which was established to relieve the injustices of material deprivation caused by marginalisation, but in doing so they are identified as part of a system which further marginalises those with whom the are dealing by depriving them of rights and freedoms that others have (Young, 1990b). Relationships between disabled people and health and social services staff can be experienced as patronising and insulting at best, and at worst abusive. Sometimes the impairment makes workers feel uncomfortable, and judgements appear to be made in terms of deserving or undeserving (Morris, 1993b).

Meeting need

Changes brought about by the NHS&CC Act for service provision can therefore exacerbate the negative approaches to meeting the needs of disabled people. The move to provide services in the independent and voluntary sector brings about criticism which resonates with the concerns expressed about the involvement of lay people in the care and support of those with mental health problems. Volunteers and unqualified workers may have romantic notions of 'helping the disabled' (Morris, 1993b: 113) and as such may be less likely to respect the autonomy of those with whom they are working.

Similarly, the changing role of disability charities, and the way that people perceive them, undermines the position of disabled people as autonomous individuals and citizens. The development of charities in the 1960s was associated with a condescending attitude which called upon public heart strings and purse strings to 'do good' for the less able; difference therefore meant dependence. The political activities which dominated the 1980s led to the involvement of some disabled people in their own right and on their own behalf, and it was this involvement which secured the political gains represented in the DDA. However, as was documented in Chapter 2, the effects of community care legislation, the introduction of the mixed economy of welfare provision meant that, to survive in the 1990s, charities had to become provider agencies.

A positive outcome of such developments might have meant that disabled people could become providers in their own right, and within that provision special, or different needs, could be responded to. Dalley, for example, argues that all-women collective residential provision would ensure that women did not have to be maintained in stereotypical roles, caring for men in mixed sex provision (Dalley, 1988).

However, the significance of this point was lost in the interchange about the implications of Dalley's willingness to consign disabled women to residential care to relieve non-disabled women of the burden of care (Morris, 1993b). Dalley's response counters that Morris's own view is too narrow, coming as it does from a 'fit' lobby of disabled people, often younger men and women who, in the strength of their own arguments, have ignored the needs of those who are 'frail', namely older disabled people, the majority of whom are female. In asking for recognition of the 'heterogeneity of dependence' (Dalley, 1996: 27), Dalley suggests that it is possible to challenge the assumed homogeneity of categories such as disabled people, older people and people with mental health problems, all of which are further cross-cut by class, race and sexual orientation. It is in the complex arrangements for meeting need that these differences become significant. The various calls for independence, or to have services provided in ways which will faciliatate independence, highlight the way that gender is implicated.

Collective action for services

For some groups therefore there are multiple strands to their simultaneous oppression, and in the political project of gaining recognition it is difficult to know with whom to identify, or which aspect of their identity is paramount. For disabled women, opportunities to join forces with other women have been constrained by the tensions associated with caring. As was discussed in Chapter 4, the position and perception of adult women in our society is often defined by their caring capacities. The function of caring has clearly been seen to have a negative impact on the status of women, and has influenced their movement in and out of the paid workforce, and their position in it. Nevertheless undisabled women, while suffering oppression and discrimination, may find some satisfaction in roles and relationships within the domestic arena. The early feminist social policy discussions around caring appeared to make assumptions that this recognition was not equally available to disabled women. While the debates that ensued have appeared to be bitter, they have made an enormous contribution to a wider understanding of discrimination by recognising that distinctions within groups are as important as those between groups.

For this reason, the emphasis of the disabled lobby on the way services can be organised to enable and empower disabled people to take responsibility for their own lives has demonstrated aspects of provision of care which have the potential to be neither controlling nor oppressive. Personal assistants, independent living and direct payments are some of the initiatives which have accompanied community care reforms. But the potential of such initiatives will only be realised if a balance is reached between universal provision and identified individual needs.

Independent living

The counter to a dependent welfare model of provision is to ensure that the means are available to facilitate independent living. This requires changes to infrastructure such as buildings, transport and communication systems. It also requires economic changes to enable disabled people the freedom to make choices about how and from where any necessary care is obtained.

Criticisms of independent living are that there are only certain people who can assert control over their lives and an overarching policy can raise expectations inappropriately. Such a stance is dominated by the perspectives and values of undisabled people, especially health and social service professionals who are expected to assess capability, risks, acceptable behaviour and desirable outcomes. However, in doing so they may reveal differences in perception of who is deemed capable and what are the desirable outcomes. In defending their position, which is informed by their care and concern for those for whom they are responsible, proponents of independent living have been criticised that they only address the concerns of young, fit, predominantly wheelchair users. This has been countered by Morris who challenges the distinction:

> If we accept all human life has value – then it is difficult to deny that the human and civil rights that younger fitter, more articulate disabled people are claiming for themselves should be accorded to those who are older/less articulate. (Morris, 1993b: 151)

While this position is obviously to be supported, what is more complex is how it is to be achieved. Independence includes the freedom to choose, and that choice might mean not living alone and not having to purchase services directly.

If independence means having control over one's life in order to achieve goals, then there is significant debate about which goals are appropriate for individuals to pursue. For example, in her discussion of independent living Morris applauds the fact that receiving personal assistance allows disabled women to become care givers themselves, to achieve femininity: 'being a woman in our society is so tied up with care-giving, the ability to use personal assistance in this way is obviously very important to many disabled women' (Morris, 1993b: 91). But this achievement in itself might constrain women's independence.

First, as has been discussed elsewhere, the automatic equating of women with caring has ben subject to much analysis, and it is questioned whether it is a necessary or positive association. Second, disabled men may achieve fulfilment in providing care, but this is not seen to be an appropriate goal, based on the assumption that caring is not a male activity. If giving emotional and physical support is part of human relationships (Morris, 1993b), then it should be possible for all disabled people to achieve potential in this area. For Morris these 'human' relationships are female, as evidenced by her examples, indicating how gendered assumptions are perpetuated in assumed norms of behaviour.

It is in the identification of *appropriate* goals that sex role stereotyping may be most influential in the provision of resources in the care package. Women may be given support in order to help them provide caring for others in a way that men may not. Conversely, women may be denied levels of personal assistance which would enable them to take up more active engagement with society (including paid employment), on the assumption that this was not necessary. In times of limited resources it may be seen as more appropriate for men to have access to employment because of assumptions about 'normal' masculinity.

As has been indicated, the constructions of male and female behaviour and the response of services to their needs have been predicated on notions of normalcy; what is normal for women and men to do and feel, and what are normal expectations of disabled people. That these notions are at times contradictory is highlighted by the work that has been undertaken on normalisation for people with learning difficulties.

A clear example of where attempts to create independent living have had different outcomes for women and men is in services for people with learning difficulties. In studies of the opportunties offered it is shown that women's lives were more restricted and involved domestic duties and watching television rather than engaging in social activities. Men were encouraged to go to vocational centres, learn skills and use public transport (Williams, 1992). In both cases the assumptions of normality and appropriate behaviour were based on gender stereotypes and denied individuals choice.

Normalisation

The understanding of the term and the process of 'normalising' people has been highly contentious and only recently is there acknowledgement that there are gender implications of work designed specifically for people with learning difficulties (Williams, 1992; Clements *et al.*, 1995).

Within normalisation programmes patterns of life and conditions of everyday living are introduced which are as close as possible to the regular circumstances and way of society. The focus is twofold. The first is on the environment, both the provision of 'normal' surroundings and encouraging the person to participate in activities – as consumers and citizens. However, the alleged benefit for people with learning difficulties is the opportunity to 'live as normal a life as possible' – which means that the focus is on the person. Practising normal skills of living will help to 'normalise' people (Ryan and Thomas, 1993: 242); they have to achieve a degree of competence.

Normalisation has been influenced by a psychological framework, especially on non-medical services such as education and social work, and it places substantial emphasis on enhancing social skills and competence rather than the person's sense of well being: 'Normalisation implied that, what is meant to be human and have rights respected, was to be "normal" to have normal experiences and opportunities' (Simpson, 1995: 89). However, the lack of specific reference to self-determination or to self-control over life decisions in the UN charter (1991) illustrates the limitations of such an approach. When a person has demonstrated competence in some particular endeavour, when they do the right thing, make the right choice or say appropriate things, they may do as they wish when they have demonstrated that they can perform correctly; if they are not responsible, they cannot be allowed to choose to do it – there is little scope for self-directed 'deviant' living.

While the emphasis is on societal tolerance of competence to do marketable tasks, to enhance social acceptability, the ascription of deviance to behaviours and attitudes which are seen to challenge 'normal' gendered expectations have implications for the way that the lives of women and men with learning disabilities are both constructed and assessed. Decisions about being competent will be made in the context of gendered expectations; both the what and the how have gendered connotations (Simpson, 1995). The desired passivity of women and the assumed assertiveness of men can become part of the 'how'.

However, as was discussed in Chapter 5, the impact of community care involves a greater number of people in assessment and this impacts on the understanding of the behaviour of those who are recipients of community care. Understandings of what is normal and/or acceptable is subjective and determined by the interpretations and attributions of those without learning difficulties. The fallibility of this process is not acknowledged, there are few checks on the possible biases and distortions, yet the consequences for people with learning difficulties can be profound (Clements *et al.*, 1995).

In gendered terms, arguing for a right to normality can mean greater pressure for people with learning difficulties to adjust to prevailing custom and standards, including recreating the familial models in community living arrangements. It is this which underpins the expectation that residents undertake the roles they would have in a normal family, the women doing the domestic chores and assisting in the day-to-day care of the children and the men going out to work, or at least to purposeful activity at day centres and training centres.

Normalisation has therefore been subject to criticism. From the outset it was presented as a value preference with a strong moral strand embedded in it. The preferred values were reflective of highly individualised non-competitive lifestyles, with stress on mutual support. Ramon (1991) argues that these were counter to the ethos of middle-class lifestyles in North America and Northern Europe and therefore not necessarily normal. Others noted that power resides in the care worker(s) who defines normality. In attempting to 'liberate' people with learning difficulties by teaching them competence, it was suggested that professionals come to 'own' the situation (Simpson, 1995: 94). Emphasis on technical competence, independent functioning and the individual as the focus for change is also said to reflect male values in service provision, and does not pay attention to the process of the relationship in which skills and competence are practised (Clements *et al.*, 1995).

Social role valorisation

It was in response to criticisms that the term normalisation was replaced by social role valorisation (SRV). This reformulation was intended to reflect that positive social revaluation of people with a disability can be achieved by their performance of socially desirable roles and through being treated as valued people by society (Wolfensberger, 1983). This goes further than enhancement of personal competences and includes 'enhancement of social image'. But, like behaviour and technical competence, social image is never ungendered and many of the roles performed by women are rarely socially desirable. Significantly, those roles that arguably are valorised, i.e. mothering, are actively denied women with learning disabilities. Equally, the concepts of masculinity which involve paid employment are frequently denied disabled men. While Ramon (1991) argues that people improve their level of functioning because of encouragement offered by others, and because of the close relationship between self and others' expectations, she acknowledges the need for culturally relative definitions of what is socially valued. Such cultural relativism has to include differentiated gender expectations.

Based on such values as respect for persons and rights to self-determination, normalisation and SRV are said to reflect notions of citizenship: 'Having social roles is a universal attribute of human autonomy, notwithstanding the diversity of cultural expectation about how they are defined and allocated' (Doyal and Gough, 1991: 185). However, for health and social care professionals there is a continuing tension between the need to have responsibility for, to care for, to protect those who are receiving services and to allow levels of self-determination which might involve the right to fail, however that failure might be described. The emphasis on risk assessment in social and health care practice means that disabled people may be given restricted choices denying them the 'dignity of risk' (Perske, 1972).

Throughout the critique of normalisation there is the tension between the desire to afford equal rights, and the need to recognise how existing material, psychological and cultural inequalities differentially influence individual situations. Also, in making available a greater range of life experiences, care must be taken not to reinforce existing inequalities, but to challenge them. However, this may be confusing for users of community care who may want to be accepted as part of a given community or population, which may have implications for their right to be different. Rights to participate include the right to choose to behave in an unconventional way, to reject exploitation and oppressive standards: 'many people choose to live in various unconventional ways – to reject certain standards of conventional dress and typical sex-role behaviour, and mentally handicapped [sic] people might choose to do so too' (Ryan and Thomas, 1993: 246). However, as Ryan and Thomas go on to point out, the pressure to organise, to conform, to forge a common identity as a united front to medical and administrative dominance in fact leads to a loss of identity.

The need to establish difference is therefore problematic in the face of an approach which is derived from symbolic interaction schools of psychology and sociology, and accepts the basic tenets of labelling theory. The purpose of the health or social care intervention is to achieve either a normalcy, or an acceptance and valorisation which will be based on conformity, preventing further labelling as deviant (Ramon, 1991). Gendered notions of deviance and conformity are relevant when considering, for example, the reactions to the behaviour of women with learning difficulties (or, at times, the social construction of their behaviour) which does not conform to the social construction of femininity (Williams, 1992). This is particularly so when so-called challenging behaviour is identified as expressions of aggression and thus associated with acceptable masculine behaviour rather than femininity, leading to more controls being exercised on women who display such behaviour (Clements *et al.*, 1995).

The notion of social roles is also a functionalistic position which is in some ways counter to any notion of difference: 'To gain and hold self esteem, a man or woman must perform skilfully and conscientiously the social roles assigned to him or her by the culture' (Naroll, 1983: 136). But if that culture is imbued with social constructions of both masculinity and femininity it is difficult for SRV to be used effectively to bring about change. Moreover it suggests that in any cultural group there are universal norms of behaviour. More significantly, it assumes that everyone should accept the roles assigned by the dominant culture.

Challenges to such cultural dominance have been presented by discussions of different expectations which are incumbent upon Black women and men who have learning difficulties. While some argue that there is a convergence of stereotypes of people with learning difficulties and Black and other minority ethnic groups (Baxter, 1989), others warn against pushing the comparisons, or the convergences too far, pointing out that the processes may be similar and may give rise to a shared understanding, but different oppressions have different histories, different roots and different paths: 'These simultaneous oppressions of women with learning difficulties, and specially black women, do not just operate in parallel forms, but they compound and reconstitute the experience of oppression for women with learning difficulties in specific ways' (Williams, 1992: 152).

Williams argues that the principles of normalisation ought to be able to incorporate a critical awareness of the need to avoid replicating the gender and racial inequalities of the 'normal' world. But if, as Nirje suggested, normalisation offers: 'the same patterns of life and conditions of everyday living which are as close as possible to the regular circumstances and ways of life of society' (Nirje, 1970), the priorities established by the service practitioners and managers may well reflect a white male middle-class view of the world (Williams, 1992).

The expectations of women and men with learning diffciulties within an understanding of normal therefore highlight that they may be treated, reacted to and served differently because constructions of maleness and femaleness influence perceptions of ability or normality.

Constructions of gender and disability

That gender and disability operate as structures of oppression differently for disabled men and women is evidenced from a variety of sources. A common theme is that dependence/independence are key parts of the social meaning of what it means to be a man or a woman. Dependence is also a key part of the social construction of disability. Hence women's powerlessness is confirmed by disability; masculinity is denied by disability. For disabled men this can contribute to feelings of being status-less and role-less, in fact mirroring the experiences of some women, disabled and undisabled. Significantly, disabled women are assumed to accept this confirmation of their womanliness or femininity, while disabled men may deny their disabilities and attempt to use masculinity as a way of resisting the disabled role (Morris, 1996a: 89). The strength of their reactions to their impairment may differ according to the degree of dependence which is constructed because of the removal of physical ability to do 'male' activities, for example, to be in paid employment.

Disability and masculinity

As discussions of hegemonic masculinity earlier in this text high-lighted, the male position is portrayed as generally dominant, active, authoritative with the female as the object (Wetherall, 1984). But understandings of masculinity are not reducible to a single and primary cause; different patterns of dominant masculinities and subordinate femininities are produced in different spheres of life – family, workplace, state etc. (Connell, 1987), and between different groups of disabled men. However, underlying many of the assumptions of masculine identity are conditions which it is difficult for many disabled men to achieve: 'meanings which are embedded in the habitual authority, technical expertise, sexual assertiveness and economic advantage of men in the day to day functioning of institutions like the workplace and trade unions as well as the family (Segal, 1990: 97). Put more simply, the three structures underlying relationships between men and women, the constructs of hegemonic masculinity – labour, power and desire (Connell, 1987) are denied disabled men. Just as feminism was slow to react to the needs of disabled women, the confusions of masculinity for disabled men are rarely addressed in writings on masculinity or disability.

Social work and social care literature has consistently ignored both, and stereotypical gender assumptions permeate the provision of services at residential and day-care level and in the interventions devised to enable people to live independent lives within the community. This is particularly apparent in the way in which services are offered. So, for example, the assumption that disabled women are discriminated against in the provision of community care facilities, because they are perceived to be in less need of positive and meaningful activities than their male counterparts, is based on constructions of femininity. However, confusions arise when, given expectations of their role within the family, disabled women are likely to want help with carrying out all the tasks associated with running a home and bringing up children. Do assumptions of the naturalness of these tasks mean that disabled women are not offered such help, and are therefore deemed unnatural for not being able to perform them? Or are they given services and support to perform these womanly functions?

Such dilemmas, accompanied by assumptions about women's incompetence with technology, or suggestions that they have less need for mobility, have denied women access to services both in terms of equipment they may be given to aid mobility and training and other opportunities offered to help access to the workplace. Again, paradoxes arise when the tasks that are made available in both sheltered workshops and the paid workplace involve routinisation and micro-skills which are peformed better by women than men.

For men, many tasks which are assumed to be their contribution to the home, for example DIY, are provided by others, or not performed at all (Morris, 1993b). Failing to be able to do these tasks is constituted a failure of masculinity. Work which raises self-esteem is seen to be constitutive of masculinity and this has direct implications for disabled men, as evidenced by the example of a disabled man who had obtained his first job for 20 years and claimed that his counsellor 'really made me feel I was a man and should apply for this job' (Segal, 1991: 89).

The conundrum for disabled people, and those working alongside them, is whether advocacy for independent living should be to fulfil the stereotypical expectations, or to challenge them. One of the major sites of contestation for the right to choose has been in the area of sexual behaviour. It is here that the potent assertion of identity is not only to have normal sexual relations, but to reproduce oneself in childbirth. The paradox is that advocating for the right of disabled people to parent may be constraining them to traditional roles and behaviour.

Parenting

Disabled women experience resistance in many ways to their desires, or even their wish to explore their desires, to parent. Questions are raised about the capabilities of disabled women to perform tasks and duties associated with 'normal' female behaviour. These questions may relate to actual physical abilities, but may also be based on prejudices that, whatever the level of their ability, disabled women are unfit for motherhood. Women who receive support and services for their disability might be deterred or dissuaded from considering mothering because they may require additional support to perform some of the physical tasks. The role of partners in such situations becomes crucial. However, even a woman with an undisabled partner may be disadvantaged because of the ambivalence of social care workers to the involvement of fathers in child care tasks.

Situations where single disabled women have become pregnant raise further questions about the legitimacy of motherhood for disabled women. In those cases the necessary support will not be available from a partner and resources will have to be found. The cost of these resources has led to suggestions that the child should be taken into care, hence problematising the disabled woman in a way that an undisabled pregnant single woman would not necessarily be problematised.

But the emphasis on achieving motherhood as a fulfilment of femininity can be counter-productive and may compound explanations of normal female behaviour and desires to parent as an essential characteristic. A possible consequence of this is that disabled women who cannot parent, or exercise an active choice not to, then become labelled as not women. Questioning the ability and desirability of disabled women to mother may be seen to challenge the female identity of disabled women and deny them the means to achieve fulfilment. This represents the violation and oppression of disabled women in the context of unequal power relations and oppressive ideologies (Morris, 1993a).

While the consequence might be that disabled women should have the right to choose motherhood, this is confounded by suggestions that within disability there is a perceived hierarchy of rights to motherhood. Women with learning difficulties are deemed least competent to mother and therefore subjected to greater controls and intervention, including sterilisation (Heginbotham, 1987; Jenkins, 1989). Ironically, this is seen as a direct consequence of community care. Once the options of institutionalisation and segregation were removed by policies of care in the community, the use of sterilisation as a means of controlling women with learning difficulties became more common. The competing rights between the right to live in the community and the right to reproduce and participate in motherhood, carry with them explicit assessments of who is 'fit' to be a mother (Williams, 1992). Moreover, as with the sexuality of undisabled women, this intervention is designed to protect women from the consequences of male behaviour.

The emphasis on disabled women's wish to parent, to be mothers, pays scant attention to the role and function of disabled men in the parenting process. When attention is paid to disabled men they are perceived as sexual beings with few assumptions that they have the emotional capacity or desire to wish to 'father' in more than the sexual sense. More confusingly, for some, even that sexuality is questioned, or thought to be not relevant.

Sexuality and disability

The concentration on motherhood as a consequence of sexual behaviour means that a disproportionate emphasis is put on the behaviour of women. This apparently denies that sexual activity involves males, either those with whom disabled women enter into relationships, or those who abuse disabled women. As with teenage girls, the risk of pregnancy in disabled women means that it is their bodies which have to be invaded; attempts to deal with male sexual behaviour are not part of the agenda (Hudson, 1985). This has major significance for the attitudes inherent in programmes for disabled people, especially work with people with learning difficulties, which are said to help achieve 'normalisation'. How cruel that normalisation programmes might work on assumptions of women's 'natural' inclination to be mothers – and then deny the right to fulfil the inclination.

Alternatively, if normalisation involves some notion of hegemonic masculinity then there is a challenge in that 'normal male behaviour' will involve overt heterosexual activity on the part of males with learning difficulties. Arrangements for their daily living will mean that the objects of their sexual attention are likely to be women with learning difficulties. If their sexual interests are demonstrated elsewhere this is likely to be seen inappropriate, deviant and, at times, criminally offensive. Heterosexual masculinity therefore becomes problematised.

Similarly confusions around femininity and sexuality which permeate society impact on disabled women in community care provision. Sexual activity in women with learning difficulties is often interpreted as an inability to control their own sexual urge (Williams, 1992). Obsession with physical image and body shapes in society leads to assumptions that disabled women are asexual and as being in some ways non-persons. This asexuality is compounded by treatment in health and social care settings where requirements to strip publicly are not unusual. Attention to issues of feminine hygiene and bodily functions such as menstruation are not treated with privacy and respect. All of these deny disabled women their dignity.

This lack of dignity can be compounded by the sexual abuse experienced by disabled women by male and female carers when in situations of physical disadvantage because of their disability. This emphasises that they may be treated as objects of the sexual behaviour of others, even if they themselves are assumed to be asexual.

That disabled men do not have the same experiences, they are assumed to have sexual needs irrespective of looks or ability, resonates with a hegemonic masculinity which espouses innate heterosexual drives and expects men to be sexually active. However, disabled men may also experience humiliation from having to undress in public, and are also victims of abuse. Their masculinity might be further confounded because of expectations that the assumed passivity of disabled people mean it is not appropriate for disabled men to comment or complain.

All of which is predicated on assumptions that disabled men and women will conform to some normal understanding of sexual behaviour which is inherently heterosexual. Writing about the experiences of people with learning diffciulties Clements *et al.* (1995) argue that the pervading view in the professions of health and social care is one of heterosexuality, which can oppress both staff and users. Staff are reluctant to address issues for gay men and lesbian women for fear of reprisals. At best homosexual women and men with learning disabilities are denied access to the gay and lesbian community, at worst they are labelled as having a lower development level or as being abnormal and perverted.

Thus in the area of sexuality the expression of difference can have negative consequences leading to freedoms being curtailed, stigmatisation and increased surveillance. Also, exploring the potential for difference within the category 'disability' illustrates the challenges for those who wish to take political action on the basis of assumed commonalities between those labelled as disabled.

Difference

To argue for the rights of disabled people as a group or a movement is justified when challenging oppressive stereotyping and labelling which leads to the marginalisation of members of that group. However, if the consequences of such political activism is to assume that all within the group share a common identity, a common set of experiences, then this can be equally oppressive. The recognition of difference, while necessary and important, is complex. Assumptions of homogeneity of particular groups lead to stereotyping and denial of difference which has been a feature of discriminatory and oppressive behaviour, but can also be a consequence of actions which are meant to be anti-oppressive. Young points out that social groups mirror the differentiation of wider society and that individuals within any group need to be able to recognise and have recognised their different group affinities and relations, their different identities (Young, 1990b). This is not to challenge the effectiveness of both feminism and the disability movement to argue for shared experiences and oppression based on those experiences, but, as writers on race and disability reflect, other identities are not necessarily recognised or valorised (Stuart, 1994).

More significant is the need to have difference recognised in a positive way. The emphasis on the negative aspects is highlighted by Stuart: 'Theoretical conceptualisation of disabled people from minority ethnic communities as merely victims of racism suggests they will continue to receive inadequate services (Stuart, 1996: 89). However, to valorise the particular and multiple differences within any identified group may weaken the political cause. In a process described as 'divide and rule' Freire (1972) argues that oppressor groups will highlight differences between those who are oppresssed. Taking a focalised view of the problem, keeping groups divided creates a sense of weakness; unity and organisation can create a transforming force.

To fail to recognise differences, the way that the circumstances of being disabled might impact differently on, for example, men and women or people from different socio-economic groups or ethnic backgrounds, is to perpetuate other forms of oppression.

However, it is not sufficient to recognise difference and to argue that oppression on the basis of, for example, being a woman, being Black or being disabled is either multiple oppression or a hierarchy of oppressions, a competition to identify which identity or experience is the more oppressive. Begum argues that it is not possible, or desirable to identify a single source of oppression; one single oppression cannot be prioritised to the exclusion of others (Begum *et al.*, 1994). In Young's analysis of the five faces of oppression she sees a need to recognise similarities between different oppressed groups as well as differences to avoid competition: 'because different factors, or combination of factors, constitute the oppression of different groups, making their oppression irreducible...it is not possible to give one essential differentiation of oppression' (Young, 1990b: 42). By pluralising the category of oppression the exclusive and over-simplifying effects of reductionism can be avoided. Reductionism to a single category of oppression such as disablism, racism or sexism fails to accommodate similarities and differences in the oppression of different groups and it falsely represents the experiences of people in the category or group as being the same.

It is the opportunity offered by the work of writers on disability to explore this model, to understand not only the experience of oppression by certain groups but also that what is learnt can be applied to other groups, analysed in the light of their experience and either developed or discarded, which is the significant process offered by an analysis by gender as opposed to an analysis of sexism.

Conclusion

This chapter has emphasised the contribution that feminist and disabled people's activism and writing has made to debates within community care which emphasise the need to recognise difference. Taking as a starting point the complex identities of those who are users of community care, it is recognised that there are competing tensions between the need to draw attention to the oppression of particular groups, because of the way that they are defined within the care arrangements, and the importance of recognising diversity and difference. This is true not only for disabled people, but also for older people and those with mental health problems.

It has been argued that the overwhelming emphasis on the category of user can have discriminatory outcomes, especially when specific interventions reinforce assumed normalcy of particular behaviours and hold them up as goals to be achieved. In particular arrangements for service delivery which are imbued with welfare overtones and negative understandings of caring constrain disabled people in passive and dependent roles.

The political lobbying of the disability rights movement has brought about change. The introduction of discrimination legislation, while limited in scope, is one response to recognising the citizenship rights of disabled people by giving them the 'Right to develop a unique disabled people's perspective on the world and the opportunity to contribute to its future shape' (Finkelstein, 1993: 41). As well as recognising the uniqueness of disabled people's perspectives, attention to gender illustrates that each different form of discrimination has its unique characteristics, but they should not be dealt with in isolation. Equally, the specific circumstances of individuals will continue to require a variety of responses from health and social care; what is required is that in dealing with individual differences services can recognise the unique strengths within these situations, rather than negatively ascribing problems to the individual within them.

While changes in community care legislation have provided some opportunities for this different perspective for working with disabled people, it is apparent that further changes are required which will enable health and social care professionals to respond to disabled people as citizens in their own right, as well as users of community care services. Such changes are necessary throughout the organisation of community care and depend on a balance being struck between the attention to individuals and their specific needs, and the circumstances, systems and structures which impact on particular groups.

These changes may involve a radically different approach to practice, but this has to be based on a reappraisal of some of the principles which have provided the value base of social work and social care practice. It is this reappraisal which provides the conclusion to this text.

8

Identity, Difference and 'Just' Practice

Introduction

At the outset this text explored the contribution that feminist theory has made to recognising and celebrating difference. Initially concentrating on the experiences of women, it has been argued that widening the focus to the ways in which women's and men's experiences are constructed and interpreted has significant implications for understanding community care from the perspectives of both service providers and those who are recipients of services.

In the more detailed analysis of different user groups what emerges is that the complex identities of users are rarely responded to by those providing services, and the ways in which services are delivered reflect assumptions of both policy makers and practitioners about the homogeneity of groups for whom they have a statutory responsibility. Such approaches are not necessarily the fault of the workers. Community care practice involves a set of ambiguities. While the rhetoric is about individualised packages of care, the reality is about commissioning services which will meet universal need. For example, a service provided to help people get out of bed focuses on the practical difficulties people may have in getting out of bed, not on the characteristics of the person who needs the service, be that their specific illness or disability or their race, class or gender. Gender as a dimension is often lost or denied when the focus is on the predominant characteristic of the group as identified by the administrative categories of community care provision. More significantly, attention to gender, if it does occur, often involves treating women and men differently. In doing so, men and women who are in receipt of community care are frozen into fixed identities which are prescribed by stereotypical assumptions about masculinity and femininity.

Diversities are rarely addressed directly by practitioners. Where they are, the dominant identity responded to is often that prescribed by stereotypical assumptions about particular groups held by workers. This is not to criticise, because the recognition of commonalities has been a powerful analysis in writing on anti-oppressive and empowering practice. To identify the way that particular groups are stigmatised and to work with them to give voice, self-determination and choice is reflective of the value base which has been at the core of social work practice for decades (Biestek, 1961; Plant, 1973). As part of empowering practice academic and other writings designed to assist practitioners may confuse by privileging one particular set of experiences for analysis. That is not to say that the specific experiences of any one group should not be acknowledged. The challenge is to recognise diversity in ways which neither privilege nor negate any one set of experiences. This has to be part of a set of values based on respect for persons, and a set of practices which includes acceptance of, and working with, for example, perpetrators, abusers and oppressors as part of the remit of social care and social work.

But recognising and accepting difference brings further challenges for practitioners. In documenting the feminist critique of social work and social care practices in Chapter 1 it was argued that social work and social care have to focus on both individuals and their environment. In this concluding chapter it is suggested that social work and social care operate at the borderlands of individuals and their environment in many senses: between individuals, between individuals and families, groups and communities; between individuals and other organisations. It explores how social work has to respond to the challenges presented by critiques of individualised practice and the opportunities presented by community care for working at these borderlands. The response is not necessarily a new social work practice, but a refocusing on social work processes, whatever the context, informed by understandings and principles of social justice.

Identity and difference as problematic

It is apparent from the preceding chapters that in any arrangements for community care there is rarely one defining identity, or if there is it is not necessarily the one to which the providers of community care services may be responding. Within feminist theory and postmodernism the fixed nature of identity has been questioned, and assumptions about the construction of behaviours and attitudes as feminine or masculine have been challenged (Butler, 1990; Flax, 1992; Williams, 1996). Focusing on a fixed identity of an individual within a particular category of user group may foreclose on recognising or identifying with those in other categories or groups who may share similar experiences. In debates about empowerment and social and community development there has been an emphasis on solidarity, recognising the commonality of experience of oppression or discrimination of those within particular groups. The work of the disability rights movement, advocacy groups for those experiencing mental health problems and pressure groups and non-governmental organisations (NGOs) set up by, and on behalf of, carers are examples of this very important strand of political activism in community care. It is based on a commonality of experience, as is the recognition by international workers of the significance of the national or religious affiliations of those with whom they collaborate.

Within these activities it is sometimes feared that expressions of difference might deny groups the means and the will to move forward in a political sense on what is shared and common. However, while social and community development, campaigning for rights and changing service delivery are important foci for social work, work with individuals remains crucial to all of these. Social workers work at the borderlands between individuals and their local, national and international circumstances, but just as significantly between individuals and the particular group in which their perceived or declared identity situates them.

Borderlands

These borderlands are uneasy territory for those employed within statutory social services whose response is proscribed by policies designed to streamline services and reduce the economic burden of care provision on the state. Jordan argues that social work has become increasingly coercive and that part of 'new orthodoxy' is that workers have to recognise the clash of interests between the moral majority and the deviant minority (1990: 12). In perceiving service users as deviant he suggests that social work is in danger of becoming the instrument of exclusion and injustice and what is needed is a recognition of the citizenship rights of users of community care services.

Similarly Parton (1999), in focusing on the 'social', suggests that social work developed at a midway point between the individual initiative and the all-encompassing state. In this context the notion of the 'social' assumes that the individual is an ensemble of social relations and therefore becomes the 'site' of interactions. The conclusions of this text similarly argue that social work legitimately operates at the interface of the individual's diverse experiences and they way that these are presented. Good practice should therefore recognise the complexity of identities that can be asserted, acquired, assumed by or attributed to individuals who are in need of community care provision. Often it is the assertions or attributions by social workers which have been paramount and which have led to the characterisation of difference on the basis of group identity rather than individual meaning. But these attributed identities are always partial, the structure of identity remains open.

To avoid ossifying, maintaining the person in one position, it is important to recognise and understand the complex relations of power within and between the identified differences which impact on the experiences of all those involved in working with and within them. So, for example, the assumptions of passivity on the part of those receiving care, be they older people or disabled people, impacts differentially on women and men, because for the former it is seen to be the extension of feminine behaviour, while for the latter it is at odds with some notion of hegemonic masculinity, but for both it may mean a loss of power.

This position is not without problems. First, there are concerns that recognising individual difference might involve freezing a fixed identity within a particular category which forecloses on recognition of, or identification with, others in other categories or groups. Second, the expression of difference at the individual level might deny groups the means and the will to move forward in a political sense on what aspects are shared and common, especially if, as Williams argues, the identities are subject to change 'The fragmentation of politics involves a constant freezing and melting and reconstituting of identity' (Williams, 1996: 72). Such fluidity creates concerns for some user groups who have focused campaigns on what is common and shared and fear that fragmentation might limit their political power.

Fragmented identities

Community care policies have ascribed to notions of particular 'user' groups but in doing so have created sets of binaries, two characteristics which are perceived as opposites, as dichotomous categories. In community care such binaries include: carers/cared for; undisabled/disabled; young/old; mentally well/ill. These can be added to already acknowledged differences such as male/female, white/Black. In these categorisations it is assumed that the binary oppositions in some way reflect some natural order, that they are fixed, rather than being constructed by historical and social conditions (Weedon, 1999). Also within the binaries there exists hierarchical relations of power with the first description assumed to be the norm, the unproblematic and indeed the privileged. Practice operates on the basis that the categories are opposites between which individuals cannot move, creating a hierarchy of oppression and requiring that individuals are responded to according to the identified need which is codified according to managerial definitions which are constructed by, and construct, the binary opposites.

To challenge such binary oppositions requires transformations which fragment what might be seen as meta-categories of age, disability, gender, sexuality, class, ethnicity, race, and nationality. This fragmentation, however, is not just a theoretical device, it represents shifts in personal identities which are part of human development. Recognising such shifts already occurs in practice, but often in negative ways which can undermine the sense of self. The loss of a stable sense of self is unsettling for those involved: 'This set of double displacements – decentring individuals both from their place in the social and cultural world, and from themselves constitutes a "crisis of identity" for the individual' (Hall, 1992: 277). So, for example, a retired professional woman can be categorised as 'old Ms Jones' on becoming a recipient of community care because of ill health in old age with none of her former expertise and status recognised.

Hence social workers and social care workers do not consciously impose sets of characteristics on, or assume group identity of, users of services, they merely reflect ways in which organisations and their institutional practices constrain and discipline those for whom they have responsibility. Becoming a 'user' of social services in itself can precipitate a crisis of identity; aspects of the self have to be presented in order to gain the attention of the agencies. Often this does not necessarily represent the overriding concern of the person requiring assistance. The older man who requires practical care may be more troubled by the crisis of becoming dependent on his adult children than the intricacies of whether he needs a day centre place or meals on wheels.

In good practice what has to be established is which aspect of the person's identity is most significant for them, but to understand that this may change at different points in a person's contact with social work and social care service and, indeed that there may be multiple identities. As the previous chapters have documented challenges come from the caring man or the user who is also the provider.

Working with individuals, although a long-standing traditional method for social work, can constitute a dilemma for social workers. On the one hand, social workers have been subject to criticism that they have focused on the individual in a negative way. As Jordan argues, there is a further complexity if the focus is solely on the individual relationship between users and social workers, and denies the wider social relations which contribute to injustice, inequality and exploitation (1990: 82). On the other had, the recognition of oppression of certain groups with whom social work deals has led to coordinated responses to individuals within those groups. In the area of gender this has been both helpful and contentious; it is possible to criticise the way that women have been treated as objects of, or subjects within, the social work process, but at the same time acknowledge that attention to the experiences of women has illustrated that the category women is not homogeneous. To work with women and men at the individual level might be in their interests, but individual work has to contribute to wider understandings of women and men, femininity and masculinity and of the interplay between these categories.

Crisis of individualisation

The 'crisis of individualisation' centres around the distinction between two opposing meanings. In one the subject is 'indivisible' – an entity which is unified within itself and cannot be further divided; in the other, it is also an entity which is 'singular, distinctive, unique' (Williams, quoted in Hall, 1992: 282). In social work and social care the emphasis has been on the latter but the uniqueness has sometimes been confounded by the use of theory which has attempted to assist practice by giving formulae to predict what is required. Such predictions are made on the basis of, for example, problem definition, risk assessment or ways of intervening.

Social workers have been subject to criticism for their interventions at the level of the individual because if attention is not paid to the diversity of individual needs, experiences and definitions then, according to the analysis of this text, social work is failing. But in being attentive they have to avoid both simplistic categorisations, and grand claims which assume that they know the causes of, and the solutions to human problems. Such claims, making has been associated by some with aspects of high modernity, of regulatory practice which secures conformity in the users of services through self-regulation brought about by the interventions of workers: 'by the legitimate interventions of "secular priests" in the resolution of personal malfunction' (Webb, 1996: 177).

Ironically and confusingly, while claims-making and grand theorising can be challenged, the very process of questioning, of being reflexive is seen by others to have therapeutic outcomes. For Giddens, writing about what he calls high modernity, the institutional order can positively contribute to a sense of self and therapy, the often derided activity of social work is an expression of the reflexivity of the self: 'abstract institutions become centrally involved not only in the institutional order of modernity, but also in the formation and continuity of the self' (Giddens, 1991: 33). So, while social work is being removed, or is removing itself from involvement in the therapeutic, the search for self becomes a much wider therapeutic activity. If self-identity is not something that is given it has to be routinely created and sustained in the reflexive actions it is discursive, it is arrived at at any one time by the sense that a person makes of their biography (Giddens, 1991).

Making sense of biography is a significant activity in the many interventions used by social workers. The discussion of reminiscence in Chapter 6 is a clear example of making sense of biography, and in problem-solving, task-centred casework helps individuals by focusing on their individual problems and problem-solving mechanisms which are part of their biography.

In community care, to respond to need without recognising biographies becomes problematic. For example, as has been repeatedly documented, to constantly relate to women as mothers and/or carers frames all women in a particular set of essential characteristics, and by implication all men in opposite and opposing characteristics. The complex interplay that the differences of race, class, sexuality, age and disability bring to women's experiences provides opportunities to recognise the individual, and not just the collective, as the site of political activity: 'to develop more complex enquiries into the relationship between identity, subjectivity, subject position and political agency' (Williams, 1996: 68). Doing so can facilitate detachment from the categories and meanings imposed by policy makers, welfare managers and others, and the pursuit the biographies of women and the diversity within those biographies: 'what the categories "single mother", "the old" "the disabled" and so on mean to those who inhabit them' (Williams, 1996: 68) but the power of bureaucratic procedures should not be underestimated.

These bureaucratic procedures include the focus on needs-led assessment of individuals and their situations, but also require that data is aggregated to facilitate commissioning of services defined by user category. In these processes the individual is situated in a wider context where what is individual and unique might be subsumed into categories for purposes other than meeting individual needs. At one level this must be so; for truly needs-led assessments attention has to be paid to the particular circumstances of particular individuals, drawing on information and knowledge about how differences such as gender, class, race and sexuality might impact on those circumstances. However, working with difference means that each individual's circumstances will produce more information about users and impact further on understandings and knowledge in a truly iterative process. The danger is that the information collection becomes the *raison d'être* of the practice.

'Disciplining' community care

With emergent systems for provision of community care, social workers have at the same time to respond to the shifting understandings of subject, individuals and their many and complex needs, but work within amanagerial discourses which classify and regulate. Social work, although emanating from the various needs of the state to make provision for citizens, has struggled to resist becoming a site of disciplinary power. Disciplining in this sense has been explained as focusing on individuality, recognising that power fixes the objective individuality in the field of writing (Foucault, 1977). However, as has been said, documentation such as record keeping, risk assessment and problem checklists contribute to the measurement of overall phenomena, description of groups, characterisation of collective facts, and the calculation of gaps between individuals and their distribution in a given population which is part of that disciplining.

Commenting in general on institutions of late modernity Hall (1992) points out the paradox that the more collective and organised is the nature of the institution, the greater is the isolation, surveillance and individualisation of the individual subject. Care management in community care has introduced techniques of disciplinary power and knowledge through surveillance. Constant observation of all those subject to control means that they are individualised by the process. This is apparent in the assessment processes of care management which recognise the need for multi-agency assessment, but mechanisms for these have produced schedules which depend on the technicalisation of the process. Information systems which can be shared and involve the means to collect individual data and produce aggregate analysis to be used for a number of different purposes become part of the surveillance. Such systems discipline individuals but they also limit social work activity because the immediacy of the need for a decision and the demands on communication processes in such circumstances fail to take into account the limitations to communication brought about by, for example, both physical and mental illness. So while focusing on the individual for the necessary data, they do not recognise or take into account the ways in which different experiences and circumstances of individual users of community care have to be recognised and validated.

While attempting to engage in a relationship with individual users for the purposes of assessment, using diverse communication channels, social workers or care managers are constantly overtaken by the instrumentality of the system which leads to contrasts between alleged intentions and outcome in community care. For example, there is a discrepancy between the espousal of consumer choice within the diversity of the marketised and mixed economy of provision for community care, and the way that the diverse needs which emerge are subsequently assessed and re-routed through administrative categories (Williams, 1996). There are similar contradictions between commitment to increased efficiency which conceals reduction in service levels and policies for user involvement which are little more than limited procedures for user consultation (Orme, 1996).

These criticisms, that the individualised approach is subject to the influence of the bureaucratic institutions, suggests that the needs of users may well be met by a more politicised approach which could include democratic involvement of the users of community care, lobbying, advocacy and other interventions based on identified needs of groups and communities, not individuals. Similarly, the loss of power created by negative labelling highlights that narrow definitions of identity deny differences and diversities among oppressed groups (Young, 1990b), but valorising differences can be empowering. Within both participation and oppression the individual experience is paramount, both in its own right and as part of a collective experience (Braye and Preston-Shoot, 1995). At any one time, depending on experience, an individual can describe him or herself in different ways and identify with different groups or collectives. Social work has to find the means to recognise and validate the interplay between complex understandings of the individual and his or her relationship with particular groups, communities, social movements and global developments.

Community/social development

Paradoxically, the fragmentation of individual identities brought about by the bureaucratisation of community care provision has been accompanied by attention to processes of globalisation. Within social work there have been suggestions that traditional approaches should be replaced by social and community development in order to avoid the negative aspects of individualisation and unite users, and those who might be in need but are excluded from services, in a political project.

It is these predicted organisational changes and the managerial responses to community care policies which have led to assumptions that social work as an activity is doomed (Clarke, 1996). This is not a necessary outcome, but highlights another borderland, that between individuals who have expressed or identified needs and the context in which that need is perceived and responded to. This response is framed both by the state, which sees itself as having a role in meeting those needs, to greater or lesser degree depending on the dominant political ideology, and by social work agencies through which the state's response is mediated. The dilemma for practitioners is: do they approach potential users of services as individuals whose complex identities and needs require special attention which are constructed by legislation, services and continued involvement of an agent of the state, or do they regard them as autonomous agents in their own right with the potential to meet their own needs, given the right conditions, or indeed as having no special needs – as merely being 'different' by virtue of their particular circumstances?

Both these perspectives require that the worker engage at the level of societal change, or community development. But to do so is no less contentious than individual work. As was documented in Chapter 2, responses in the past have included community action, moving outside the statutory sector to work with collectives to empower, or to make provision which was not dependent upon the bureaucratic state. But when social work has defined itself as a process of mediation between client and community, with an emphasis on the social context in which people live, social workers have found themselves 'caught between client and community, and constantly frustrated by forces that undermine their efforts at every turn' (Hartman, 1989: 387).

Other criticisms of community-based approaches have come from a variety of theoretical and political perspectives, including those adopted and championed by users of the services which were being provided. One set of reactions is to question the relevance of political and liberatory activity to those whose circumstances make them unable or unwilling to participate in political activity, which is seen to be the domain of middle-class educated people who are not caught in the net of welfare. This can deem users of social services to be less capable of being involved in such activities by virtue of the circumstance which have brought them to the attention of, or to request aid of, the welfare services. Alternatively, it is assumed that because service users are part of the welfare net they are less deserving of involvement as citizens, and have given up, or have had removed their rights to involvement. Either way, simple responses fail to recognise the complex ways in which becoming a user of community care services denies people agency, and citizen rights.

A further criticism is that community, collective and empowering approaches have by definition to categorise people, to relate to them as members of a particular group whether that be defined by gender, race, geographic location (local and national, as in the literature on social development), disability, age, etc. They assume a 'shared subjectivity' and represent a desire to see people in unity with each other as part of a shared whole. As such the assertion of community is seen to be the logical consequence of rejecting individualism (Young, 1990a: 229–30). But this often means that the interventions are not meaningful to those individuals within these categories whose construing of their own experiences may mean that their dominant identity may be other than the one to which the worker or the service is responding at that particular time. According to Young, this division between individualism and community represents another unnecessary dichotomy, and she argues that what is needed is mutuality and reciprocity: 'social differentiation without exclusion' (1990a: 238).

This position is supported by Lane who, offering an alternative perspective to the negative, neutralising effect of community, argues that understandings of community can be liberating:

> Emphasis on a subjective negotiated community, rather than a belief in community as an objective reality (which imposes identity upon people), allows people to construct their own identity and promotes the inclusion of previously excluded voices in decision-making. The tensions and conflicts associated with recognition of diverse values and interests are not denied but rather acknowledged and made part of the negotiating process. (Lane, 1999: 145)

She does not see this as a simple task but one that requires a repertoire of skills which include questioning, listening, encouraging and responding. Importantly, it recognises the need to respond to the diversity of needs represented within communities as a response to globalisation which is precipitating individuals into identifying themselves as belonging to particular ethnic groups, and structuring nation boundaries within more solid borderlands or boundaries. It recognises that individuals need to construct their own identity.

The importance of self identity

As has been highlighted, self-identity is shaped, altered and reflexively sustained in relation to rapidly changing circumstances in social life on both a local and global scale. This is always part of individual biography. While it is apparent that changes for individual users of community care services impact on them as autonomous individuals, either in the assessments made of them, or in the way that services are offered, changes brought about by different political and welfare ideologies have also impacted. The question is whether it is possible to retain the notion of the individual, with its many complexities, in political and economic situations which might require at more macro level interventions of social development.

A reflexively ordered narrative of self-identity provides a means of giving coherence to the finite lifespan, given changing external circumstances be they local or global. This is not to suggest that the old parody of casework needs to be invoked, that feelings about a situation, whether that be the need for personal care, the experiences of famine or war, have to be the initial, immediate or sole focus of the intervention of social workers and social care workers. In any situation, whether delivering a package of care, community development in war-torn regions or providing aid in conditions of poverty and/or famine, those within the situation need to realise a notion of autonomous self. The tyranny of the caseworker in the individual relationship interpreting and re-interpreting individuals' experiences can be repeated in the tyranny of social and community development. The colonisation of the means of each country to develop its welfare systems, to be insensitive to the needs of the particular socio-political circumstances which impact upon the needs of individuals within those situations, is part of anti-dialogical action (Freire, 1972) which keeps oppressed group within conditions of oppression.

For feminism these dilemmas highlight how personal circumstances are structured by public factors and vice versa; the personal is the political. However, while for some the consequence of this analysis has been that personal problems can be solved only through political action, for others there is a recognition that within political action there is a need for private and individual interventions. The equation is therefore more complex: 'the personal is not the political, the two spheres are interrelated dimensions of a future democratic feminist order' (Pateman, 1989: 131). It is this democratic order which can contribute to new understandings of social work but it requires collective approaches, and the participation of women at all levels. But if the suggestion is that the collective means that *all* women's experiences have to be perceived as conforming to a particular predefined explanation of oppression, there is a direct conflict with the well-established definitions of individualisation in social work and with the argument here that to empower women (and disabled people, older people and those with mental health problems) they should not be assumed to conform to some preordained norm. However, the assertion that what is needed is participation is part of the way forward.

Positive interventions

It was noted at the outset of this chapter that it is not helpful to produce false dichotomies between and within groups who might participate in community care. There is a continuum of individual circumstances and abilities that requires that social workers and social care workers employ a combination of skills framed by a variety of perspectives to recognise and respect the diversity of experience. While the responsiveness of systems and the sensitivity of the worker to the circumstances of the individual remains paramount, the range of interventions is broad.

Individual identities as the focus for intervention

At one end of the continuum the focus stays with the individual and notions of empathy; the cornerstone of casework is an example where the individual's understanding and experience of the world is paramount. At the other end, equal opportunities initiatives recognise oppression on the basis of group identity but make available processes and procedures for individual redress.

Positive use of empathy

Social workers and social care workers are in an invidious position because they have to be able to recognise the objective circumstances of those that they work with, but be prepared to accept and respect the subjective wishes of the individual. For example, the limitations of choice of supported places of residence for women with mental health problems because of underfunding for women's services might anger the worker, but a woman user of mental health services who moves into any community-based accommodation might see this as personal progress and express gratitude and relief.

This presents a paradox: that if users of services are to be afforded full citizenship workers should respect their judgement and perceptions. But, as has been argued consistently, being a user of community care services impinges negatively on citizenship rights (Jordan, 1990). While recognising the pressures of instrumental social policy on the practice of social work, Blaug urges workers to remain focused on the basic insight that care involves people and is most properly conceived as a communicative practice oriented towards mutual understanding, which will involve people talking face to face (Blaug, 1995). These sentiments art supported by Stuart who, in acknowledging that the heterogeneous nature of Black and other minority ethnic users of community care services might be daunting, suggests that difficulties can be mitigated by 'careful listening to the views of both users and carers' (Stuart, 1996: 103).

This communication, through talking and listening, have been core skills in social work and are consistent with respect for persons. Such respect, requires social workers to make relationships with those with whom they are working, and in doing so to express empathy. As Jordan suggests, this is vital if the individual's understanding of their experiences is to be heard and responded to:

> Words like 'genuineness' and 'empathy' in accounts of successful and effective practice indicate a moral dimension to the encounter, where the issues are serious, and involve value and commitments which are central to the clients' beliefs and hopes about themselves and their relationships. (Jordan, 1990: 177)

But the concept of empathy is not unproblematic. It involves communication and understanding. According to Fransella (1995), problems in communication between individuals are inevitable because individuals place their own constructions upon the 'reality' that they perceive; they construct their own reality. At its worst, therefore, individual work can fail to recognise the differences in perception. The consequences are that it either negatively labels the person, or is constituted by missed communication. Either way, the outcome is disempowering for both worker and service user.

Often the effects of caring are that workers express sympathy and assume that the circumstances which have brought someone into the ambit of community care are negative. An alternative is to recognise that individuals may frame their circumstances as a challenge, and to take responsibility for change. This requires recognising that the person has to be understood within their social contexts and that they may have been limited by their circumstances, but not victims of them. In community care the writings of disabled women highlight that many have not simply accepted the labels of disability and the construction of their impairments as illness but have made active choices, as evidenced by Morris's introduction to *Pride Against Prejudice*: 'For me this book is both a personal exploration of the sources of my anger and a celebration of the strengths which have come from realising that I am now part of a movement which is making fundamental challenges to the kind of society in which we live' (Morris, 1996b: 10). But would it be unrealistic to expect that every disabled person becomes an activist, all sufferers of mental illness have to become involved in advocacy, and all older people have to join grey power organisations? Is it any more helpful for a woman to know that she is oppressed rather than depressed? If she interprets her experiences as depression, then that is where the work has to begin. To avoid miscommunication a balance has to be struck between understanding how people construe their experiences, and their own part in them; between the worker interpreting these experiences in the light of their own understandings and construing, and being paternalistic.

However, while it is necessary for the worker to accept the person's own description of their state, they must be alert to, and explore with the person all that impacts on that state. Such explorations must avoid the processes of anti-dialogical action which include producing inauthentic myths (Freire, 1972). Examples of such myths operating in community care have been highlighted throughout this text, and include the myths of feminine behaviour which have been used as yardsticks in mental health and, equally powerful, the myths of masculinity which might deny men the capacity to express their caring selves.

In classic empathy the worker suspends his or her own values and listens only to the client's or user's. To be able to do so enables the worker to operate in a way that is sensitive to the person's experience and which is not influenced by the worker's own cultural values. Being truly empathic means that workers are culturally sensitive, anti-discriminatory and anti-oppressive. But suspending a value system might also involve having to be equally accepting of racist or sexual construing by the user. This constitutes some of the limitations of empathy.

Limitations of empathy

It is this notion of undiscriminating acceptance that has meant that understandings of empathy have been the focus of feminist analysis (Brook and Davis, 1985; Hanmer and Statham, 1988) and are discussed in detail in Chapter 4. A further limitation is that empathy may have much the same effect as the disciplining procedures of care management. It may create an atomised, individualistic and socially isolated notion of self suggesting that there is no political project.

Attention to the individual is therefore not enough, especially in discourses of community care where assumptions of both caring and community suggest some notion of relational beings, with the possibility that individuals have attachments and responsibilities, on which they can rely for stability and continuity of being, of a sense of self.

In stressing these relational aspects of the constitution of the self, individual work is challenged by feminists who argue that the notion of self is never totally subjective, it is always the object of others' construction: 'Feminists displace unitary, essentialist and asocial ahistorical ideas of self by analysing the way gender enters into and partially constitutes both self and our ideas about it' (Flax, 1992: 196). But, in recognising that gender is part of the 'constitution of self', it is also possible to accept that other aspects of individual identity are equally constitutive of self, and that attention to those can and should be part of understanding how individuals construe their own world. Which aspect of their identity operates within the world, or is paramount in their experiences at any one time, is reflective of the world as it is being experienced. For a person requiring community care, it might not be the fact that they are old or disabled per se which is paramount, but the way that age or disability has affected their perception of themselves, or the way that others perceive them as non-active or worthless because of age or disability.

Also, while the notion of self is important it is not possible for workers to concentrate only on the individual. They have a responsibility to others who may be the providers of care, be they family, friends and volunteers who provide direct care or the taxpaying public who make indirect provision of care resources. Working in a statutory agency social workers have to allow for individual choice within a framework of equality and access (Jordan, 1990).

It is to these confusions in notions of individualised empathy, and to the need to address inequalities in access to service provision, that work in the area of equal opportunities has sought to provide a different kind of solution.

Emancipatory practice

The highly individualised focus on self-identity has been counter-acted by equally conflictual understandings of equal opportunities in social work. Acknowledging current imperatives for attention to notions of citizenship, participation, community presence, equality, anti-oppressive practice and empowerment and/or user control at one level seems to deny the individual, but to do so might conflict with some notion of equality:

> the danger that when every individual is seen as unique and self determining, collective need experienced by groups of people is overlooked and barriers to 'fulfilment' experienced as a result of structural inequality are ignored. If everyone is unique, everyone is, in effect, the same and provided equal access is offered to the same facilities, people are being fair; or are they? (Braye and Preston-Shoot, 1995: 37)

Understandings and theories of equal opportunities come from both liberal and radical perspectives. In various arenas women, Black and ethnic minority groups and disabled people have sought a notion of equality, often in the sense of equal treatment. Liberal understandings equated equality with notions of sameness, women had to eliminate differences, to cease being female, to be like men, before entering the public world to be citizens. As was discussed in Chapter 7 the disability movement sought radical strategies to challenge this, calling for differences to be recognised, and for the public world to adapt. However, like care management and community care these political imperatives for equality became highly procedural in their implementation.

As a means of dealing with the borderlands between the individual and the collective, equal opportunities policies have been both criticised for presenting oppressor groups as universal reductionist categories (Sibeon, 1991–2), and commended as part of the discourse of diversity and difference in the restructuring of welfare: 'They have grasped the administrative categories (or subject positions) imposed upon them by policy makers, administrators and practitioners and translated these into political identities and new subjectivities' (Williams, 1996: 75). Equal opportunities policies have therefore been seen by some in social work to be important in raising issues of discrimination and facilitating collective organisation and advocacy groups to emerge from emancipatory movements of gender and race, but they also have the potential to 'freeze' or to ossify differences into categories which are seen as rigid and essential (Williams, 1996). This both sets up a hierarchy of competing needs and makes it difficult to identify common needs between groups.

In equal opportunities, as in community care, everyone has the right to be heard, for their position to be understood, but not necessarily accepted. What is required is a means of achieving communicative fairness, free from distortions of power described by some as the ideal speech situation (Blaug, 1995). This is achieved not through processes of individual empathic communication described above but through a form of emancipatory politics. Ironically, for some, such a politics seems to lead inexorably to a focus on the individual: 'The more social circumstances approximate to an ideal-speech situation, the more social order based on the autonomous action of free and equal individuals will emerge' (Giddens, 1991: 213).

For Giddens equal opportunities is a form of institutional reflexivity which involves the regularised use of knowledge about circumstances of social life as a constitutive element in its organisation and transformation. His notion of emancipatory politics is concerned with liberating individuals and groups from the constraints which adversely affect their life chances and consists of two elements: 'the effort to shed the shackles of the past to permit a transformative attitude towards the future and the aim of overcoming the illegitimate domination of some individuals or groups by others' (Giddens, 1991: 211). As such it works with hierarchical notions of power, where power is the capacity of an individual or group to exert its will over others, and the aim is to reduce or eliminate exploitation, inequality and oppression by making primary the imperatives of justice, equality and participation.

The mobilising principle of behaviour behind most versions of emancipatory politics is autonomy. But for Jordan (1990) this is problematic. He contends it is impossible to deny that social workers have power and argues this power is legal, procedural and moral. What is important is how social workers recognise their power, and how they attempt to share it. However, finds he no clear guidance in social work theory, which he sees as lacking a form of moral or ethical reasoning. Unlike the codified values that social workers usually cite as the moral base of their work (e.g. self-determination, respect for persons, acceptance, etc.), such moral reasoning does not imply universality of principles which once identified can apply in any set of circumstances.

For example, within theories of justice and theories of communication, how individuals will behave is left open with little indication
of what choices will have to be made. This involves identifying both
individual and collective needs in ways which do not blame,
pathologise, oppress, discipline or deny. It is here that understandings of social justice can enhance social work practice in community
care.

Social justice

Users of community care services comprise an infinite number of
human beings with expressed or identified needs competing for
limited resources. The social work project is to ensure that a
response to these recognises both individual and collective needs,
and the right to have these needs met to a greater or lesser extent:
'both needs and rights need to be understood as tiered, embracing
both the universal and the differentiated, and standing in dynamic
relationship to each other through a "politics of needs interpretation"' (Lister, 1997: 41). This politics of needs interpretation is not,
and never can be, universalistic but is subjected to different cultural,
and historical interpretations (Doyal and Gough, 1991). It involves
pragmatism which is both congruent with postmodern projects and
with the project of social work (Davies, 1985). But pragmatism itself
is not unproblematic:

> The political problems intrinsic to pragmatism include: how to resolve
> conflict among competing voices; how to ensure that everyone has a chance
> to speak; how to ensure that each voice counts equally; how to assess
> whether equality or participation is necessary in all cases or in which
> cases; how to effect transition from the present in which many voices cannot
> speak, or are necessarily included or are not heard, to a more polyvocal one;
> how to instil and guarantee a preference for speaking over the use of force;
> and how to compensate for the political consequences of an unequal dis-
> tribution and control of resources. (Flax, 1992: 198)

That such criteria are necessary for community care is evidenced
not only by the competing voices of users of community care, but
also by the responsibility of social workers and social care workers
to ensure the appropriate allocation of services and resources while
acknowledging their responsibility to the taxpayers who have provided the means for the resources.

Distributive justice

This notion of distributive justice assumes that goods will be shared according to some equitable process, but decisions about what is equitable or fair remain problematic (Jordan, 1990). Often the principles behind some notion of sharing goods and resources are transformed into forms of procedural justice. In community care the detailed assessment schedules designed to capture every detail of individuals' lives which might influence the allocation of resources are often accompanied by, or counteracted by formal and informal eligibility criteria. These may be more to do with prevailing public concerns about risk or political agendas about resources than they are to do with the involvement of those requiring services in the decisions about their allocation.

However, conceptions and understandings of justice are complex and problematic and cannot be assumed to translate into prescriptions for practice (Lovelock, 1998). The distributive paradigm of justice is questioned by Young (1990a), whose concern is that some theorists and practitioners have suggested that distributive rights can go beyond material goods and can extend to social goods such as rights, opportunities and self-respect. Her criticism is relevant to social work and social care in that the bland repetition of the principles of casework does seem to suggest that it is enough assert self-determination, respect for persons and acceptance without questioning the implications for practice. For Young the distinction is between the public and the private. The latter she equates with autonomy, and the values espoused by casework may be seen to relate to an autonomous and atomised individual. Empowerment is public and involves participation. Echoing Pateman (1989) she argues that 'justice requires that each person has the institutionalised means to participate effectively in the decisions that affect her or his action and the conditions of that action' (Young, 1990a: 251). What is problematic is that Young relates her understanding to notions of citizenship, where individuals can be involved in communicative ethics, deliberating about problems and issues. In community care the problem is twofold. One is that the notion of citizenship can exclude those who are users of care services, or, more accurately, being in receipt of services disqualifies individuals and groups from recognition as citizens. Second, it is often assumed that the provision of care services occurs in situations of crisis, and that decisions have to be made quickly, which removes the opportunity for workers to deliberate the complexities of the situation with users and carers.

Justice as a process

However, if social justice is understood as a process and not merely an outcome, it can operate at both the level of the individual and of the collective. Involving individuals in decision making enables them to recognise that they are simultaneously public and private, lone and in relation to others, desiring and interdependent. It focuses on their private and particular needs, but recognises that these may be shared with others, and that others might have a whole variety of means of dealing with them, or providing for them. However, for this to be a just process the individual must be able to express their needs in a public context.

This feeds into just processes at the collective level, where the individual is situated not only in the context of a particular user group, but also in the consequences of previous organisational contexts:

> justice is one way groups manage the strain of mediating between individual subjectivities of which they are composed and the objectivities such as limited resources, past traditions and the consequences of past decisions and practices which these individuals did not create but to which they must respond. (Flax, 1992: 205)

Flax's notion of justice as a process therefore facilitates an understanding of what has to be done at the borderlands of individuals within their context, whether that context be their membership of a group of services users (e.g. disabled people), their gender, ethnic, race or class identity. Diversities may have to be reconciled but this is achieved in a spirit of reciprocity which precludes domination and avoids hierarchies of oppression. It is not the bureaucratic categories which dictate the relationship between people but the sense of acknowledging the legitimacy of others and identifying with the other to imagine the experiences of concrete others and yet maintaining distance between groups, to think about the more abstract needs of the collectivity as a whole. This has to happen not only in the face-to-face work between worker and users and carers, but also between users.

If justice is necessarily connected to an active notion of citizenship, a transitional practice which helps manage the strain between the subjective and objective worlds, then social work has to be seen to mediate and not dominate. Justice demands attention to individual identity as well as political and community action. It involves the transformation of private need into public action which in turn, according to Flax, requires three processes which address the borderland between the individual and the community the notions of self and identification with others which can help formulate a role for social work as mediators between the individual and their perception of self; the construction of the identity of individuals by the agencies of community care; and the interventions which are required in those agencies. Those processes therefore have to operate at all levels of the organisation and not only in the face-to-face work with users and carers. In this way the emphasis is not just on the crisis which precipitates someone to request services, it is on the very way the services are designed and made available. Justice has to operate in community care planning, within organisations, and between organisations. More importantly, in the methods of communication between statutory organisations and individuals the diversity of need and the variety of responses has to be recognised.

To do this, in the first instance it is necessary to see a need as publicly actionable. However, in bringing a private need to the public, the spirit in which this is done must itself be transformed. The 'I want' must be transformed into the 'I and others are entitled to'. There is then both the recognition of the individual, and the potential for identification with diverse groups. This necessarily situates the individual as a member within a public which is shared by others. In some ways these others are similar and yet each person, even those who may share a claim, is not exactly alike. Thus the individual becomes part of a community which is self-defined and which can collectively act to change its joint practices. But justice demands that in taking action it is necessary not only to take responsibility in a meaningful way, but also to be seen to be able to take responsibility in a meaningful way (Flax, 1992). It is this process that social work and social care have to facilitate without dominating either the individual or the group.

Domination is made possible by rendering some of the community's members, and the consequences of individual or collective actions, invisible. This can be done by workers, with the best of intentions, acting on behalf of groups or by ignoring their voices. It is therefore necessary for actions and decisions to be transparent and justifiable. The danger here is that justice, like community care and equal opportunities, becomes procedural by focusing on the rules, by, for example, dictating with whom consultation should take place and the modes of consultation. But justice as a process gives people the freedom to change the rules. If the aim of social work is redefined as both meeting needs, and influencing the way that the needs are met, then the rhetoric of user involvement in community care has to be part of just practice. But in truly just practice there is no end state, the process of being involved means that identities and diverse ways of being change as a result of participation (Freire, 1972). Struggles for recognition involve struggles for democratisation. The disability rights groups have led the way in trying to change the rules of participation, but by that very participation highlight that other groups should be similarly involved, and that they need to be in dialogue with those other groups. There has to be participatory diversity – groups can participate equally, but not identically with others (Tully, 1999).

'Just' practice

For social work in community care therefore, while working with individuals involves recognising their unique individuality, the challenge is not to be individualistic in response but to facilitate through a range of practice skills immediate relief of the identified problem, this very identification reflecting the way that the person construes their individual experience. These is also a requirement to work with users and others to change the way that the person and their needs are constructed by agencies, policy makers and other citizens. As such, social work in community care is a political project which draws on micro-skills of intervention, in particular the ability to communicate by both listening and by articulating the choices that individuals have to make. This involves recognising the potential for change, rather than being reactive, disciplining and bureaucratic.

Conclusion

In this chapter, synthesising the implications of the analysis of gender throughout the text, the notion of borderlands has been seen as significant for social work and social care practice. Globalisation is said to transcend state borders but many international disputes take place over those very same borders as individuals and groups attempt to establish both their space and their identity as nation states, religious or ethnic groups, confirming that the politics of identity remains powerful, and indeed may become reinforced by the proximity of difference. Similarly, in the micro-practice of social work, it is argued that borderlands are important. The introduction of community care, and social work's response to it, attempted to break down definitions of problems in terms of individual pathologies by grouping users into categories such as older people, disabled people and those with mental health problems, but in doing so organised services into individualised care packages. A gendered perspective highlights that within these packages the complexity of people's needs and resources were not recognised, and users were not necessarily enabled to define their own identity; they were colonised.

The argument of the text therefore is that gender is one aspect of identity which is either denied or colonised within community care policies and practices. In much of the literature of community care the differences between men and women have been ignored, or when they are addressed they are set in opposition to each other, a process which is understandable in view of the long history of oppression and domination of women by men. However, to ignore gender is to make women invisible and to fail to recognise their continued oppression within the provision of community care services. Once the experiences of women within community care are documented, it becomes apparent that borderlands can be created between women, as well as between women and men. The complex processes of oppression and identification on the basis of, for example, age, disability and mental ill heath, of being a carer and being cared for, can both reinforce similarities of experience and exacerbate differences on the basis of gender. Throughout, examination of the expectations of both providers and users of community care services has helped construct understandings of gender identity which confirm that categorisation of femaleness and maleness, femininity and masculinity as dichotomous opposites does not reflect the lived experience of users of community care services.

Finally, social work has a tradition of working with individuals, but such work has continually denied the complexity of identities, or when it has recognised difference it has been experienced as oppressive. Social work in community care can be informed by the wealth of literature which has addressed issues of gender in both discourses of practice and theory and it can become much more meaningful to the diverse populations whose needs have to be met. At the same time social work and social work theory in its 'applied' status, have the capacity to translate and mediate the meta theories into the realm of individual and interpersonal. This is not just the application of theories, it is the construction of other discourses which translate, reflect on and reformulate existing theories to produce other narratives which neither prove nor negate, but enrich. It is this discursive tradition of social work theory which enables it to address both the individual and the social and gives it claim to its place in the academy, but equally gives it a role in informing and forming practice.

Bibliography

Abbot, P. and Sapsford, R. (1987) *Community Care for Mentally Handicapped Children* (Milton Keynes: Open University Press).

Abrams, P. (1977) 'Community care: some research problems and priorities' *Policy and Politics*, **6**(2): 125–51.

ADSS/CRE (1978) *Multi Racial Britain: the Social Services Response* (London: CRE).

Ahmad, W.I.U. and Atkin, K. (eds) (1996) *'Race' and Community Care* (Buckingham: Open University Press).

Allan, G. (1983) 'Informal Networks of Care: Issues raised by Barclay', *British Journal of Social Work*, **13**: 417–33.

Allan, G. (1988) 'Kinship, responsibility, and care for elderly people', *Ageing and Society*, **8**: 249–68.

Allen, H. (1986) 'Psychiatry and the construction of the feminine' in Miller, P. and Rose, N. (eds) *The Power of Psychiatry* (Cambridge: Polity).

Allen, H. (1987) *Justice Unbalanced Gender Psychiatry and Judicial Decisions* (Milton Keynes: Open University Press).

Anthias, F. and Yuval-Davis, N. (1992) *Racialized Boundaries* (London: Routledge).

Arber, S. and Gilbert, N. (1989) 'Men: The Forgotten Carers', *Sociology*, **23**(1): 111–18.

Arber, S. and Ginn, J. (1991) *Gender and Later Life* (London: Sage).

Arber, S. and Ginn, J. (1992) 'Class and Caring: A Forgotten Dimension', *Sociology*, **26**(4): 619–34.

Atkin, K. and Rollings, J. (1996) 'Looking after their own?' in Ahmad, W. I. U. and Atkin, K. (eds) *'Race' and Community Care* (Buckingham: Open University Press).

Audit Commission (1986) *Making a Reality of Community Care* (London: HMSO)

Audit Commission (1994) *Finding a Place: A Review of Mental Health Services for Adults* (London: HMSO).

Aves, G. (1964) 'The relationship between homes and other forms of care' in Slack, K. (ed.) *Some Aspects of Residential Care of the Elderly* (London: National Council of Comunity Service).

Aves, G. (1983) *Eileen Younghusband Lecture* (London: National Institute for Social Work).

Baldock, J. and Ungerson, C. (1994) *Becoming Consumers of Community Care: households within the mixed economy of welfare* (York: Joseph Rowntree Foundation).

Baldwin, S. and Twigg, J. (1991) 'Women and community care' in Maclean, M. and Groves, D. (eds) *Women's issues in Social Policy* (London: Routledge).

Bailey, R. and Brake, M. (1975) *Radical Social Work* (London: Edward Arnold).

Barclay, P. (1982) *Social Workers: Their Role and Tasks* (London: Bedford Square Press).

Barnes, M., Bowl, R. Fisher, M. (1990) *Sectioned: Social Services and the 1983 Mental Health Act* (London: Routledge).

Barnes, M. and Maple, N. (1992) *Women and Mental Health: challenging the stereotypes* (Birmingham: Venture Press).

Barrett, M. (1987) 'The Concept of Difference', *Feminist Review*, **26**: 29–42.

Baxter, C. (1989) 'Parallels between the social role perception of people with learning difficulties and black and ethnic minority people' in Brechin, A. and Walmsley, J. (eds) *Making Connections: Reflections on the Lives and Experiences of People with Learning Difficulties* (Sevenoaks: Hodder and Stoughton).

Begum, N., Hill, M. and Stevens, A (1994) *Reflections: views of disabled people on their lives and community care*, Vol. Paper 32.3. (London: CCETSW).

Bell, C. and Newby, H. (1971) *Community Studies* (London: Allen & Unwin).

Beresford, P. and Croft, S. (1986) *Whose Welfare: private care or public services* (Lewis Cohen Urban Studies Centre).

Biehal, N. (1993) 'Changing Practice: Participation, Rights and Community Care' *British Journal of Social Work*, **23**: 443–58.

Biestek, F. (1961) *The Casework Relationship* (London: Allen & Unwin).

Biggs, S. (1993) *Understanding Ageing* (Buckingham: Open University Press).

Blau, P. (1968) *Exchange and Power in Social Life* (New York: Wiley).

Blaug, R. (1995) 'Distortion of the Face to Face: Communicative Reason and Social Work Practice', *British Journal of Social Work*, **25**: 423–39.

Blieszner, R. (1993) 'A socialist-feminist perspective on widowhood', *Journal of Aging Studies*, **7**: 171–82.

Bond, J. and Coleman, P. (1990) *Ageing in Society: an Introduction to Social Gerontology* (London: Sage).

Boniface, D. and Denham, M. (1997) 'Factors influencing the use of community health and social services by those aged 65 and over', *Health and Social Care in the Community*, **5**(1): 48–54.

Bordo, S. (1990) 'Feminism, Postmodernism, and Gender Scepticism' in Nicholson, L. J. (ed.) *Feminism/Postmodernism* (New York: Routledge).

Bornat, J. (1993) 'Anthology: Charters' in Bornat, J., Pereira, C., Pilgrim, and Williams, F. (eds) *Community Care: a reader* (Basingstoke: Macmillan/ Open University).

Bowl, R. (1986) 'Social Work and Older People' in Phillipson, C. and Walker, A. (eds) *Ageing and Social Policy* (Aldershot: Gower).

Bradley, H. (1993) 'Across the Great Divide' in Williams, C. L. (ed) *Doing "Women's Work" Men in Nontraditonal Occupations* (California: Sage).

Braye, S. and Preston-Shoot, M. (1995) *Empowering Practice in Social Care* (Buckingham: Open Universty Press).

Brearley, P. (1975) *Social Work, Ageing and Society* (London: RKP).

Brook, E. and Davis, A. (eds) (1985) *Women, the Family and Social Work*, Tavistock Library of Social Work Practice (London: Tavistock).

Broverman, I.K, Broverman, D.M., Clarkson, F.E., Rosenkrantz, P.S. and Vogel, S.R. (1970) 'Sex Role Stereo-types and Clinical Judgement of Mental Health', *Journal of Consulting and Clinical Psychology*, **34**: 1–7.

Brown, G.W, and Harris, H. (1978) *Social Origins of Depression* (London: Tavistock).

Bulmer, M. (1987) *The Social Basis of Community Care* (London: Allen & Unwin).

Bunch, C. (1982) 'Copenhagen and Beyond: Prospects for Global Feminism', *Quest: A Feminist Quarterly*, **5**(4).

Busfield, J. (1996) *Men, Women and Madness: Understanding Gender and Mental Disorder* (Basingstoke: Macmillan).

Butler, A. and Pritchard, C. (1983) *Social Work and Mental Illness* (Basingstoke: BASW/Macmillan).

Butler, J. (1990) *Gender Trouble: feminism and the subversion of identity*. (London: Routledge).

Bytheway, W. (1987) *Informal Care Systems: an exploratory study with the families of older steel workers in South Wales* (York: Joseph Rowntree Memorial Trust).

Carby, H. (1982) 'Black feminism and the boundaries of sisterhood' in CCCS (ed.) *The Empire Strikes Back: Race and Racism in 70s Britain* (London: Hutchinson).

Cavanagh, K. and Cree, V.E. (1996) *Working with Men: Feminism and Social Work, The State of Welfare* (London: Routledge).

Challis, D., Chesterman, J., Darton, R. and Traske, K. (1993) 'Case Management in the Care of the Aged' in Bornat, J., Pereira, C., Pilgrim, D. and Williams, F. (eds) *Community Care: a reader* (Basingstoke: Macmillan in association with the Open University).

Charlesworth, A., Wilkin, D. and Durie, A. (1984) *Carers and Services: a Comparison of Men and Women Caring for Dependent Elderly People* (Manchester: Equal Opportunties Commission).

Chesler, P. (1974) *Women and Madness* (London: Allen Lane).

Chodorow, N. (1974) *The Reproduction of Mothering* (Berkeley: University of California).

Church, J. and Summerfield, C. (1995) *Social Focus on Women* (London: Central Statistical Office).

Clarke, J. (1996) 'After social work?' in Parton, N. (ed.) *Social Theory, Social Change and Social Work* (London: Routledge).

Clarke, L. (1995) 'Family Care and Changing Family Sstructure: Bad News for the Elderly' in Allen, I. and Perkins, E. (eds) *The Future of Family Care for Older People* (London: HMSO).

Clements, J, Clare, I. and Ezelle, L. (1995) 'Real Men, Real Women, Real Lives? Gender issues in learning disabilities and challenging behaviour', *Disability & Society*, **10**(4): 425–35.

Coleman (1990) 'Ageing and Life History: The Meaning of Reminiscence' in S. Dex, (ed.) *Life and Work History Analysis* (London: Routledge).

Collins, B. (1986) 'Defining Feminist Social Work', *Social Work*, May–June: 214–19.

Commission for Social Justice (1994) *Social Justice: strategies for national renewal* (London: Vintage).

Connell, R.W. (1987) *Gender and Power* (Cambridge: Polity Press).

Coote, A. (ed.) (1992) *The Welfare of Citizens* (London: Institute for Public Policy Research/Rivers Oram Press).

Dalley, G. (1988) *Ideologies of Caring*, 1st edn (Basingstoke: Macmillan).

Dalley, G. (1996) *Ideologies of Caring*, 2nd edn (Basingstoke: Macmillan).

Davies, M. (1985) *The Essential Social Worker: A Guide to Positive Practice*, 2nd edn (Aldershot: Gower).

De Beauvoir, S. (1972) *The Second Sex* (Harmondsworth: Penguin).

DoH (1981) *Growing Older* (London: HMSO).

DoH (1989) *Caring for People* (London: HMSO).

DoH (1992) *Health of the Nation* (London: HMSO).

DoH (1993a) *Code of Practice. Mental Health Act 1983* (London: HMSO).

DoH (1993b) *Health of the Nation: Key Areas Handbook – Mental Health* (London: HMSO).

DoH/SSI (1993c) *Key Area Handbook – Mental Illness* (London: HMSO).

Dominelli, L. (1997) *Sociology for Social Work* (Basingstoke: Macmillan).

Dominelli, L. and McLeod, E. (1989) *Feminist Social Work* (Basingstoke: Macmillan).

Doyal, L. and Gough, I. (1991) *A Theory of Human Need* (Basingstoke: Macmillan).

Equal Opportunities Commission (1981) *Behind Closed Doors* (Manchester: Equal Opportunities Commission).

Etzioni, A. (1993) *The Spirit of Community: The Reinvention of America* (New York: Touchstone Books).

Evans, J. (1995) *Feminist Theory Today* (London: Sage).

Evers, H. (1981) 'Care or Custody? The experiences of women patients in long-stay geriatric wards' in Hutter, B. and Williams, U. (eds) *Controlling Women. The Normal and the Deviant* (London: Croom Helm).

Featherstone, B. and Fawcett, B. (1995) 'Oh No! Not More Isms: Feminism, Postmodernism, Poststructuralism and Social Work Education', *Social Work Education'*, **14**(3): 25–43.

Fernando, S. (1988) *Race and Culture in Psychiatry* (London: Croom Helm).

Finch, J. (1984) 'Community care: developing non-sexist alternatives', *Critical Social Policy*, **9**.

Finch, J. (1990) 'The politics of Community Care in Britain' in (Ungerson, C. (ed.) *Gender and Caring: Work and Welfare in Britain and Scandinavia* (Hemel Hempstead: Harvester Wheatsheaf).

Finch, J. (1995) 'Responsibilities, Obligations and Commitments' in Allen, I. and Perkins, E. (eds) *The Future of Family Care for Older People* (London: HMSO).

Finch, J. and Groves, D. (eds) (1983) *A Labour of Love: Women, Work and Caring* (London: RKP).

Finch, J. and Groves, D. (1985) 'Old girl, old boy: gender divisions in social work with the elderly' in Brook, E. and Davis, A. (eds) *Women, The Family and Social Work* (London: Tavistock).

Firestone, S. (1971) *The Dialectic of Sex* (London: Jonathan Cape).

Finkelstein, V. (1993) 'Disability: a social challenge? in Swain, Finkelstein, J., French, V. and Oliver S.M. (eds) *Disabling Barriers –*

Enabling Environments (London: Sage in association with the Open Univeristy).

Fisher, M. (1994) 'Man-made Care: Community Care and Older Male Carers', *British Journal of Social Work*, **24**: 659–80.

Fisher, M. (1997) 'Older male carers and community care' in Bornat, J., Pereira, C., Pilgrim, D. and Williams, F. (eds) *Community Care: a reader* (Macmillan: Open University).

Flax, J. (1992) 'Beyond equality: gender justice and difference' in Bock, G. and James, S. (eds) *Beyond Equality and Difference: citizenship, feminist politics and female subjectivity* (London: Routledge).

Forbes, I. (1991) 'Equal Opportunity: Radical, liberal and conservative critiques' in Meehan, E. and Sevenhuijsen, S. (eds) *Equality Politics and Gender* (London: Sage).

Ford, J. and Sinclair, R. (1989) 'Women's experience of old age' in Carter, P., Jeffs, T. and Smith, N. (eds) *Social Work and Social Welfare Yearbook* (Basingstoke: Macmillan).

Ford, P. and Hayes, P. (eds) (1996) *Educating for Social Work: Arguments for Optimism* (Aldershot: Avebury, in association with CEDR.

Foucault, M. (1977) *Discipline and Punish: the Birth of the Prison* (Harmondsworth: Penguin).

Fox, N. (1995) 'Postmodern perspectives on care: the vigil and the gift', *Critical Social Policy*, **15**: 107–25.

Fransella, F. (1995) *George Kelly* (London: Sage).

Freire, P. (1972) *The Pedagogy of the Oppressed* (Harmondsworth: Penguin).

French, S. (1993) 'Disability, impairment or something in between' in Swain, J., Finkelstein, V., French, S. and Oliver, M. (eds) *Disabling Barriers – Enabling Environments* (London: Sage, in association with the Open University).

Fuller, R., and Tulle-Winton, E. (1996) 'Specialism and Genericism with Elderly People', *British Journal of Social Work*, **26**(5): 679–98.

Gee, E. and Kimbal, M. (1987) *Women and aging* (Toronto: Butterworth).

Gibson, D. (1996) 'Broken Down By Age and Gender', *Gender and Society*, **10**(4): 433–48.

Giddens, A. (1991) *Modernity and Self-Identity: Self and Society in the Late Modern Age* Cambridge: Polity).

Gilhooly, M. (1984) 'The impact of caregiving on caregivers: factors associated with the psychological well being of people supporting a dementing relative in the community', *British Journal of Medical Psychology*, **57**: 35–44.

Gilligan, C. (1993) *In a Different Voice* (London: Harvard University Press).

Goffman, I.E. (1961) *Asylums: essays on the social situation of mental patients and other inmates* (Harmondsworth: Penguin).

Goldberg, D. and Huxley, P. (1980) *Mental Illness in the Community: the pathway to psychiatric care* (London: Tavistock).

Gonyea, J.G. (1994) 'Making Gender Visible in Public Policy' in Thompson, E.H.J. (ed.) *Older Men's Lives* (Thousand Oaks: Sage).

Goss, S. and Miller, C. (1995) *From Margin to Mainstream: developing user and carer centred community care* (York: JRF).

Graham, H. (1983) 'Caring: a labour of love' in Finch, J. and Groves, D. (eds) *A Labour of Love: Women, Work and Caring* (London: RKP).

Graham, H. (1991) 'The Concept of Caring in Feminist Research: The Case of Domestic Service', *Sociology*, **25**(1): 61–78.

Graham, H. (1993) 'Feminist perspectives on caring' in Bornat, J., Pereira, C., Pilgrim, D. and Williams, F. (eds) *Community Care: a reader* (Basingstoke: Macmillan/Open University).

Grant, G. (1986) 'Elderly parents and handicapped children: Anticipating the future', *Journal of Ageing Studies*, **4**(4): 359–74.

Green, D.G. (1996) *Community Without Politics: a market approach to welfare reform* (London: Institute of Econmic Affairs).

Green, H. (1988) *General Household Survey 1985: Informal Carers* (London: HMSO).

Gregory, J. (1987) *Sex, Race and the Law* (London: Sage).

Griffiths, R. (1988) *Community Care: an Agenda for Action* (London: HMSO).

Gutmann, D. (1987) *Reclaimed powers: toward a new psychology of men and women in later life* (New York: Basic Books).

Hadfield, B. and Mohamad, H. (1994) 'Women, Men and the Mental Health Act 1983', *Research, Policy and Planning*, **12**(3): 6–10.

Hadley, R. and Leidy, B. (1996) 'Community Social Work in a Market Environment', *British Journal of Social Work*, **26**: 823–42.

Hadley, R. and McGrath, M. (1980) *Going Local – Neighbourhood Social Services* (London: Bedford Square Press).

Hall, S. (1992) 'The Question of Cultural Identity' in Hall, S. Held, S. and McGrew, D. and T. (eds) *Modernity and Its Futures* (Cambridge: Polity).

Hanmer, J. and Statham, D. (1988) *Women and Social Work: Towards a Women Centred Practice* (Basingstoke: BASW/Macmillan).

Haraway, D. (1990) *Siminians, Cyborgs, and Women* (New York: Routledge).

Harding, C. and Sherlock, J. (1994) *Women and Mental Health* (London: GPMH).

Harris, J. and Hopkins, T. (1994) 'Beyond anti-ageism: Reminiscence groups and the development of anti-discriminatory social work education and practice' in Bornat, J. (ed.) *Reminiscence Reviewed: perspectives, evaluations, achievements* (Buckingham: Open Univesity Press).

Hartman, A. (1989) 'Still Between Client and Community' in *Social Work* vol **34**(5) 387–8.

Hawkesworth, M. (1989) 'Knowers, Knowing, Known: Feminist Theory and Claims of Truth', *Signs*, **14**(31): 533–57.

Heginbotham, C. (1987) 'Ethical dilemmas of sterilisation', *Social Work Today*, (13 April).

Hekman, S. (1991) *Gender and Knowledge: Elements of Postmodern Feminism* (Cambridge: Polity Press).

Hester, M., Kelly, L. and Radford, J. (eds) (1996) *Women, Violence and Male Power* (Buckingham: Open University Press).

Hewitt, P. (1993) *About Time: The revolution in work and family life* (London: IPPR/Rivers Oram Press).

Higgs, P. (1995) 'Citizenship and Old Age: The End of the Road?', *Ageing and Society*, **15**: 535–50.

hooks, bell (1984) 'Feminism: a movement to end sexist oppression' in Philips, A. (ed.) *Feminism and Equality* (Oxford: Blackwell).

Horney, K. (1932) 'The dread of women', *International Journal of Psychoanalysis* vol **13** 348–60.

Howe, D. (1987) *An Introduction to Social Work Theory* (Aldershot: Arena).

Hudson, A. (1985) 'Feminism and social work: resistance or dialogue?', *British Journal of Social Work*, **15**: 635–55.

Hudson, A. (1989) 'Changing perspectives: feminism, gender and social work' in Langan, M. and Lee, P. (eds) *Radical Social Work Today* (London: Unwin Hyman).

Hughes, B. (1995) *Older people and Community Care* (Buckingham: Open University Press).

Hughes, B. and Mtezuka, M. (1992) 'Social work and older women: where have older women gone?' in Langan, M. and Day, L. (eds) *Women Oppression and Social Work: issues in anti- discriminatory practice* (London: Routledge).

Hugman, R. (1991) *Power in Caring Professions* (Basingstoke: Macmillan).

Hugman, R. and Philips, N. (1992–93) '"Like Bees Round the Honeypot" Social Work responses to Parents with Mental Health Needs', *Practice*, **6**(3): 193–205.

James, S. (1992) 'The good-enough citizen: female citizenship and independence' in Bock, G. and James, S. (eds) *Beyond Equality and Difference: citizenship, feminist politics and female subjectivity* (London: Routledge).

Jenkins, R. (1989) 'Dimensions of Adulthood' in Brechin, A. and Walmsley, J. (eds) *Making Connections* (Sevenoaks: Hodder & Stoughton).

Jerrome, D. (1990) 'Intimate Relationships' in Bond, J. and Coleman, P. (eds) *Ageing in Society: An Introduction to Social Gerontology* (London: Sage).

Jones, K. and Fowles, A.J. (1984) *Ideas on Institutions: analysing the literature on long term care and custody* (London: RKP).

Jordan, B. (1990) *Social Work in an Unjust Society* (London: Harvester Wheatsheaf).

Kaye, L.W. and Applegate, J.S. (1994) 'The Family Caregiving Orientation' in Thompson, E.H.J. (ed.) *Older Men's Lives* (Thousand Oaks: Sage).

Kingston, P. and Penhale, B. (1995) 'Social Perspectives on Elder Abuse' in Kingston, P. and Penhale, B. (eds) in *Family Violence and the Caring Professions* (Basingstoke: Macmillan).

Lane, M. (1999) 'Community development and a postmodernism of resistance' Pease, B. and Fook, J. (eds) in *Transforming Social Work Practice: postmodern critical perspectives* (London: Routledge).

Langan, M. (1992) 'Who cares? Women in the mixed economy of care' in Langan, M. and Day, L. (eds) *Women Oppression and Social Work: issues in anti-discriminatory practice* (London: Routledge).

Langan, M. (1993) 'The Rise and Fall of Social Work' in Clarke, J. (ed.) *A Crisis in Care? Challenges to Social Work* (London: Sage, in association with the Open University).

Langan, M. and Day, L. (1992) *Women, Oppression and Social Work: issues in anti-discriminatory practice* (London: Routledge).

Lewis, J. (1991) *Women and social action in Victorian and Edwardian England* (Aldershot: Edward Elgar).

Lewis, J. and Meredith, B. (1988) *Daughters Who Care: Daughters Caring for Mothers at Home* (London: Routledge).

Lewis, J., Bernstock, P. Bovell, V. and Wookey, F. (1997) 'Implementing Care Management: Issues in Relation to the New Community Care', *British Journal of Social Work*, **27**: 5–24.

Lister, R. (1990) 'Women, Economic Dependency and Citizenship', *Journal of Social Policy*, **19**(4): 445–467.

Lister, R. (1997) 'Citizenship: towards a feminist synthesis', *Feminist Review*, **57** (Autumn): 28–48.

Lorde, A. (1984) *Sister Outsider* (Freedom, CA: The Crossing Press).

Lovelock, R. (1998) 'Social Work and Theories of Justice'. Paper presented to the Joint World Congress of IFSW and IASSW: *Peace and Social Justice – the challenges facing social work* (Jerusalem).

Manthorpe, J. (1994) 'The family and informal care' in Malin, N. (ed.) *Implementing Community Care* (Buckingham: Open University Press).

Marshall, M. (1990) *Social Work with Old People* (Basingstoke: Macmillan).

Marshall, T.H. (1950) *Citizenship and social class and other essays* (Cambridge: Cambridge University Press).

Mayo, M. (1994) *Communities and Caring: The Mixed Economy of Welfare* (Basingstoke: Macmillan).

Means, R. and Smith, R. (1994) *Community Care: Policy and Practice* (Basingstoke: Macmillan).

Michailakis, D. (1997) 'When Opportunity is the Thing to be Equalised', *Disability and Society*, **12**(1): 17–30.

Miles, A. (1987) *The Mentally Ill in Contemporary Society*, 2nd edn (Oxford: Blackwell).

Miles, A. (1988) *Women and Mental Illness: The Social Context of Female Neurosis* (Brighton: Wheatsheaf).

Miller, J. Baker (ed.) (1988) *Toward a New Psychology of Women*, 2nd edn (Harmondsworth: Penguin).

Miller, R.B. and Dodder, R.A. (1989) 'The abused-abuser dyad: elder abuse in the State of Florida' in Filinson, R. and Ingman, S.R. (eds) *Elder Abuse: Practice and Policy* (New York: Human Sciences Press).

Millet, K (1970) *Sexual Politics* (London: Virago).

MIND (1993) *Making it Happen: Developing Community Mental Health Services* (Oxford: GPMH).

Morgan, C. (1995) *Family Resources Survey Great Britain 1993/94* (London: Department of Social Security).

Morris, J. (1993a) 'Feminism and Disability', *Feminist Review*, **43**: 57–70.

Morris, J. (1993b) *Independent Lives? Community Care and Disabled People* (Basingstoke: Macmillan).

Morris, J. (1993c) ' "Us" and "Them"? Feminist Research and Community Care' in Bornat, J., Pereira, C., Pilgrim, D. and Williams, F. (eds) *Community Care: a reader* (Basingstoke: Macmillan/Open University).

Morris, J. (1996a) 'Gender and Disability' in Wain, J., Finkelstein, V., French, S. and Oliver, M. (eds) *Disabling Barriers – Enabling Environments* (London: Sage, in association with the Open University).

Morris, J. (1996b) *Pride Against Prejudice* (London: The Women's Press).

Naroll, R. (1983) *The Moral Order: an Introduction to the Human Situation* (London: Sage).

Nirje, B. (1970) 'The normalisation principle – implications and comments', *British Journal of Subnormality*, **16**: 62–70.

Nottage, A. (1991) *Women in Social Services: A Neglected Resource* (London: SSI).

Oliver, M. (1990) *The Politics of Disablement* (Basingstoke: Macmillan).

Oliver, M, and Barnes, C. (1996) 'Discrimination, disability and welfare: from needs to rights' in Wain, J., Finkelstein, V., French, S. and Oliver, M. (eds) *Disabling Barriers – Enabling Environments* (London: Sage, in association with the Open University).

OPCS (1982) General Household Survey 1980 (London: HMSO).

Orme, J. (1991) 'The Teaching of Race on a Social Work Course in a Predominantly White Area' in Divine, D. (ed.) *One Small Step Towards Racial Justice* (London: CCETSW).

Orme, J. (1992) 'Women and the Criminal Justice Act', *Probation Journal*, **39**(2): 79–81.

Orme, J. (1994) 'Violent Women' in Lupton, C. and Gillespie, T. (eds) *Working with Violence* (Basingstoke: BASW/Macmillan).

Orme, J. (1996a) 'Social Work Education: Reactive or Proactive?' in Ford, P. and Hayes, P. (eds) *Educating for Social Work: Arguments for Optimism* (Aldershot: Avebury in association with CEDR).

Orme, J. (1996b) 'Participation or Patronage: changes in social work practice brought about by community care policies in Britain', Paper read at Joint World Congress of IFSW/IASSW Hong Kong.

Orme, J. (1997) 'Research into Practice' in Mckenzie, G., Powell, J. and Usher, R. (eds) *Understanding Social Research* (Basingstoke: Falmer Press).

Orme, J. (1998) 'Feminist Social Work' in Adams, R., Dominelli, L. and Payne, M. (eds) *Social Work: Themes Issues and Critical Debates* (Basingstoke: Macmillan).

Orme, J. and Glastonbury, B. (1993) *Care Management* (Basingstoke: BASW/Macmillan).

Parker, G. (1992) 'Counting care: numbes and types of informal carers' in Twigg, J. (ed.) *Carers: Research and Practice* (London: HMSO).

Parker, G. (1996) 'The politics of disability' in Wain, J., Finkelstein, V., French, S. and Oliver, M. (eds) *Disabling Barriers – Enabling Environments* (London: Sage, in association with Open University Press).

Parker, G. and Lawton, D. (1994) *Different Types of Care, Different Types of Carer: Evidence from the General Household Survey* (York: Social Policy Research Unit).

Parton, N. (1996) 'Social work, risk and the "blaming system"' in Parton, N. (ed.) *Social Theory, Social Change and Social Work* (London: Routledge).

Parton, N. (1999) 'Some Thoughts on the Relationship Between Theory and Practice In and For Social Work', Paper presented to ESRC Seminar Series: *Theorising Social Work Research*.

Patel, N. (1990) *A 'Race' Against Time? Social services provision to black elders* (London: Runnymede Trust).

Pateman, C. (1987) 'Critiques of the Public/Private Dichotomy' in Phillips, A. (ed.) *Feminism and Equlity* (Oxford: Blackwell).

Pateman, C. (1989) *The Disorder of Women* (Cambridge: Polity Press).

Pateman, C. (1992) 'Equality, difference, subordination' in Block, G. and James, S. (ed.) *Beyond Equality and Difference* (London: Routledge).

Payne, M. (1991) *Modern Social Work Theory: a critical introduction* (Basingstoke: Macmillan).

Payne, M. (1995) *Social Work and Community Care* (Basingstoke: Macmillan).

Peace, S. (1986) 'The Forgotten Female: Social Policy and Older Women' in Phillipson, C. and Walker, A. (eds) *Ageing and Social Policy* (Aldershot: Gower).

Perkins, R. (1994) *Women in Mental Health: Good Practices in Services for Women with Long Term or Recurring Problems* (London: GPMH).

Perske, R. (1972) 'The Dignity of Risk' in Wolfensberger, W. (ed.) *The Principles of Normalisation in Human Services* (Toronto: National Institute of Retardation).

Phillipson, C. (1990) 'The Sociology of Retirement' in Bond, J. and Coleman, P. (eds) *Ageing in Society: an Introduction to Social Gerontology* (London: Sage).

Phillipson, C. and Biggs, S. (1995) 'Elder Abuse: A Critical Overview' in Kingston, P. and Penhale, B. (eds) *Family Violence and the Caring Professions* (Basingstoke: Macmillan).

Phillipson, J. (1992) *Practising Equality Women, Men and Social Work* (London: CCETSW).

Pilgrim, D. and Rogers, A. (1993) *A Sociology of Mental Health and Illness* (Buckingham: Open University Press).

Plant, R. (1973) *Social and Moral Theory in Casework* (London: RKP).

Plant, R. (1992) 'Citizenship, Rights and Welfare' in Coote, A. (ed.) *The Welfare of Citizens: developing new social rights* (London: IPPR/ Rivers Oram Press).

Qureshi, H. and Walker, A. (1989) *The Caring Relationship: Elderly people and their families* (Basingstoke: Macmillan).

Rack, P. (1990) 'Psychological and Psychiatric Disorders' in McAvoy, B.R. and Donaldson, L. (eds) *Health Care for Asians* (Oxford: Oxford University Press).

Ramazanoglu, C. (1989) *Feminism and the Contradictions of Oppression* (London: Routledge).

Ramon, S. (1991) 'Principles and Conceptual Knowledge' in Ramon, S. (ed.) *Beyond Community Care: Normalisation and Integration Work* (Basingstoke: Macmillan).

Rees, A.M. (1996) 'T.H. Marshall and the Progess of Citizenship' in Bulmer, M. and Rees, A.M. (eds) *Citizenship Today; The contmporary relevance of T.H Marshall* (London: UCL Press).

Rees, S. (1991) *Achieving Power: Practice and Policy in Social Welfare* (Sydney: Allen & Unwin).

Richards, S. (1996) *Defining and Assessing Need: an Ethnographic Study of the Community Care Needs Assessment of Older People*; Unpublished Thesis (Southampton: University of Southampton).

Rose, H. and Bruce, E. (1995) 'Mutual care but differential esteem: caring between older couples' in Arber, S. Ginn, J. (eds) *Connecting Gender and Ageing: A Sociological Approach* (Buckingham: Open University).

Rowlings, C. (1981) *Social Work with Elderly People* (London: Allen & Unwin).

Rubin, G. (1975) 'The Traffic in Women: Notes on the "Political Economy" of Sex' in Reiter, R.R. (ed.) *Toward an Anthropology of Women* (New York: Monthly Review Press).

Ryan, J., and Thomas, F. (1993) 'Concepts of Normalisation' in Bornat, J., Pereira, C. Pilgrim, D. and Williams, F. (eds) *Community Care: a reader* (Basingstoke: Macmillan).

Sapsford, R. (1993) 'Understanding People: The Growth of Expertise' in Clarke, J. (ed.) *A Crisis in care? Challenges to Social Work* (London: Sage, in Association with the Open University).

Scull, A. (1977) *Decarceration* (Engelwood Cliffs, NJ: Prentice-Hall).

Seebohm (1968) *Report of the Committee on Local Authority and Allied Personal Services*, Cmnd 3703 (London: HMSO).

Segal, J. (1991) 'The Professional Perspective' in Ramon, S. (ed.) *Beyond Community Care: Normalisation and Integration Work* (Basingstoke: Macmillan, in association with MIND).

Segal, L. (1987) *Is the Future Female?* (London: Virago).

Segal, L. (1990) *Slow Motion: changing masculinities, changing men* (London: Virago).

Sheppard, M. (1991) 'General Practice, Social Work, and Mental Health Sections: The Social Control of Women', *British Journal of Social Work*, **21**: 663–83.

Showalter, E. (1987) *The Female Malady: Women, Madness and English Culture 1830–1980* (London: Virago).

Sibeon, R. (1991–2) 'Sociological Reflections on Welfare Politics and Social Work', *Social Work and Social Sciences Review*, **3**(3): 184–203.

Simpson, M. (1995) 'The Sociology of "Competence" in Learning Disability Services', *Social Work and Social Sciences Review*, **6**: 85–97.

Skillen, T. (1995) 'The Social Justice Commssion: community and a new welfare state' in Baldock, J. and May, M. (eds) *Social Policy Review 7* (Kent: Social Policy Asociation).

Smale, G., Tuson, G. Cooper, M. Wardle, M. and Crosbie, D. (1988) *Community Social Work: A Paradigm for Change* (London: NISW).

Smale G., Tuson, G. with Bhehal, N. and Marsh, P. (1993) *Empowerment, Assessment, Care Management and the Skilled Worker* (London: HMSO).

SSI (1994) *Implementing Caring for People: Care Management* (London: HMSO).

SSI (1995a) *Social Services Departments and the Care Programme Approach: An Inspection* (London: HMSO).

SSI (1995b) *Young Carers: Something to Think About* (London: HMSO).

SSI (1999) *Workforce Audit of the Personal Social Services* (London: HMSO).

Stuart, O. (1994) 'Journey From the Margin: Black Disabled People and the Antiracist Debate' in Begum, N., Hill, M. and Stevens, A. (eds) *Reflections The Views of Black Disabled People on their Lives and Community Care* (London: CCETSW).

Stuart, O. (1996) ' "Yes, we mean black disabled people too": thoughts on community care and disabled people from black and minority ethnic communities' in Ahmad, W.I.U. and Atkin, K. (eds) *'Race' and Community Care* (Buckingham: Open University Press).

Swain, J., Finkelstein, V. French, S. and Oliver, M. (eds) (1993) *Disabling Barriers – Enabling Environments* (London: Sage, in association with the Open University).

Thomas, C. (1993) 'De-constructing Concepts of Care', *Sociology*, **27**(4): 649–669.

Thompson, E.H., Jr (1994a) 'Older Men as Invisible Men in Contemporary Society' in Thompson, E.H., Jr (ed.) *Older Men's Lives* (London: Sage).

Thompson, E.H. Jr, (ed.) (1994b) *Older Men's Lives* (Thousand Oaks: Sage).

Thompson, N. (1995) 'Men and Anti-Sexism', *British Journal of Social Work*, **25**: 459–75.

Tolson, A. (1977) *The Limits of Masculinity* (London: Tavistock).

Townsend, P. (1993) 'The Structured Dependency of the Elderly' in Bornat, J., Pereira, C., Pilgrim, D. and Williams, F. (eds) *Community Care: a reader* (Basingstoke: Macmillan, Open University).

Tozer, R. and Thornton, P. (1995) *A Meeting of Minds: older people as research advisers* (York: Social Policy Research Unit).

Tully, J. (1999) 'The agonic freedom of citizens', *Economy and Society*, **28**(2): 161–82.

Ungerson, C. (1983a) 'Why Do Women Care?' in Finch, J. and Groves, D. (eds) *A Labour of Love* (London: Routledge).

Ungerson, C. (1983b) 'Women and Caring: Skills Tasks and Taboos' in Gamarnikov, E., Morgan, D. Purvis, J. and Taylorson, D. (eds) *The Public and The Private* (London: Heinemann).

Ungerson, C. (1987) *Policy is Personal: Sex, Gender and Informal Care* (London: Tavistock).

United Nations (1991) Declaration of General and Specific Rights of the Mentally Retarded.

Ussher, J. (1991) *Women's Madness: misogyny or mental illness?* (Hemel Hempstead: Harvester Wheatsheaf).

Victor, C. (1987) *Old Age in Modern Society* (London: Croom Helm).

Vincent, J. (1995) *Inequality and Old Age* (London: UCL Press).

Wagner, G. (1988) *Residential Care: A Positive Choice*, Report of the Independent Review of Residential Care (London: National Institute of Social Work).

Wainwright, J. (1997) unpublished PhD thesis (Durham: University of Durham).

Waldman, J., Orme, J., Avison, D., Forbes, I. and Glastonbury, B (1996) 'Who Should Have a Say? Developing a Rationale for Consultation with Older Persons in Relation to Commisioning Plans', *Generations Review*, **6**(3): 6–8.

Walker, A. (1993) 'Community Care Policy' in Bornat, J., Pereira, C., Pilgrim, D. and Williams, F. (eds) *Community Care; a reader* (Basingstoke: Macmillan in asociation with the Open University.

Walker, A. and Warren, A. (1996) *Changing Services for Older People* (Buckingham: Open University Press).

Wallach Scott, J. (1988) *Gender and the Politics of History* (Columbia University Press).

Walmsley, J. (1996) ' "Talking to top people": some issues relating to the citizenship of people with learning difficulties' in Wain, J., Finkelstein, V., French, S. and Oliver, M. (eds) *Disabling Barriers – Enabling Environments* (London: Sage, in association with the Open University).

Walton, R. (1975) *Women and Social Work* (London: RKP).

Watters, C. (1996) 'Representations and realities: black people, community care and mental illness' Ahmad, W.I.U and Atkin, K. (Eds) (Buckingham: Open University Press).

Webb, D. (1996) 'The state, CCETSW and the academy', in Parton, N. (ed.) *Social Theory, Social Change and Social Work* (London: Routledge).

Webster, J. (1992) 'Split in two: experiences of children of schizophrenic mothers', *British Journal of Social Work*, **22**(3): 309–29.

Weedon, C. (1999) *Feminism, Theory and the Politics of Difference* Oxford: Blackwell).

Wenger, C. G. (1987) *Support Networks: Change and Stability* (Bangor: Centre for Social Policy Research and Development, University College of North Wales).

Wenger, C. (1992) *Help in Old Age – Facing up to Change* (Liverpool: Liverpool University Press).

Wetherall, W. (1984) 'Linguistic Repertoires and Literary Criticism: New Directions for a Social Psychology of Gender' in Wilkinson, S. (ed.) *Feminist Social Psychology* (Milton Keynes: Open University Press).

White, V. (1995) 'Commonality and Diversity in Feminist Social Work', *British Journal of Social Work*, **25**: 143–56.

Whitmarsh, A. (1995) *Social Focus on Women* (London: Central Statistical Office).

Williams, C.L. (ed.) (1993) *Doing "Women's Work": Men in Nontraditional Occupations* (California: Sage).

Williams, F. (1992) 'Women with Learning Difficulties are Women Too' in Langan, M. and Day, L. (eds) *Women Oppression and Social Work* (London: Routledge).

Williams, F. (1996) 'Postmodernism, feminism and difference' in Parton, N. (ed.) *Social Theory, Social Change and Social Work* (London: Routledge).

Wilson, E. (1977) *Women and the Welfare State* (London: Tavistock).

Wilson, E. (1980) 'Feminism and Social Work' in Bailey, R. and Brake, M. (eds) *Radical Social Work and Practice* (London: Edward Arnold).

Wilson, G. (1994) 'Elder Abuse', *British Journal of Social Work*, **24**(6): 681–700.

Wise, S. (1990) 'Becoming a Feminist Social Worker' in Stanely, L. (ed.) *Feminst Praxis* (London: Routledge).

Wolfensberger, W. (1983) 'Social Role Valorisation: A Proposed New Term for the Principle of Normalisation', *Mental Retardation*, **21**(6): 234–9.

Woolf, V. (1931) 'Professions for Women' in *Killing the Angel in the House* (Harmondsworth: Penguin).

Woolf, V. (1938) *Three Guineas*, 1992 edition, Shiach, M. (ed.) (Oxford: Oxford University Press).

Young, I.M. (1990a) 'The Ideal of Community and the Politics of Difference' in Nicholson, L.J. (ed.) *Feminism/Postmodernism* (New York: Routledge).

Young, I.M. (1990b) *Justice and the Politics of Difference* (New Jersey: Princetown University Press).

Young, M. and Willmott, P. (1957) *Family and Kinship in East London* (London: RKP).

Younghusband, E. (1947) *Report on the Employment and Training of Social Workers* (London: Carnegie UK Trust).

Younghusband, E. (1951) *Social Work in Britain* (London: Carnegie UK Trust).

Younghusband, E. (1981) *The Newest Profession: a Short History of Social Work* (Sutton: Commnity Care/IPC Business Press).

Yuval-Davis, N. (1997) 'Women, Citizenship and Difference', *Feminist Review*, **57** (Autumn): 4–27.

Index